The Bauer Thesis Examined

The Bauer Thesis Examined

The Geography of Heresy in the Early Christian Church

Thomas A. Robinson

The Edwin Mellen Press

Lewiston / Queenston

1988

Library of Congress Cataloging-in-Publication Data

Robinson, Thomas A.
    The Bauer thesis examined : the geography of heresy in the early
Christian church / Thomas A. Robinson.
        p. cm. -- (Studies in the Bible and early Christianity ; 11)
    Bibliography: p.
    Includes index.
    ISBN 0-88946-611-4
  1. Heresies, Christian--History--Early church, ca. 30-600.
2. Church history--Primitive and early church. ca. 30-600.
3. Ecclesiastical geography--Mediterranean Region. 4. Bauer, Walter,
1877-1960. Rechtgläubigkeit und Ketzerei im ältesten Christentum. I.
Title. II. Series.
Br166.R63 1988   87-28288
273'.1--dc19   CIP

This is volume 11 in the continuing series
Studies in the Bible and Early Christianity
Volume 11 ISBN 0-88946-611-4
SBEC Series ISBN 0-88946-913-X

The Edwin Mellen Press   The Edwin Mellen Press
P.O. Box 450   P.O. Box 67
Lewiston, New York   Queenston, Ontario
USA 14092   CANADA L0S 1L0

Printed in the United States of America

to
Ben F. Meyer

Contents

Preface

My interest in the question of orthodoxy and heresy and, in particular, the thesis of Walter Bauer was sparked when I started my graduate studies at McMaster University in the fall of 1980. The Department of Religious Studies at the University was in the middle of a multi-year project on Jewish and Christian Self-Definition in the Greco-Roman period. Terms like "self-understanding" and "self-identification" were very much in the air.

On my first reading of Bauer's *Orthodoxy and Heresy in Earliest Christianity,* I was, like many before me, presented with a new world. Although never becoming a full-fledged convert to "the Bauer Thesis," I could never get away from its implications. Thus attracted, Bauer's work became the focus of my attention. But the more I examined the thesis, the less convinced I became. Had Bauer really shown an adequate sensitivity for the way groups define themselves? Had he stressed diversity too much, without considering the ways in which even diverse groups can share a common and friendly world? Had he given adequate attention to self-definition as *process*? And had he proven that heretical movements were both strong and early—two points essential to his thesis?

Concentrating on the Ignatian material, I attempted to put Bauer's thesis to the test. The present volume is rooted in that investigation, and incorporates part of the material that I presented in my 1985 Ph.D. dissertation at McMaster University. My work there was done with the valued contribution of Ben Meyer, Ed Sanders and Gérard Vallée, professors in the Religious Studies Department. In particular, the friendly and learned dialogue with Ben Meyer made my studies at McMaster delightful in a way that graduate studies are often not. The windows of insight to which he has pointed numerous students over the years have opened onto horizons that stimulate and challenge. For this, I dedicate the present volume to Dr. Meyer.

The particular emphases on geography and on Koester's recent support for the Bauer thesis were suggested by Professor Herb Richardson of the Edwin Mellen Press. I thank the various persons at the press who have contributed to the technical aspects of the book.

Thomas Robinson
The University of Lethbridge
Spring 1988

Abbreviations

AB	Anchor Bible
BJRL	*Bulletin of the John Rylands University Library of Manchester*
CBQ	*Catholic Biblical Quarterly*
CH	*Church History*
ET	English translation
Exp Tim	*Expository Times*
HNTC	Harper's NT Commentaries
HTR	*Harvard Theological Review*
IEph	Ignatius *to the Ephesians*
IMag	Ignatius *to the Magnesians*
IPhil	Ignatius *to the Philadelphians*
IPol	Ignatius *to Polycarp*
IRom	Ignatius *to the Romans*
ISmyr	Ignatius *to the Smyrnaeans*
ITral	Ignatius *to the Trallians*
JBL	*Journal of Biblical Literature*
JEH	*Journal of Ecclesiastical History*
JES	*Journal of Ecumenical Studies*
JCSD	*Jewish and Christian Self-Definition*, vol 1., ed. E.P. Sanders (Philadelphia: Fortress, 1980)
JJS	*Journal of Jewish Studies*
JSNTSup	Journal for the Study of the New Testament—Supplement Series
JTS	*Journal of Theological Studies*
LCL	Loeb Classical Library
NCBC	New Century Bible Commentary
NovT	*Novum Testamentum*
NT	New Testament
NTA	*New Testament Apocrapha*
NTS	*New Testament Studies*
PolPhil	Polycarp *to the Philippians*
RelSRev	*Religious Studies Review*
SC	*The Second Century*
SE	*Studia Evangelica*
SR	*Studies in Religion/Sciences religieuses*
TS	*Theological Studies*
TheolRund	*Theologische Rundschau*
VC	*Vigiliae christianae*

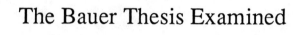

The Bauer Thesis Examined

Chapter One

The History of the Debate

I. The Problem

A. An Original Orthodoxy?

In the last century and a half of New Testament scholarship, radical changes have been made to the traditional view of the character of earliest Christianity. According to the traditional view, the earliest church was, in its initial stages, free from fundamentally diverse theological interpretations. Specifically, two points were made: first, it was contended that "authentic apostolic tradition" had been proclaimed consistently and without alteration in all areas of the primitive mission; and second, it was charged that heresy was a later phenomenon and reflected a deviation from this original apostolic tradition.[1]

Neither point is granted much credibility today.[2] It is now widely claimed that the original uniformity of Christianity argued for

---

1. A brief summary of the traditional view is provided in the introduction of the work of Walter Bauer, *Orthodoxy and Heresy in Earliest Christianity,* ed. Robert Kraft and Gerhard Krodel, trans. by a team from the Philadelphia Seminar on Christian Origins (Philadelphia: Fortress, 1971). This book is a translation of the 1964 second German edition, which contained appendices by Georg Strecker. The first edition was published in 1934 as volume 10 in the series Beiträge zur historischen Theologie (Tübingen: Mohr/Siebeck) under its now classic title: *Rechtgläubigkeit und Ketzerei im ältesten Christentum.*

2. In §II.C.5-6 of this chapter, I discuss the modern developments in more detail.

1

by the second and third-century catholic church was nothing more than an idealistic and strikingly unhistorical reconstruction of the church's earliest period. This reconstruction is said to reflect not the realities of the first century but the ambitions of the second century. It is charged that the developing catholic church excluded certain alternative (and equally ancient) interpretations of the Christian message and brought certain other formerly competing interpretations into a novel synthesis through heavy modification and alteration of their original intent. In other words, modern scholarship contends that the concept of a uniform primitive church is a product, not of the realities of the first century (in which radical theological diversity flourished), but of the wishful thinking of the early catholic element, engaged in a concentrated struggle to create a monolithic Christianity, reflecting, of course, its own biases.

The theory of an early orthodoxy in the primitive church is judged to have failed at two critical points. First, the church of the earliest period does not seem to reflect among all its propagandists and in every area of its mission a uniform message; theological diversity is a characteristic of the earliest period.[3] Second, no one particular theological perspective stands out as apostolic to the exclusion of the others: that is, no one first-century interpretation has clear connections to second and third-century orthodoxy, in contrast to all the other first-century interpretations, whose connections are with heretical movements.

There has been a failure of the traditional view, then, for two reasons. First, the view has been blind to the tolerated presence in the first century of views judged as heresy by the second-century orthodox church. Second, the view has been blind to the competing diversities in first-century theological interpretations of the Christian message, which, through a process of synthesis and modification,

---

3. Although Bauer's work did not itself deal with the diversity of first-century Christianity, much of the debate since Bauer has focused on this period. Bauer explained his decision not to address the first-century situation (4/ET:xxv). Although Bauer has been criticized for not examining the early period, Bauer's omission is understandable. Believing that he had established that heresy was the original and dominant form of Christianity throughout much of early second-century Christianity, by extension, Bauer could feel comfortable in his conclusion that the character of first-century Christianity was not markedly dissimilar.

were shaped into a novel, or significantly altered, orthodoxy of the second century. From the perspective of the modern critical historian, the traditional view is simply a historically inaccurate and theologically motivated reconstruction provided by the catholic church of the second and third centuries in its conflict with Christian groups outside of its communion.

Although this flawed traditional view clearly requires correction, its faults are, nonetheless, understandable. The flaws are largely due to the polemical and theological contexts in which it was shaped. The developing catholic church was confronted on all sides by various interpretations of the Christian message. Some of these interpretations were stark denials of fundamental elements in the catholic church's understanding of the gospel, yet these various interpretations claimed apostolic roots, just as the catholic church did. In the context of these competing claims, it is possible to make sense of the catholic church's denial that rival interpretations had credible apostolic roots. The most obvious way to challenge the apostolic roots of rival interpretations was to deny that the rival interpretations were as ancient as the catholic interpretation and to contend that there had been a uniform message at the beginning, to which only the catholic community had remained faithful.

But whatever the excuses that might be made for the way this "history" came to be written, for the historian its faults are grave; a less-biased history is required. We must admit that the repeated criticism voiced by present scholarship is substantial and sound: the traditional reconstruction of the history of the early church has undoubtedly been negatively shaped by the polemical and theo-logical concerns of the age in which that reconstruction was first put forward. Christian history cannot be left there, for such a history cannot be expected to meet the needs of the modern discussion, in which the polemical and theological concerns are radically different.[4]

---

4. It is now considered unseemly to engage in vicious attacks on the groups judged as heretical by the early catholic church. It is also considered unseemly to emphasize exclusion and purity of belief rather than inclusion and tolerance of diversity. The reasons for this are numerous, ranging from genuine sympathy for the concerns and insights of particular alternative interpretations of the Christian

B. The Traditional View

1. Eusebius

The traditional view is perhaps best represented in *The Ecclesiastical History*[5] of Eusebius, bishop of Caesarea in Palestine about the time of the conversion of Emperor Constantine. Eusebius's work reflects the basic understanding of the orthodox community during the two hundred years prior to Eusebius's time, and it shaped the view of the character of early Christianity until the modern period.

The view of the history of the primitive church controlling Eusebius's *Ecclesiastical History* was that orthodoxy had credible apostolic roots, whereas heresy lacked such primitive roots and credible parentage. In passages within that work, Eusebius stated his view explicitly: in the earliest period, there was not a diversity of interpretations of the Christian message but simply one pure apostolic proclamation; diversity was the result of the attempt by Satan to introduce false doctrine into the church after the death of the apostles (*E.H.* 3.32.7-8; 4.22.4-5). Eusebius's view posits, quite clearly, a first century relatively free of heresy (or of diversity—which was, for Eusebius, basically the same thing).

Walter Bauer, the chief critic of Eusebius and with whom most of this present work will engage, became, at times, almost enraged over what he conceived to be a blatant falsification of the history of the early church by the biased Eusebius (152-3; 161; 194/ ET:149-51; 158; 192).[6] Yet, however much Bauer may have had grounds

---

faith, to a disinterested (and sometimes lazy) tolerance, unwilling to raise the question of truth. The early fathers shared neither this sympathy nor this tolerance.

5. References in this work are to the edition of the Loeb Classical Library. Vol. 1, ed. and trans. Kirsopp Lake; vol. 2 trans. J.E.L. Oulton, from the edition by H.J. Lawlor (Cambridge, Mass.: Harvard University Press/London: William Heinemann, 1939).

6. Since extensive reference will be made throughout this work to Bauer's *Orthodoxy and Heresy in Earliest Christianity*, references to that work are included in the text rather than in the footnotes. All references are enclosed in parentheses; the page number of the second German edition is given first, then, following a diagonal stroke and the abbreviation "ET:," the page number of the English edition [e.g., (95/ET:91) is a reference to page 95 in the German edition and to page 91 in the English]. References to all other modern authors are found in the footnotes.

to distrust (or dismiss outright) the reconstruction of Eusebius, with some fairness to Eusebius it must be noted that a similar view of the purity of the early church was held by every second and third-century catholic writer whose writings are known to us. The following writers are particularly significant.

2. Irenaeus

A view similar to that reflected by Eusebius's history was used in detail by Irenaeus over a century earlier to discredit the gnostic systems that threatened the orthodox community towards the end of the second century. Irenaeus is especially well known for promoting the idea of apostolic succession. The claim to apostolic succession was designed to restrict reliable apostolic tradition to the catholic church by placing the catholic bishops, and only those bishops, in a credible and ordained line stemming from the apostles (*A.H.* 3.3.3; 3.4.1). Irenaeus's polemic is marked, as well, by other emphases. In particular, Irenaeus contrasted the unity of the catholic church to the diversity of the gnostic systems. This he did in order to make suspect the heretics' claim to valid apostolic tradition (*A.H.* 1.10; 1.11.1).

3. Ignatius

About one hundred years earlier than Irenaeus, Ignatius, the bishop of Antioch (one of the earliest Fathers whose writings can be dated with some certainty), reflected a similar understanding of primitive Christianity. Although he offered no developed view on apostolic succession and no explicit view on the matter of the unity of the orthodox in contrast to the diversity of the heretic (both of which were primary themes in Irenaeus's polemic), it is clear that Ignatius's thought could have easily developed in the direction of that reflected by Irenaeus and Eusebius. Ignatius spoke often of the unity of the church under the bishop, of the need to hold to the particular teachings taught by the bishop's church, and of the preservation of the apostolic message in the bishop's church—and only in the bishop's church.[7] Had Ignatius the choice between the

---

7. IEph 2.2, 3.2, 4.1, 5.2, 6.1; IMag 6, 7.1; ITral 2, 3.1, 7; IPhil 3.2, 4,

view of the primitive church offered by Eusebius and that offered by Bauer, it is clear where his preference would have lain.

4. The New Testament

The book of Acts is the classic example from the New Testament materials of an attempt to promote a reconstruction in which the diversity of the primitive era is reduced to a minimum. The Tübingen School had used this document as the main support in its argument for a second-century synthesis of movements that in the first century were in opposition.[8] It is not important to our question here to determine to what extent the Tübingen analysis of the thrust of the book of Acts is correct. For the purposes of the present discussion, it need only be noted that the portrait of the first-century church provided by Acts reflects little of the extensive diversity proposed by many of the modern reconstructions of primitive Christianity. The author of Acts seems to share with Eusebius a view of early Christian uniformity, as F.C. Baur, the founder of the Tübingen school, observed, noting that Paul is made to look as Petrine as possible and Peter as Pauline as possible.[9] Although the Tübingen school may have exaggerated the differences between Peter and Paul in its efforts to counter the portrait in the book of Acts, it is difficult not to agree with the Tübingen insight that the author of Acts consciously attempted to show a primitive Christianity that is basically both united and uniform. Whether the author of Acts has grossly misrepresented the character of earliest Christianity continues to be a matter of scholarly debate.[10]

8.1; ISmyr 8, 9. References to Ignatius are, unless otherwise stated, from The Loeb Classical Library edition, *The Apostolic Fathers*, vol. 1, ed. Kirsopp Lake (Cambridge, Mass.: Harvard University Press/London: William Heinemann, 1925). Reference is made, as well, to the edition of J.B. Lightfoot, *The Apostolic Fathers*, part 2, vol. 2, *Ignatius and Polycarp* (London: Macmillan, 1889-1890); reprint ed. Grand Rapids: Baker, 1981.

8. See §II.C.1 of this chapter for a more full discussion of the Tübingen School.

9. A brief review of the discussion is given in Stephen Neill, *The Interpretation of the New Testament 1861-1961*, The Firth Lectures 1962 (London: Oxford University Press, 1964), 21-27.

10. Although the majority of scholars seem hesitant to accept Acts as a good source for the history of the earliest church, it is perhaps to be considered a good source in light of what little else we have. Martin Hengel, *Acts and the History*

As for other material in the New Testament, it is a matter of some dispute how to interpret the numerous comments that might be relevant to our question—especially those comments about truth and tradition. Scholars who think that a sense of orthodoxy came late tend to judge the sometimes sharp lines drawn by Paul and John,[11] for example, in terms of ethics rather than of doctrine, or in terms of practice rather than of belief.[12] Scholars who believe that a sense of orthodoxy was early tend to find in these same sharp drawing of lines clear evidence for an early sense of orthodoxy.[13] Each side seems unconvinced by the other's reading of the material. The disagreement on this point reflects a fundamental disagreement among scholars regarding the self-understanding of the primitive community. This is a large question in itself, and the problem is to be addressed elsewhere.[14]

---

of Early Christianity, (Philadelphia: Fortress, 1979), has demonstrated how a critical historian can make fruitful use of Acts. Also see Ward W. Gasque, *A History of the Criticism of the Acts of the Apostles* (Grand Rapids: Eerdmans, 1975).

11. Paul can use such language as "false brothers" (Gal 2.4) for those who contradict his message, and he can call down curses and hurl insults not only on his Judaizing opponents but on straying angels as well (Gal 1.8-9; 2 Cor 11.13-15). John has some equally colourful language for his opponents: "anti-Christ" and "liar" among the more memorable (1 John 2.18, 22; 4.3).

12. This was Bauer's claim (236-7/ET:234-5). See, too, Maurice Goguel, *The Birth of Christianity*, trans. H.C. Snape (London: George Allen & Unwin, 1953), 431. This is, as well, the thesis of Martin Elze, "Häresie und Einheit der Kirche im 2. Jahrhundert," *ZTK* 71 (1974): 389-409.

13. For example: Leonhard Goppelt, "The Plurality of New Testament Theologies and the Unity of the Gospel as an Ecumenical Problem," in *The Gospel and Unity*, ed. Vilmos Vajta (Minneapolis: Augsburg, 1971), 106-30, especially the section titled "Paul's View of the Limits of Diversity in Terms of Heresy." Ernst Käsemann, "The Canon of the New Testament and the Unity of the Church," in *Essays on New Testament Themes*, trans. W.J. Montague, Studies in Biblical Theology 41 (London: SCM, 1964), 100, says that only doctrinal differences can account for the conflict in Acts 6. Käsemann has argued often that irreconcilable theological diversity is rooted in the canon itself, and he, like Luther, believes he knows which of the diversities should be normative (p. 100). C.F.D. Moule, *The Birth of the New Testament*, 3rd ed. HNTC (San Fransisco: Harper & Row, 1982), 247, thinks that 1 and 2 John reflect a consciousness of orthodoxy. I. Howard Marshall, "Orthodoxy and heresy in earlier Christianity," *Themelios* 2 (1976): 7 says: "Granted that there is diversity and development in the theologies expressed in the New Testament, the question is whether this is the same thing as saying that no distinction between orthodoxy and heresy was being made, or that this concept did not exist prior to the development of a vocabulary to describe it."

14. In a volume to follow the present one, I intend to address methodological

5. Origen: An Exception?

Some have argued that Origen was the one early churchman who held a more critical view of the diversity of the primitive period.[15] But however more refined Origen's view may have been than that of many in his time, his is, nonetheless, hardly a voice in support of a view like Bauer's over against that of Eusebius. Origen, as clearly as any church Father, denied to the heretics of the second and third centuries any right to their claim to authentic tradition or apostolic parentage,[16] and that, in itself, widely separates Origen from an understanding of primitive Christianity like that offered by Bauer or by those influenced by him.

II. The Current Discussion of Primitive Diversity

A. The Assumption of Diversity

As has already been pointed out, modern historians of the early church (over whom the figure of Walter Bauer towers head and shoulders) have generally dismissed the traditional reconstruction of church history. Quick censure is assured to any reconstruction that

---

issues in the debate regarding orthodoxy and heresy. There I will offer a detailed examination of the nature of diversity—not just the diversity of early Christianity but of diversity of ideological positions in general, especially as that impacts on the self-understanding of an ideological community.

15. Marcel Simon, "From Greek Hairesis to Christian Heresy," in *Early Christian Literature and the Classical Intellectual Tradition,* ed. William R. Schoedel and Robert L. Wilken, Théologie historique 53 (Paris: Beauchesne, 1979), 107, says that Origen only abandons to his adversaries sects such as the Orphites and the Cainites who "do not share with us even the name of Jesus." But the heretics to whom he will allow the label "Christian" to be applied are still heretics, nonetheless. As Simon says, these heretics play a role in helping to discriminate between true and false Christianity (p. 107). Such a position is Eusebian enough. R.A. Markus, "The Problem of Self-Definition: From Sect to Church," in *JCSD* 1:8, says that Origen alone was aware of the complexities of the primitive Christian community. See, too, Norbert Brox, "Häresie," in *Reallexikon für Antike und Christentum,* ed. Theodor Klauser *et al* (Stuttgart: Anton Hiersemann, 1984), 13:267-8. The strongest passage from Origen's writings that would seem to suggest a fairly generous attitude by Origen towards heretics is *Contra Celsum* 3.10-13. But see n. 16 below.

16. Note in particular, *Contra Celsum* 5.61-4; 8.14-6. As well, Origen's role as a defender of the catholic position should be considered (described in detail in Book 6 of Eusebius's *Ecclesiastical History*).

posits a uniformity in the early Christian proclamation and denies to the heretics valid claim to apostolic tradition while granting it to the orthodox. We can note the increasing confidence with which the Eusebian scheme has come to be challenged. Even in 1963, when Arnold Ehrhardt could complain that Bauer's work had not been given the attention it deserved, Ehrhardt was, nonetheless, able to say without fear of serious challenge that there was likely no original uniformity in the primitive Christian community.[17] In the more recent McMaster Project on Jewish and Christian Self-Definition in the Greco-Roman period,[18] George MacRae notes that "diversity is now assumed."[19] In that same volume, R.A. Markus describes the Eusebian scheme as "notorious," something he recognizes he is free to do because of the impact of the Bauer Thesis.[20]

B. Preliminary Challenges to the Eusebian Scheme

1. The Gnostic Complaint

We have seen that orthodox leaders of the post-apostolic age were persistent in their claim that they represented the original and apostolic form of Christianity; views not conforming to those in the bishop's church were, they contended, deformed and late. Of course, those who were committed to these diverse interpretations disagreed, and disagreed quite strongly.[21] But their claims came to

---

17. Arnold Ehrhardt, "Christianity Before the Apostles' Creed," *HTR* 55 (1962): 78.

18. The McMaster Project in Judaism and Christianity was a research project of the Department of Religious Studies of McMaster University. The project ran from 1976-81 and resulted in the publication of a number of books on themes related to the orthodoxy/heresy debate. Besides the three volumes of collected papers in *Jewish and Christian Self-Definition*, ed. E.P. Sanders *et al* (Philadelphia: Fortress, 1980-2), there have been two books of particular relevance to our question: Gérard Vallée, *A Study in Anti-Gnostic Polemics: Irenaeus, Hippolytus, and Epiphanius*, Studies in Christianity and Judaism 1 (Waterloo: Wilfrid Laurier University Press, 1981), and Ben F. Meyer, *The Early Christians: Their World Mission and Self-Discovery*, Good News Studies 16 (Wilmington: Michael Glazier, 1986).

19. George W. MacRae, "Why the Church Rejected Gnosticism," in *JCSD* 1:127.

20. R.A. Markus, "The Problem of Self-Definition," in *JCSD*, 1:3-4.

21. Gnostics are frequently reported to have argued that their position was not fundamentally different from the orthodox position, and when they were forced to show the antiquity of their beliefs, they apparently quite freely appealed to a

appear less and less credible as catholic Christianity increasingly forced uniformity of belief through the weight of church councils and the political force of a Christian empire equally dedicated to the concept of uniformity.

From the late second century onwards, almost all of the writing we possess suggest that the heretics were in the minority.[22] (Whether the heretics had once been in the majority is, of course, the fundamental question raised by the Bauer Thesis.) Given the minority status of the heretics by the end of the second century, it is natural to find that this minority frequently challenged the basis upon which the orthodox majority attempted to justify the authority they exercised. In that sense, we might say that the traditional view of church history has always come under fire. It is not my intention to investigate these kinds of challenges to the traditional view. Such challenges are clearly polemical and apologetic, and they stand in marked contrast to the descriptive and neutral stance taken by most modern critics of the traditional reconstruction.

Another reason for not examining the various early criticisms that were raised by minority groups against the claims of the orthodox is that most of these criticisms are not, strictly speaking, challenges to the traditional, or Eusebian, scheme. Throughout the history of Christianity, there have been fringe groups that have spoken against the church of the orthodox majority. The objections of these discontents were rooted, however, in the problems of the orthodox (or catholic) Christianity of their day. Given the pressing situation of their own time, these fringe groups did not generally have the leisure nor the historical perspective to focus their strong criticism of the catholic tradition of their day back on its second and third-century roots. In order to establish whether a particular challenge to the majority group is a challenge as well to the Eusebian scheme, one must determine the point at which the critic claims that the orthodox have deviated from apostolic tradition and direction. If

---

secret tradition which had been passed on from the apostles to men spiritually qualified. See Elaine Pagels, *The Gnostic Gospels* (New York: Random House, 1979): in particular, chapters 2 and 5.

22. Even on Bauer's own analysis of the literature, the orthodox win. See especially his chapter 5.

the critic marks it with Constantine, for example, then the view is basically Eusebian up to that specified point of deviation. In fact, any scheme that proposes a pure apostolic period—regardless how far they extend that period of purity into later centuries—is Eusebian at its heart.

But the modern debate is of a different character. It is distinctive, not in identifying a different point at which deviation is seen to have begun (as is generally the case for groups that have opposed the Roman church throughout history), but in refusing to admit a specific point of deviation at all. The modern debate is uncomfortable with the language of "deviation" and prefers to grant to a variety of theological perspectives both primitive and apostolic roots. What formerly were classed as deviations have been rehabilitated by modern church historians into the fold of authentic and apostolic Christianity. This stands in contrast to the variety of older protesting groups that, regardless of their complaint against the church of their day, nonetheless assumed a normative and uniform character to the earliest apostolic tradition.

2. The Reformation

Those who have examined Bauer's contribution to this new understanding of primitive Christianity have often pointed to his Protestantism as one factor that could explain the roots of his thinking.[23] Indeed, in the early years of the discussion of Bauer's theory, the debate about early orthodoxy and heresy sometimes was little more than defensive posturing by German Protestants and Roman and Anglo-Catholics.

Given such a context for the initial discussion of Bauer's work, I will begin my examination of the challenge to the Eusebian scheme with the Protestant Reformation. I do so, not hoping to find a clear challenge to the Eusebian scheme in the Reformation, but merely to probe for roots that might account in some way for the perspective of a man like Bauer.

---

23. In Appendix 2 of the reprinting of Bauer's *Orthodoxy and Heresy*, the editor divides his discussion of the reception of Bauer's book basically in terms of Protestant-Catholic groupings: "Continental Protestant Reviews," "English Language Reviews," and "Roman Catholic Reviews."

The Reformation, even with its stinging attack on Roman Christianity and its elevation of scripture over tradition, was primarily concerned with the defects of the Christianity of the 1500s. Any challenge that the Reformers may have raised to the Catholic claim to apostolic tradition was more a challenge to the principle of tradition *for establishing truth* than to the principle of tradition *per se*. Their attack on tradition was not necessarily an attack on the basic concept of an orthodox Christianity extending from the days of the apostles into later centuries. Although the Roman church of the 1500s was itself seriously castigated, Luther was open to a concept of orthodoxy that could admit significant development over the centuries, at least of external forms. Tradition remained important so long as it could support dogma believed to be established by scripture. The catholic church of the early centuries and its theologians of repute were held by sixteenth-century Protestants, as much as by Roman Catholics, as a positive part of the Christianity of which they believed themselves to be a part. This is clearly a Eusebian position.

Yet, an opening was made by the Reformation for the kind of sustained attack on tradition that could be carried back from the sixteenth century into the early centuries of the developing church. In some ways, Bauer's critique of tradition was different more in degree than in kind from that of the Reformation. Luther challenged the claim of the sixteenth-century church to credible links with the Christianity of the apostles; he repudiated the appeal to tradition that was used to support the authority of the Roman church. Bauer simply examined the links and evaluated the basis of authority of an earlier stage of the catholic church. Yet Luther does differ from Bauer in one fundamental way: unlike Bauer, Luther is basically Eusebian in his perspective. He has no quarrel with the catholic church of the early period and, unlike some of the Reformers, he has no difficulty with various developments that had taken place within that church.

Less openness to the developments within the church of the first few centuries is seen in the thrust of the non-Lutheran branches of the Reformation. Zwingli found in the Bible, and in the Bible alone, the pattern for church organization. That approach challenged development in a way that Luther's did not. Roland Bainton sums up the difference: "Luther would...allow whatever the Bible did not prohibit, whereas Zwingli would reject whatever the Bible did not enjoin."[24] Zwingli's approach was less able to take account of development; his perspective would lead more quickly to a criticism of the post-apostolic church than would Luther's.

3. The Radical (Anabaptist) Reformation and Pietism

An even more sustained attack on tradition and a more marked return to the form of primitive Christianity is reflected in the Anabaptists. Seeking to recover the pattern of the primitive church, the Anabaptists found themselves unable to adapt to a society in which Christianity was the dominant culture. Whereas the initial reform movement in Germany and Switzerland was quite happy to take over the role once played by the Roman church, the more radical reform found nothing attractive in such a role. The true church was not simply a non-Roman Christian society; rather, it was the small element of the faithful in the midst of a non-Christian society. The Radical Reformation found itself more comfortable sharing the status of a minority in the society (like the early Christians in the Roman empire) than in taking over from the Roman Catholics the role of members in a society that was Christian.

The pietists as well, dissatisfied with the results of the Reformation, were attracted to the form of Christianity they found in the New Testament. One of the more extreme of the pietists, Gottfried Arnold, wrote a history of the Christian church.[25] In this

---

24. Roland H. Bainton, *Christendom: A Short History of Christianity and Its Impact on Western Civilization*, Harper Torchbooks (New York: Harper & Row, 1966), 2.31.

25. Gottfried Arnold, *Unparteyishe Kirchen-und Ketzer-Historie* (Frankfurt a. M., 1699). This book was published shortly after Arnold's *Die erste Liebe*, in which he showed his predisposition for the simplicity of the primitive church in contrast to developments that had occurred within the catholic community. As Patrick Henry notes: "Scholarship itself is proposing what the most radical of the sixteenth-century Reformers (or even Marcion, for that matter) declared polemically: that the 'Fall of the church' and the origin of the church are simultaneous events" ["Why is Contemporary Scholarship so Enamored of Ancient Heretics," in *Proceedings of the 8th International Conference on Patristic Studies*,

work (ET: *Impartial History of the Church and of Heretics*), Arnold found in the condemned heretics of the church, not deformed Christianity, but authentic Christianity. In doing so, Arnold introduced a new perspective in his historical reconstruction: not only was he attracted by the purity of first-century Christianity (as were all the Reformers to some extent);[26] he discovered a warmth of authentic Christianity in movements judged as heretical by their catholic opponents, and in this he is closer to Bauer—though Bauer himself seemed not particularly concerned to discover what was "authentic Christianity," but only to give the heretics a fairer hearing.

4. Bauer: A Son of the Reformation?

We have just reviewed some of the tendencies of the Reformation that led to adjustments in the way the history of the Christian church came to be viewed. But Walter Bauer, the revolutionary historian of the primitive church, was only remotely connected to these forces. It was not from reading Arnold's work that Bauer was led to reevaluate the claims of the heretics; it was not from sharing the Anabaptist desire to return to an original ecclesiastical purity that Bauer questioned the links of second-century catholic doctrine to first-century apostolic teaching; it was not by sharing Luther's insight into the corruption of the Roman

---

1979, ed. E.A. Livingstone (Oxford: Pergamum Press, 1980), 124-5].

26. Among all streams of the Reformation, there was conceived to be a period in the past in which the church was more pure than the contemporary church, and an attempt was made to move from the present state of deformity and corruption to the purity of the church in its primitive period. Whether that period of purity was restricted to the first century or extended far beyond, the principle of tradition as an infallible vehicle for the preservation of truth was discarded. As with any attempt to return to the purity of the "apostolic age," this approach has, built-in, a general dissatisfaction with the developments that have taken place within the church. Development is judged negatively. This opens the way for criticism of the trend toward catholicism that is evidenced in the second and third centuries (though often the focus of criticism is directed to a much later stage of the Catholic church). See Thomas H. Olbricht, "Understanding the Church of the Second Century: American Research and Teaching 1890-1940," in *Texts and Testaments: Critical Essays on the Bible and Early Church Fathers,* ed. W. Eugene March (San Antonio: Trinity University Press, 1980), 251. Observe, for example, that Protestant scholars are much more quick to criticize Ignatius of Antioch than are Catholic scholars.

church that caused Bauer to be suspicious of second-century catholicism.[27]

Thus to connect Bauer to the Reformation would be misleading. Bauer simply did not work under the historical forces that were pressing at the time of the Reformation. For Bauer, there was no face-to-face death struggle with the Roman Catholic church, and his work is generally free of the kind of polemic that shaped the Reformation (though in Bauer's making of the church at Rome the bogeyman of second-century Christianity, we doubtlessly see a historian who had not completely freed himself of the influence of his roots within Protestantism).

It is really as a son of the Enlightenment, especially the enlightenment as reflected in the biblical criticism of the nineteenth century, that Bauer is to be best understood.

C. The Main Challenge to the Eusebian Scheme
1. F.C. Baur and the Tübingen School

Ferdinard Christian Baur, and under his influence the Tübingen school, asserted that radical diversity existed in the primitive church during its earliest years. F.C. Baur (not to be confused with Walter Bauer) contended that the view of the primitive Christian community reflected in the book of Acts and in other later works represented a synthesis of what, in the first century, had been opposing movements.[28] Numerous refinements and serious qualifications

---

27. Even in Luther's finding of theological diversity in the early church, the heart of the matter is of a different character from Bauer's similar claim. Luther's awareness of significant theological diversity is well known. He was prepared to find in the New Testament theological perspectives that did not pass muster. James, Jude, Hebrews and Revelation were judged inferior. But Luther's judgments were basically tied to his polemic against the sixteenth-century Roman church. It was Pauline Christianity that was Reformation Christianity; all else was depreciated. But Bauer, in contrast to Luther, would not have been interested in the categories of "inferior" and "superior." He would have agreed with Luther here only in regard to the identification of the *fact* of theological diversity, not in an evaluation of the diversities. We find in Bauer no defense of Paulinism. We find no selection of a particular element in the range of first-century theological diversity as the normative to which all must be subject. For Bauer, the search for a normative Christianity is over. And that search is over not because the normative form of Christianity has been found; it is over because no such form ever existed to be found.

28. For a review of F.C. Baur's contribution to New Testament scholarship,

were made, and continue to be made, to the Tübingen view, but its basic thrust remains unchallenged:[29] the catholic church of the second century is judged to reflect a unity not found in the first century and to consist of a reconciliation or synthesis of major first-century interpretations of the Christian message, which in the first century stood apart—perhaps even in stark opposition.

Some students of Walter Bauer's novel historical reconstruction have found substantial roots for Bauer's theory in the Tübingen perspective. Such is the opinion of Jerry Flora, who in a doctoral dissertation in 1972, attempted to locate Bauer's theory in the context of the evolution of scholarship.[30] Others agree with the Tübingen roots of Bauer's reconstruction.[31] But this view requires modification. The Bauer Thesis, at its heart, does not seem to share in a substantial way the perspective of the Tübingen school in regard to heresy. That is not to say that the Tübingen reshaping of our view of the primitive church did not have some impact on Bauer. It would have at least contributed in that it made radical reconstructions of the early church's character acceptable within the circle of scholars. And it would have contributed, as well, in calling attention to primitive diversity. Little more than this, however, seems to have been contributed by the Tübingen perspective to the

---

see Stephen Neill, *Interpretation*, ch. 2. "The New Testament and History"; also Werner Georg Kümmel, *The New Testament: The History of the Investigation of its Problems*, trans. S. McLean Gilmour and Howard C. Kee (Nashville and New York: Abingdon Press, 1972), part IV, "The Consistently Historical Approach to the New Testament."

29. Neill, *Interpretation*, 59, points to the observation of Johannes Munck (*Paul and the Salvation of Mankind*, 1959, 69 ff.) that, though the literary results of the Tübingen thesis have been generally abandoned, the historical results based on those literary result still are widely accepted.

30. Jerry R. Flora, "A Critical Analysis of Walter Bauer's Theory of Early Christian Orthodoxy and Heresy," (Th.D. diss., Southern Baptist Theological Seminary, 1972), 82-3.

31. Hans Dieter Betz, "Orthodoxy and Heresy in Primitive Christianity: Some critical remarks on Georg Strecker's republication of Walter Bauer's *Rechtgläubigkeit und Ketzerei im ältesten Christentum*," *Interpretation* 19 (1965): 305, points out that Bauer's prior conclusion about there being a Petrine and a Pauline interpretation of the new message of Jesus shows that his work on orthodoxy and heresy is rooted in past conclusions. Flora, "Analysis of Bauer's Theory," 83, also sees Bauer's work on orthodoxy and heresy rooted in the work of the Tübingen school.

kind of thesis Bauer put forward.

In contrast to Bauer, the Tübingen school was prepared to see in the history of the Christian church natural and necessary developments. Thus the development of the primitive church into the catholicism of the second and third centuries was viewed positively as part of the working out of *Geist*. As Philip Hefner pointed out, for Baur, all of history is theological; the history of the church is self-propelling.[32] One might say that for Baur, what happens should happen. In its proper place and time, any of the significant and successful developments within Christianity can be considered natural, necessary, and good. Other movements, of course, have a role to play, providing the antithetical backdrop upon which a new synthesis can be viewed. As such, heresy can have a positive role.

One must wonder, however, whether the Tübingen school, given its commitment to the Hegelian dialectic (or to something similar),[33] had the resources and motivation to evaluate the various movements within the history of Christianity in any substantial way. Indeed, one must wonder whether the Tübingen school was prepared to accept any responsibility to evaluate the various movements of the historical past. Did not this divinely directed history itself provide the evaluation of the movements within Christian history? Was the duty of the scholar not simply to accept the judgments of history itself? Whatever worked out for itself a niche in the dialectical process was positive and fundamental; whatever failed to work out a niche was certainly secondary, and perhaps irrelevant.

But in the kind of discussion about orthodoxy and heresy that has arisen since the days of Walter Bauer, at the core of the debate is the assumption that the credibility and authenticity of various elements of the Christian movement has little—and perhaps nothing—to do with their survival. The victorious party may have

---

32. Philip J. Hefner, "Baur Versus Ritschl on Early Christianity," *CH* 31 (1962): 273.

33. It is not clear when F.C. Baur became a conscious follower of the thought of Hegel. See E. Earle Ellis, "Dating the New Testament," *NTS* 26 (1980): 495 n.45.

been misdirected; it may have been in error; it may have not represented authentic Christianity. In other words, catholicism may have been less authentic than gnosticism. But, one wonders: could the Tübingen school ever have reached such a conclusion? Given its commitment to the Hegelian dialectic, it seems that the Tübingen school was incapable of ever concluding that catholicism was, in its own time and place, fundamentally inadequate.[34] The current discussion of orthodoxy and heresy requires, however, that this be a possibility.

So, then, the Tübingen contribution to the debate regarding orthodoxy and heresy must be judged as minimal. Only in its general contention that first-century Christianity was diverse and that second-century orthodoxy represented a change of some sort from the first century has it left anything to the current debate. Its positive evaluation of the catholic developments align it more with the Eusebian viewpoint than with the anti-Eusebian thrust of Bauer's reconstruction.

2. Albrecht Ritschl

A powerful critic of the Tübingen understanding of the history of Christianity was found in Albrecht Ritschl. He dismissed the dialectic with which F.C. Baur had been so engaged; for Ritschl, there were only slight differences among the apostles. It was in the catholicism of the second and third centuries where Ritschl found "deviation" from apostolic ways of thinking.[35]

Unlike Baur, Ritschl believed that it was necessary to evaluate each stage in the process of Christian history. There was no natural and necessary character to development. Each stage was to be judged in terms of the normative message of Jesus.[36] As a

---

34. Hefner, "Baur Versus Ritschl," 273, with high words of praise for Baur's insights, saw the Tübingen commitment to the Hegelian dialectic overriding the commitment to the Reformation. Rather than catholicism being judged critically, it was viewed as proper in its place in the dialectical framework of history; Protestantism, coming later, and standing in tension with Roman Catholicism, was simply granted a higher place in the process.

35. Hefner's article, "Baur Versus Ritschl," is a useful discussion of fundamental differences between the two approaches.

36. This is the thesis of Ritschl in, *Die Entstehung der altkatholischen Kirche* (Bonn: Adolph Marcus, 1857). See Hefner, "Baur Verses Ritschl," 272.

committed Protestant, Ritschl found no obstacle in positing a discontinuity between apostolic Christianity and catholic Christianity.

In this lies firmer support for the substantial kind of criticism Walter Bauer brought against the second-century catholic thrust. Like Ritschl, Bauer dismissed the Tübingen dialectic that would have compelled him to modify his criticism of the catholic development. History, for both Ritschl and Bauer, could go wrong. Although Bauer did not emphasize a rediscovery of authentic Christianity in the Reformation, or a reestablishing of continuity broken by Catholicism, as Ritschl did, Bauer was like Ritschl in that both were capable nonetheless of a negative assessment of catholicism in a way the Tübingen school, bound by a view of the naturalness of development in history, was not.

Ritschl's contribution to the Bauer Thesis was, however, indirect. Ritschl had no agendum to defend heretics, as Bauer seemed to have; he had no drive to find radical diversity in the primitive movement, as Bauer had. But in providing a sustained critique of the novel Tübingen view of history, Ritschl retained for the historian the right to evaluate the flow of history, and to assess certain of its developments negatively. Had this right been lost to a Hegelian dialectic with its basically uncritical acceptance of the past developments in history, a thesis like that proposed by Bauer would have been, if not impossible, certainly less than likely.

3. Adolf Harnack

In many ways, shadows of the coming Bauer Thesis can be seen in the work of Adolf Harnack.[37] This is true, in spite of the fact that Bauer disagreed sharply with the perspective of his old teacher.[38]

---

37. For a general introduction to Harnack's thought, see L. Michael White, "Adolf Harnack and the 'Expansion' of Early Christianity: A Reappraisal of Social History," *SC* 5 (1985-6): 97-127.

38. Flora, "An Analysis of Bauer's Theory," 87, notes Bauer's general disregard for the perspective of Harnack, and he repeats a comment that Bauer was an antipode of Harnack, made by Wilhelm Schneemelcher, "Walter Bauer als Kirchenhistoriker," *NTS* 9 (1962-1963), 12-13. Flora (p. 83) believes that Bauer possibly presented a better interpretation of the evidence by following the Tübingen approach than that of Harnack.

Harnack's criticism of Catholicism, even early catholicism,[39] is not wholly unlike the explosive attack on second-century catholicism that marked Walter Bauer's work. And Harnack's positive, but not wholly uncritical, evaluation of the arch-heretic Marcion,[40] pointed to the coming concentrated defense of the heretics of the second century put forward by Bauer. Much of Harnack's criticism is shaped by his intense dislike for tradition. Given this dislike, the Roman Catholic church and the Eastern Orthodox church both came under Harnack's stinging criticism. Of the transformation to Greek Christianity, Harnack laments that there was no sadder spectacle of the Christian religion.[41] And of the "outward institution" of the Roman Catholic church, Harnack charges: "It is a case, not of distortion, but of total perversion."[42]

But besides Harnack's general dislike for tradition, which prevented him from being generous towards Roman and Greek orthodoxy, Harnack's view of history provided a basis from which such criticism became possible. Rejecting Hegel's positive view of the direction of history driven ever to new heights by an almost divinely guided dialectical process, Harnack was open to the possibility that the flow of history could be misdirected. People could make wrong decisions. Change need not be natural. It need not be necessary. It need not be good.[43] This evaluation of the historical process sets Harnack against Hegel and the Tübingen school, and whatever criticisms that might be levelled against Harnack's view,

---

39. Adolf Harnack, *What is Christianity?* trans. Thomas Bailey Saunders (New York: Harper & Brothers, 1957), 216, concludes that there can be justified criticism of the Old-Catholic Church, though the Gospel was not yet stifled there, as would later be the case.

40. Adolf Harnack, *Marcion: Das Evangelium vom fremden Gott* (Leipzig, 1921).

41. Harnack, *What is Christianity?* 238.

42. *Ibid.*, 262.

43. See Wilhelm Pauck, *The Heritage of the Reformation*, rev. ed. (Glencoe: Free Press, 1961), 340, says that Harnack did not believe in the continual process of history; there was, for Harnack, the possibility of a lapse into barbarianism. See, too, Henry, "Contemporary Scholarship," 124. Henry notes that under Hegel, change was natural and necessary and good, but for Harnack change did not always have these qualities, for as Harnack says, "No religion gains anything over time; it only loses." But that does not mean that Harnack was not open to the possibility of development: see Pauck, "Harnack's Interpretation of History," 348.

Harnack did possess the potential to evaluate the historical process in a way that the Tübingen school was not capable.

Some have charged that Harnack was too critical of the developments in Christianity. For example, H.E.W. Turner thought that Harnack did not seriously enough consider the possibility that Hellenism was more a veneer on Christianity than a dilution of it.[44] In other words, the change to catholicism (assumed to result from a Hellenistic environment) was one of outward form; it did not affect the essential character of the Christian religion. But whatever the case, it is not my concern here to defend Harnack's evaluation of particular movements in the historical process. I wish only to show that Harnack's rejection of the Hegelian dialectic is a necessary step before the kind of criticism raised by Walter Bauer is possible. At the heart of Bauer's work is the assumption that the successful movements of history are not necessarily the most authentic movements. Ritschl and Harnack are the powerful voices prior to Bauer that make this assumption a credible one. Hegel and the Tübingen School were too confident in the historical process for that kind of assumption to have been made by them.

4. History of Religions School

Positions even more extreme than Harnack's were being argued. Some historians even argued that there was no significant continuity between the New Testament and later orthodoxy.[45] The History of Religions School went even further, making a break between the teachings of Jesus and the interpretations provided by the earliest Christian communities, thus making credible the theory of early and radical theological diversity. Further, in finding the heart of Christianity in "religiousness," the History of Religions school provided a more ready openness to peripheral movements discarded as heretical by the early catholic community. All this hits at the heart of the Eusebian scheme, and much of it was brought over into Bauer's novel and influential reconstruction.

---

44. H.E.W. Turner, *The Pattern of Christian Truth: A Study in the Relations between Orthodoxy and Heresy in the Early Church*, Bampton Lectures 1954 (London: A.R. Mowbray & Co., 1954), 18-19.
45. *Ibid.,* 20.

5. Walter Bauer

Whatever changes in the way of viewing primitive Christianity that took place in the decades prior to Walter Bauer, little prepares us for the revolutionary view of primitive Christian history proposed by Bauer.

In spite of the changes brought to a study of early Christianity by the Tübingen school, and the corrections to that scheme proposed by men of an entirely different philosophy of history, it was Walter Bauer, in the first third of the twentieth century, who was working out the most significant contribution to the repudiation of the traditional view of the character of earliest Christianity. His *Rechtgläubigkeit und Ketzerei im ältesten Christentum* convinced many that the widely accepted view of early Christian history was without credible defense. Bauer was judged to have shown that theological diversity was reflected in the church from its earliest stages, and that the catholic church of the second and third centuries had no better claim to apostolic tradition than had various so-called heretical forms of Christianity.

The importance of Bauer's work in focusing the current debate concerning orthodoxy and heresy does not mean that the previous challenges from Harnack or the Tübingen School to the traditional reconstruction of church history were of little consequence; it simply means that it was Bauer's posing of the question that brought the full significance of early theological diversity to general recognition.

Whatever the influences behind Bauer—and doubtless they were many and varied—Bauer was a pioneer in his perception of the character of the early church. He is universally recognized, by both friend and foe (and there are many of both), as the person responsible for the radically new and explosive way of viewing the history of the early church. Words like "seminal,"[46] and "stimulating,"[47] were not uncommon in the reviews. G.T. Burke described Bauer's work as "one of the most influential monographs on

---

46. R.A. Markus, review of *Orthodoxy and Heresy in Earliest Christianity*, by Walter Bauer, *New Blackfriars* 54 (1973): 283.

47. F.W. Norris, "Asia Minor before Ignatius: Walter Bauer Reconsidered," in *SE* VII (1982): 365.

Christian origins to appear in this century."[48] R.A. Markus thought that, even forty years after the publication of Bauer's work, its importance was "far from exhausted."[49] James McCue, one of the most convincing critics of parts of Bauer's thesis, years after the publication, said that "the work remains one of the great pieces of undigested scholarship."[50] James Robinson described the work as "epochal";[51] Helmut Koester as "ingenious."[52] And Robert Wilken got at the heart of the matter when he said that Bauer created "a new paradigm."[53]

Although serious qualifications have been offered to specific parts of Bauer's work, Bauer's attack on the Eusebian view of early church history is generally accepted as valid, if not in details, certainly in its basic thrust. Markus, in his contribution of the McMaster project on Christian self-definition, stated that a project like the McMaster one was possible only as the Eusebian scheme broke down, and he credited Bauer's work with providing "the severe jolt that the notorious Eusebian scheme needed."[54] That judgment cannot be disputed, nor in this day would the attempt be made. Even Patrick Henry, who has some sympathy for the Eusebian scheme, agreed that the Eusebian scheme does not shape the scholar's view of primitive Christianity to the extent it once had. He said:

> In much current writing about Christian origins, the Fathers are no longer put on par with the heretics; they are put on the defensive, and it is assumed that the heretics are the true religious geniuses...The historian is not content to assure the heretics a fair hearing; the historian has become an advocate in their cause.[55]

---

48. G.T. Burke, "Walter Bauer and Celsus: The Shape of Late Second-Century Christianity," *SC* 4 (1984): 1.

49. Markus, Review, 283.

50. James McCue, "Orthodoxy and Heresy: Walter Bauer and the Valentinians," *VC* 33 (1979): 118.

51. Robinson, in James M. Robinson and Helmut Koester, *Trajectories through Early Christianity*, (Philadelphia: Fortress, 1971), 16.

52. Helmut Koester, *"Gnomai Diaphoroi:* The Origin and Nature of Diversification in the History of Early Christianity," *HTR* 58 (1965): 280.

53. Wilken, "Diversity and Unity in Early Christianity," *SC* 1 (1981): 103.

54. Markus, "The Problem of Self-Definition," 4.

55. Henry, "Contemporary Scholarship," 124-125.

Wilken, in reviewing the influence of Bauer's work, cited this passage from Henry. Of course, Henry was exaggerating, as Wilken pointed out. But Wilken, himself one of the translators of the English edition of Bauer's work, admitted that Henry had a point.[56]

Although Bauer's work is now over fifty years old, for a number of reasons it remains at the centre of the current discussion of the character of primitive Christianity. In part, the reason for the present prominent position of Bauer's work is a quirk of the publishing industry. Bauer's work was not translated into English until 1971. It is usually recognized that Bauer's thesis did not have an impact proportionate to its brilliance until this time, or perhaps a few years earlier, when, in 1964, the second German edition appeared.[57] Arnold Ehrhardt, in his own significant contribution to the debate published just two years earlier, had complained that Bauer's work had found "far too little of the attention it so richly deserved."[58] The next few years changed that. The second German edition was released, which Robert Wilken described as "the single most important factor in the study of early Christianity in the last generation in the United States."[59] (Wilken wrote that in 1981.) The English translation was completed by a number of recognized scholars of early church history: Achtemeier, Kraft, Krodel, O'Rourke, Wilken, to name some.[60] Seminars were organized to wrestle with the issues raised by Bauer. One such study group was held in Edinburgh, sparking the interest of James Dunn, whose work, *Unity and Diversity in the New Testament: An Inquiry into the Character of Earliest Christianity,*[61] has done much to

---

56. Wilken, "Diversity and Unity," 105.

57. *Ibid.,* 101-2. The history of the publication of Bauer's work runs thus: first German edition (1934); second German edition with added appendices by Georg Strecker (1964); and the English translation of the second German edition (1971).

58. Ehrhardt, "Apostles' Creed," 93.

59. Wilken, "Diversity and Unity," 101.

60. For a list of the eleven translators, see Bauer, *Orthodoxy and Heresy,* xviii.

61. James D.G. Dunn, *Unity and Diversity in the New Testament: An Inquiry into the Character of Earliest Christianity,* (Philadelphia: Westminster Press, 1977), xi.

disseminate, or at least to reinforce, Bauer's ideas, though that may not have been Dunn's intention.[62] I refer to these (the second German edition, the English translation, the recent seminars), and I cite from recent authors, to show that even today Bauer's work still bears directly on much of the debate.

But from the perspective of Bauer's publisher, Bauer's book was not a striking success. In fact, scholars interested in a reprinting of the work had to convince the publisher that copies of a new edition would not remain on the shelves of the stockroom for as long as had copies of the first edition.[63] After the first edition, Bauer himself had put aside his work on Christian origins, giving his attention to a new and time-consuming work, his lexicon of early Christian literature,[64] for which he became the more widely known. He did continue to think about the question of the character of primitive Christianity and made notes in the margin of his copy of *Rechtgläubigkeit und Ketzerei im ältesten Christentum*. These notes were used in the second edition, published four years after Bauer's death. But Bauer published nothing more on the theme of his classic work after the appearance of the first edition of *Rechtgläubigkeit und Ketzerei im ältesten Christentum*, except for a *précis* of his work in the same year.[65]

---

62. Dunn's emphasis on the unity, as well as the diversity, of the New Testament documents sets Dunn apart from Bauer, but it could be argued that Dunn's minimal common core of the traditions (i.e., the confession that Jesus is Lord) does not provide a common confession much different from that allowed by The Bauer Thesis, taken at its most extreme.

63. James M. Robinson, "Basic Shifts in German Theology," *Interpretation* 16 (1962): 77.

64. Walter Bauer, *Griechisch-Deutsches Wörterbuch zu den Schriften des Neuen Testaments und der übrigen urchristlichen Literatur*, known in the English world as *A Greek-English Lexicon of the New Testament and Other Early Christian Literature* (Chicago: The University of Chicago Press, 1952). The English translation was from the fourth German edition. A new English translation of the fifth German edition has been made. See Robinson, "Basic Shifts," 77 n. 1, for a comment on the history of the translation, and the failure of the English edition to give deserved credit to Bauer.

65. See Flora, "An Analysis of Bauer's Theory," 31-35, and Bauer, *Orthodoxy and Heresy*, xii. The précis appeared in *Forschungen und Fortschritten*, X (1934): 99-101, and was reprinted in a volume of collected writings: Walter Bauer, *Aufsätze und Kleine Schriften*, ed. Georg Strecker (Tübingen: J.C.B. Mohr [Paul Siebeck], 1967), 229-233.

What Bauer had put aside, others took up. Very little published on the character of primitive Christianity in the last few decades does not show the clear impact of Bauer's thesis,[66] though there is the rare learned exception.[67]

6. Helmut Koester

The man who stands above all others as one committed to the refinement and advancement of the Bauer Thesis is Helmut Koester. His writings include several articles that deal with the problem of heresy,[68] and he, along with James Robinson, published a collection of essays under the title of *Trajectories in Early Christianity*. In that work, an attempt was made to supply the Bauer Thesis with first-century support, something that Bauer had passed over.[69] More recently, Koester presented his massive

---

66. See Bauer, *Orthodoxy and Heresy*, appendix 2, "The Reception of the Book," for a list of those who favour Bauer's approach. Also, see Betz, "Orthodoxy and Heresy," 299-311; Daniel J. Harrington, "The Reception of Walter Bauer's *Orthodoxy and Heresy in Earliest Christianity* During the Last Decade," *HTR* 73 (1980): 289-293; Helmut Koester, "Häretiker im Urchristentum," *Die Religion in Geschichte und Gagenwart*, 3rd ed., (Tübingen: J.C.B. Mohr [Paul Siebeck], 1959), III.14-21; and F.W. Norris, "Ignatius, Polycarp, and I Clement: Walter Bauer Reconsidered," *VC* 30 (1976): 23, n. 1. Finally, in an article in which B. Drewery reviewed ten books relevant to our question, all published in 1970 or 1971 (the year of the publication of Bauer's *Orthodoxy and Heresy* in English), one can gain a capsule of the debate that has been shaped by Bauer's work [Drewery, "History and Doctrine: Heresy and Schism," *JEH* 23 (1972): 251-66.

67. Robin Lane Fox, *Pagans and Christians* (New York: Alfred A. Knopf, 1987), 276, says: "An older [sic] view that heretical types of Christianity arrived in many places before the orthodox faith has nothing in its favour, except perhaps in the one Syrian city of Edessa." This is probably the first time that Bauer's view has been called the "older" view. See also Peter Brown's review of Fox's *Pagans and Christians* under the title "Brave Old World," *The New York Review of Books* 34 (March 12, 1987): 24-7.

68. Helmut Koester, "*Gnomai Diaphoroi*," 279-319. This article has been reprinted in James M. Robinson and Helmut Koester, *Trajectories through Early Christianity* (Philadelphia: Fortress, 1971), 114-57. In this volume, a number of essays confront head-on the problem of orthodoxy and heresy. Also, Koester, "Häretiker im Urchristentum"; "The Theological Aspects of Primitive Christian Heresy," in *The Future of our Religious Past: Essays in Honour of Rudolf Bultmann*, ed. J.M. Robinson (London: SCM, 1971), 65-83.

69. See Georg Strecker, "On the Problem of Jewish Christianity," in Bauer (242/ET: 241). Also see n. 3 of this chapter.

Introduction to the New Testament,[70] and did so in terms that ideally suited the Bauer Thesis.[71] Koester's contribution, as the most significant and consistent support for this kind of reconstruction of early Christianity, will be considered throughout my work.

D. Directions for the Continuing Debate

Given the general acceptance of Bauer's critique of Eusebius and the widespread acceptance of Bauer's own reconstruction (however modified), it is clear that one must take Bauer's theory seriously today. And so I, in turning to the question of the character of primitive Christianity, turn, too, to the Bauer Thesis.

But my attention to the Bauer Thesis should not imply acceptance. I am convinced that Bauer's understanding of orthodoxy and heresy does not provide the kind of insight into the character of earliest Christianity that is widely attributed to it. Admittedly, Bauer must receive a considerable share of the credit for the attention now being focused on the character of primitive Christianity. And his concern that the heretics be heard as much as possible from their own perspectives[72] calls us to a more responsible evaluation of the various interpretations of the Christian message proclaimed in the early period. These are worthy contributions to our field.

But Bauer's work is limited at fundamental points. For one thing, it provides a serious challenge only to the Eusebian recon-

---

70. Koester, *Einfürung in das Neue Testament im Rahmen der Religions-geschichte und Kulturgeschichte der hellenistischen und römischen Zeit,* (Berlin and New York: Walter de Gruyter, 1980). The English edition, translated by Koester himself, appeared in two volumes under the general title: *Introduction to the New Testament* (Philadelphia: Fortress/Berlin and New York: Walter de Gruyter, 1982). It is vol. 2, *History and Literature of Early Christianity,* that is of particular importance to the discussion of orthodoxy and heresy.

71. Wayne Meeks, review of *Einfürung in das Neue Testament im Rahmen der Religionsgeschichte und Kulturgeschichte der hellenistischen und römischen Zeit,* by Helmut Koester, *JBL* 101 (1982): 446, says that Koester "is still working to reformulate the legacy of Walter Bauer."

72. As Bauer states in the second paragraph of his work (xxi). But one could wonder whether Bauer acted as an impartial judge of the heretics or as their vigorous advocate, a concern noted in the English edition of Bauer's work (p. 313, n. 29).

struction of early church history; it does not provide significant insights into the fundamental character of orthodoxy and heresy or of early Christianity. Too much credit is given to Bauer's work by the comment of Bultmann:

> Bauer has shown that that doctrine which in the end won out in the ancient church as the "right" or "orthodox" doctrine stands at the end of a development or, rather, is the result of a conflict among various shades of doctrine, and the heresy was not, as the ecclesiastical tradition holds, an apostasy, a degeneration, but was already present at the beginning—or, rather that by the triumph of a certain teaching as the "right doctrine" divergent teachings were condemned as heresy...[73]

Many scholars besides Bultmann have accepted Bauer's reconstruction and accepted, too, the assumption that the "antiquity" of heresy or the lack of uniformity in the proclamation of the Christian message in the first century is adequate cause to reject "orthodoxy" as a meaningful concept to describe any particular tendency of the first century. In other words, "orthodoxy" is, for many, merely a word that describes what comes out of the Rome-dominated drive towards theological uniformity in the second and third centuries; its application to the church of the first century is misplaced and reflects theological and polemical concerns, not historical reality. But such a conclusion requires more support than Bauer's work supplies. That work provides an adequate basis for no conclusion other than that early Christianity was diverse and that the Eusebian scheme is defective as history.

Two questions must be posed in regard to the Bauer Thesis. First, has that thesis demonstrated an adequate grasp of what diversity entails? In other words, can the mere discovery of early diversity bear the weight of the thesis built upon it? Second, has the Bauer Thesis really shown that heresies were not only early (as is certain) but strong as well (as is less clear)? That is required of the thesis. The early heresies must be strong; they must provide a significant challenge to the catholic movement—not in the mid-

---

73. Rudolf Bultmann, *Theology of the New Testament*, trans. K. Grobel (New York: Charles Scribner's Sons, 1955), 2.137.

second century, but considerably earlier.[74] It is my contention that the Bauer Thesis does not stand up well on either point.

First with regard to diversity. In light of the indisputable evidence for marked diversity in the early period, as long as the debate about orthodoxy and heresy defines its focus in terms of uniformity, the Bauer Thesis will appear to offer a coherent analysis of the history of the early church. There is, however, a problem with this view. Any theory that demands uniformity within the sphere of a credible orthodoxy cannot hope to offer a satisfactory reconstruction of the primitive Christian movement, for such a theory lacks sufficient sensitivity for the way in which diverse elements can be united into a noncontradictory unity.[75]

---

74. Bauer's thesis is that the heresies provided a valid (or at least credible) option for early Christians. But if the heresies had only a few adherents in the earliest period, one could question just how credible that option appeared to the early Christians. If we move to a later period (midsecond century) and there witness a large number of heretics but fail to find such representation for the earlier period, that would reflect a situation not unlike that contended by the orthodox churchmen of the second century. For them, heresy was a late arrival and had only recently come to appear credible to elements within the Christian church. Bauer's thesis is that orthodoxy, even in its early form, was not more credible (either in numbers or in undisputable apostolic connections) than other forms of the Christian message—forms that the orthodox element judged as heretical. In fact, Bauer makes the orthodox a minority throughout most of early Christianity.

75. I intend to address this issue in detail in a later volume. It seems to me that the fact of early diversity cannot be properly understood unless we have some sensitivity to the way that diverse groups draw lines of inclusion and exclusion. Difference does not always mean exclusion, though often it might. We would have a better appreciation of the relevance of early diversity to our problem of orthodoxy and heresy were we to investigate the early diversity in terms of what I suggest we call a "pool of acceptable diversity," for it is within such a pool that religious and ideological groups comfortably live (see chapter 2, n. 4). Related to this matter, see Brice L. Martin, "Some reflections on the unity of the New Testament," *SR* 8 (1979): 143-152. Martin accuses the German discussion about orthodoxy and heresy of having failed to recognize a middle position in diversities. Between the complementary (harmonizable) and the incompatible (contradictory), there is the noncomplementary but compatible position (pp. 150-1). Martin's work reflects various of the writings of Bernard J.F. Lonergan, whose insights need to be applied more often to our question. See too, I. Howard Marshall, "Orthodoxy and heresy," 5-14; and Brevard S. Childs, *The New Testament as Canon: An Introduction* (Philadelphia: Fortress, 1984), 29-30.

III. Terminology

Finding adequate and acceptable terminology is a problem in itself. Our terminology must not only be descriptive, it must be purely descriptive (i.e., neutral, nonpolemical, and free of prejudgments).

For many scholars, the terms "orthodoxy" and "heresy" fail on both points. They take the terms to be intrinsically polemical (and thus offensive); in their view, the terms assume an idealistic and historically inaccurate black-and-white distinction between sound and suspect belief (and thus are misleading). James D.G. Dunn, for example, argued that the terms "begged too many questions, are too emotive, provide categories that are far too rigid."[76]

While the terms "orthodoxy" and "heresy" are hardly above criticism, the terms suggested as replacements have provided no attractive alternative. Consider the terms Dunn offered. He chose "unity" and "diversity."[77] These terms certainly are more neutral, but they remove us further from the language of the early church (which may not be bad) and, perhaps, further from the concerns of the early church (which may not be good).

Another term that is often suggested is "centre."[78] But this is as loaded as is the term "orthodoxy." And it is as relative. What is conceived as the centre of the early Christian proclamation is a matter of some dispute, in itself, and even if scholars could come to some agreement on the issue, it is unlikely that they would have done justice to the way early Christians understood their movement.

In spite of the general discomfort with the words "orthodoxy" and "heresy," some scholars have maintained that this vocabulary can continue to be employed in the discussion of the character of early Christianity.[79] Perhaps a less loaded use of the terms is still

---

76. Dunn, *Unity and Diversity*, 5-6. See a discussion of the problem in Bauer, *Orthodoxy and Heresy*, 312-314.

77. *Ibid.*, 6.

78. Wilken, "Diversity and Unity," 105.

79. G. Clarke Chapman, Jr., "Some Theological Reflections on Walter Bauer's *Rechtgläubigkeit und Ketzerei im ältesten Christentum:* A Review Article," *JES* 7 (1970): 570-1, argues that the term "orthodoxy" remains a "defensible and necessary term, once it has been loosened from its Eusebian oversimplifications."

possible, as Bauer had thought.[80] I find that criticism of Bauer for his use of these terms is misdirected, for it is possible to qualify the use of these terms in such a way that they make sense from the perspective of the historian, without demanding the historian's submission to the theological implication of these terms from the perspective of the catholic church.

My proposed limitations are brief. "Orthodoxy" is to be used for those theological positions that came to be incorporated into the developing catholic church. "Heresy" is to be used for those theological positions that were excluded from the developing catholic church. In other words, whatever is judged by the catholic community to be true, that I call orthodox; whatever is judged by the catholic community to be false, that I call heretical. It is another matter whether these terms, as used historically, specify as well what beliefs are true and what beliefs are false from any perspective other than that of the early catholic community. As the editors of the second edition of Bauer's work have argued in a somewhat different context:

> [T]here *is* a strictly historical legacy left by Bauer—the obligation to ask each participant in the drama how he sees his role and how it relates to other participants. This is a descriptive task. Where it deals with evaluations, they are the evaluations of the participants in their own time and place, not of the investigator. The theological aspect is unavoidably present, but it concerns the "theology" of the participants, not of the investigator. If one *then* wishes to make theological judgments about the participants from his own modern perspective, or to derive from some of them theological principles to be applied today, or to trace back into an earlier period theological outlooks that are appealing today, or in some other way to join the theological to the historical approach, that is his business; but it is not an inevitable or necessary adjunct to the descriptive-historical task.[81]

Having failed to find useful terminology in what has been

He dismisses attempts to produce more objective terminology, such as "mainstream Christianity," "catholic tradition," and "the Great Church" as replacements for orthodoxy.

80. Bauer, *Orthodoxy and Heresy*, xxii-xxiii.
81. *Ibid.,* 312-313.

offered by others and not being convinced that the terms "orthodoxy" and "heresy" cannot be used in a purely historical investigation of the character of primitive Christianity, I propose to use these terms in such a way that the theological question is left unaddressed.[82] I recognize that the theological question was a primary one for the groups I am studying, and I recognize that my use of the terms reflects how these terms would have been used by one group, in particular, and not by others. Such a use of these terms will not satisfy some readers. It is my contention that widespread agreement on terminology is not likely to be reached until the end of the debate. If my impression is correct, we are but in the middle of it.

IV. Summary

Finally, we cannot address the issue of orthodoxy and heresy without becoming aware of the theological question that lies at its roots. Raymond Brown pointed to:

> an increasing chorus of objections that Bauer's hypothesis...leaves unanswered fundamental questions. For instance, was what emerged from the diversities by "winning out" more faithful to what Jesus of Nazareth taught and represented than were the Christian views that lost the struggle?[83]

Although Brown's statement is laden with qualifications (each of which is probably necessary), his point cannot easily be set aside. The theological question remains. The Bauer Thesis has not been able to dismiss it.

---

82. McCue, "Walter Bauer and the Valentinians," 119 n. 4, discusses his use of the terms "orthodoxy" and "heresy." He recognizes that the terms, as commonly used, are judgmental, and he limits his own use of the terms to the way that Bauer tried to limit the terms, and as I have proposed for my own work. McCue says: " Like Bauer, I wish to abstain from the judgments implied, but fear that to introduce an alternative and more neutral-sounding vocabulary will simply confuse matters."

83. Raymond E. Brown, *The Epistles of John*, AB 30 (Garden City: Doubleday, 1982/London: Geoffrey Chapman, 1983), 55.

But it is not the theological question that I address in this work. I am concerned here with a purely historical question. It is this. Were the movements that were judged as heretical by the early catholic community both early and strong, as the Bauer Thesis requires? An answer to that question may have serious implications to the theological question, but it is not my intention here to address these implications, crucial as I judge them to be. I am, however, in full sympathy with the warning from Robert Wilken:

> If the net effect of Bauer's book has been to spawn a generation of scholars who are disinterested in [the theological] question or even embarrassed by it, his inheritance will be sad indeed.[84]

With this conclusion, a number of scholars consent.[85] This takes the debate well beyond Bauer's work.

---

84. Wilken, "Diversity and Unity," 106.

85. Chapman, "Theological Reflections," 571, puts forward a good case for keeping the theological question at the centre of the debate. He says that the theological question is "not only feasible, but unavoidable." Also see Betz, "Orthodoxy and Heresy," 311. And Harrington, "Reception," 298, offers a sound critique of the Bauer Thesis, saying that there is "still need to explore the theological significance of orthodoxy's eventual triumph...Bauer's own description ('a curious quirk of history') is hardly adequate."

Chapter Two

Geographical Areas
and Theological Diversity

I. The Attention to Geography

The traditional view of early Christianity—blind to obvious diversity—insisted on thinking only in terms of a monolithic first-century church. Over the past century and a half, that view has deservedly suffered injury from which it cannot recover. In the initial deadly thrust, Ferdinand Christian Baur and the Tübingen school argued that the uniformity once assumed to have been the character of the primitive church was actually a compromise achieved in the second century between two formerly warring parties, one favouring the conservative Jewish sympathies of James (and Peter) and the other favouring the liberal thrust to the gentiles by Paul.[1]

Various refinements were made to the Tübingen theory. Baur's observation that there was a division in first-century Christianity was, upon closer examination, altered, so that considerable division

---

1. A brief discussion of the work of F.C. Baur has been provided in Werner Georg Kümmel, *The New Testament: The History of the Investigation of Its Problems*, trans. S. McLean Gilmour and Howard C. Kee (Nashville/New York: Abingdon, 1972), 126-143. Also see Peter C. Hodgson, "The Rediscovery of Ferdinand Christian Baur: A Review of the First Two Volumes of his *Ausgewälte Werke*," *CH* 33 (1964): 206-214.

even within these two primary divisions was posited.[2] No longer could one speak simply of Jewish Christianity and Pauline Christianity—and even less of New Testament Christianity—one spoke now of the theologies of numerous distinct parties. With only slight exaggeration, one could charge that scholarship had begun so to divide primitive Christianity that each first-century church leader had his own movement and each first-century document its own devotees. Raymond Brown's recent work, *The Churches the Apostles Left Behind,* reflects this tendency. In this work, Brown identifies seven distinct theological communities in the last third of the first century—three of them Pauline![3]

Such fragmentation of primitive Christianity (or of any movement) is perhaps extreme and is considerably more likely to reflect not the coherent self-understanding of individual communities but the overly microscopic analysis of documents that stem from a complex and dynamic movement.[4] Brown himself admits the "serious methodological problem" in the attempt to identify distinct theological communities in the primitive church: the historian is forced to reconstruct the communities solely from isolated documentary evidence, and this raises the question whether the theological perspective of a document is peculiar to the author or is

---

2. Kümmel, *History of Investigation,* 162-184. Also see Philip Hefner, "Baur Versus Ritschl on Early Christianity," *CH* 31 (1962): 259-278.

3. Raymond E. Brown, *The Churches the Apostles Left Behind,* (New York/ Ramsey: Paulist, 1984), 19-30.

4. A key question is the self-understanding of the primitive Christian community itself. We do not get at the heart of the significance of early Christian diversity until we understand how the early Christians themselves viewed this diversity. The fundamental question that needs to be considered is this: did the early Christians identify as diversity everything the modern critical scholar has judged as diverse? In other words, is the same sense of contradiction or opposition shared by the primitive community and the modern scholar? It is my contention that the proper perspective from which to evaluate early Christian diversity is one that is sensitive to the kinds of distinctions the early Christian groups would have, themselves, found intelligible. Groups seem to exist in what I would call a "pool of acceptable diversity." It is this pool that defines for them the limits of their "friendly" or "kindred" world. That is to say: groups generally are not uncomfortable and intolerant towards all diversity. Some diversity is tolerated; other diversity is not. Mere identification of differences is but a preliminary step in the evaluation of the diversity of the early Christian movement, and it is a far step from the heart of the primitive church's own understanding.

characteristic of a clearly defined community.[5] Frederik Wisse offers a similar warning.[6]

Walter Bauer is chiefly responsible for a different approach to the problem, shifting the investigation of diversity away from microscopic analysis of documents and imaginative invention of distinct communities to a less fragmenting approach.[7] This was done unintentionally, it seems, by Bauer's calling attention, not mainly to documents, but to geographical areas.[8] Bauer seems to have worked with the assumption that in most major geographical areas a large element of the Christian church there would have held a uniform belief, though not necessarily the same belief as that held by

---

5. Brown, *Churches,* 29-30. In another work, in which Brown was discussing the opponents reflected in the Johannine letters, Brown said: "It seems an appropriate occasion to apply 'Ockham's rasor': Postulated entities should not be multiplied without necessity" [Brown, *The Epistles of John,* AB 30 (Garden City: Doubleday, 1982/London: Geoffrey Chapman, 1983), 50]. One wonders whether Brown employed Ockham's razor with sufficient rigour in his reconstruction of early Christian diversity.

6. Frederik Wisse, "The Use of Early Christian Literature as Evidence for Inner Diversity and Conflict," in *Nag Hammadi, Gnosticism, and Early Christianity,* ed. Charles W. Hedrick and Robert Hodgson, Jr. (Peabody: Hendrickson, 1986), 181, is worthy of extensive quote. Speaking of the problem of analyzing early Christian literature, Wisse says: "...one may not assume that the views advocated in these writings reflect the beliefs and practices of a distinct group. There are, of course, documents commissioned by a larger group which represent community views. These, however, are relatively rare and the reader is normally informed of the special background of the document. If these clues are absent from the texts the burden rests upon the historian to give sufficient reasons as to why the text in question ought to be taken as representative of a larger group or faction. In practice this means that one must show compelling reasons as to why the author reflects in the writing the beliefs and practices of a wider community."

7. Brown, *Churches,* 18-19, credits Kirsopp Lake with a different reconstruction of the early period. Lake concentrated on city centres, contending that a volatile Ephesus and a conservative Rome were the two major centres of early Christianity [Lake, *Landmarks in the History of Early Christianity* (London: Macmillan, 1920)]. Bauer's concentration on geographical areas is similar enough to Lake's concentration on cities to put them in the same camp. Frederick W. Norris, "Ignatius, Polycarp, and I Clement: Walter Bauer Reconsidered," *VC* 30 (1976): 37, thinks that the geographical presentation is one of the strong points of Bauer's work, and Robert L. Wilken, "Diversity and Unity in Early Christianity," *SC* 1 (1981): 104, notes that as a result of Bauer's work, we are inclined to think in terms of distinct geographical areas.

8. Bauer dealt with large geographical areas: Egypt, Syria, western Asia Minor, and even when he spoke of particular cities (e.g. Edessa, Corinth, Rome), he had in mind the larger area of which that city was a centre.

Christian groups in other geographical areas.

Bauer's concentration on distinct geographical areas provided us with two things: first, with a new way to investigate the character of primitive Christianity; and second, with a basis for assigning particular documents to particular locales. Our conclusion that a document is Syrian, for example, often depends solely on the assumption that there is such a thing as an identifiable Syrian Christianity. Take the Gospel of Matthew. Few would argue that this gospel was not from Antioch or Syria.[9] Why? Because we believe we know what kind of Christianity was dominant in this area.[10] The underlying assumption, perhaps not yet adequately tested, is that the churches in distinct geographical areas would have developed distinct theologies even in the early period.

This shift in our understanding of diversity is in some ways reflected in the difference between previous introductions to the New Testament that were divided into an examination of various theological groups (Johannine, Hellenist, etc.) and the approach by Helmut Koester, a confessed devotee of Bauer, who made his divisions along the lines of geography.[11] Whether this will be the beginning of a trend is difficult to say, but it is almost certain that no work in the future will dare neglect geographical distinctions entirely.

In spite of this new attention to geography, it is not my intention here to work out the various geographical areas that have their own distinctive interpretation of the Christian message. Several problems must be faced by any who would attempt this. First, few of the areas have substantial literature from the early period, and the justification for assigning some of the literature to particular areas

---

9. For a recent reconstruction that places Matthew in the situation of the late first-century church of Antioch, see John P. Meier, "Antioch," Part One, in Raymond E. Brown and John P. Meier, *Antioch & Rome: New Testament Cradles of Catholic Christianity* (New York/Ramsey: Paulist, 1983).

10. There are other reasons, too, that are put forward to support the Syrian locale for the composition of Matthew. One of the main ones is that Ignatius, bishop of Antioch, is the earliest witness to the Gospel of Matthew. See W.G. Kümmel, *Introduction to the New Testament,* (Nashville and New York: Abingdon, 1975), 119.

11. Helmut Koester, *Introduction to the New Testament,* vol. 2 (Philadelphia: Fortress, 1982).

depends in advance on a conclusion about the character of Christianity in that area. (Colin H. Roberts' warning in this regard is well worth consideration.[12]) Further, a case can be made for considerable movement of Christians in the early period, and rigid geographical boundaries can be credibly assumed only where isolation can be demonstrated (perhaps in the case of Samaria, and maybe of Phrygia). In fact, it might be argued that any major centre would have had numerous house-church communities, each reflecting one part of the fully represented spectrum of the theological options available to early Christians.[13] These matters are still quite debatable.

What I wish to do here, amidst the unsettled state of this question, is to determine which geographical areas appear potentially the most rewarding for our questions about orthodoxy and heresy. This is in line with Bauer's structuring of his investigation. I do differ with Bauer, however, in regard to which areas I judge to be potentially fruitful areas of investigation, given the present state of our knowledge of early Christianity. And further, unlike Bauer seems to have done, I make no assumption that a particular form of Christianity will dominate any particular area.

---

12. Colin H. Roberts, *Manuscript, Society, and Belief in Early Christian Egypt*, The Schweich Lectures of the British Academy for 1977 (London: Oxford University Press, 1979), 53-54.

13. One factor that may alter the assumption that distinct theological forms dominated particular geographical areas is the house church. If the house church was the primary structure for regular corporate worship, the whole spectrum of early Christian diversity may have been represented somewhat equally in many areas. Perhaps distinct theological forms can be safely attributed only to *isolated* groups, and then not to geographically isolated groups but only to groups ethnically isolated. In other words, it might be more safe to speak of a distinct Edessan form of Christianity than of a distinct Antiochene form, and more safe to speak of a Phrygian form than of an Ephesian form. These matters are still unsettled. See Brown's comment in *Churches*, 23. James F. McCue, "Orthodoxy and Heresy: Walter Bauer and the Valentinians," *VC* 33 (1979): 124, cautions against exaggerating the importance of geographical differences, for churchmen seemed to have travelled extensively.

II. Chief Geographical Areas of Early Christianity
A. Primary Areas

Several areas have been judged to be distinctive and significant in early Christian history. Although we frequently speak of cities in this regard rather than of larger political units, the idea is the same, for in most areas the church in the major city seems to have dominated the other churches.[14] Thus we could speak of Jerusalem, Antioch, Edessa, Ephesus and Rome without overlooking any significant, novel interpretation of the Christian message distinctive to a surrounding area. Of Alexandria, we might wish to limit its influence somewhat and allow for a fairly independent, and perhaps markedly different, Egyptian Christianity too.[15] And we might wish to add a Samaritan and Galilean Christianity apart from Jerusalem (which is perhaps more justified for Samaria than for Galilee).[16] As well, a distinction between Roman and Latin Christianity can be credibly argued.[17] The form of Christianity in Achaia and Macedonia is more difficult to assign to a particular dominant city; the situation there would not necessarily follow the pattern of other areas. Nonetheless, for the most part, we can direct our attention to key cities.

---

14. Cities were the centres of Greek culture and Roman law throughout the empire. Greek cities had been established throughout the eastern Mediterranean area, and the Romans, as their empire grew, established their own colonies in the east too (Corinth and Philippi are examples). The countryside may not have been significantly influenced by the Greek and Roman element. See Chester G. Starr, *The Roman Empire: 27 B.C. - A.D. 476* (New York: Oxford University Press, 1982), 91-108. The distinction between city and country from the perspective of studies of early Christianity is reflected in Wayne A. Meeks, *The First Urban Christians*, (Philadelphia: Fortress, 1983), 14-6.

15. See Alan L. Bowman, *Egypt after the Pharohs: 332 B.C.-A.D. 642*, (Berkeley: The University of California Press, 1986), 122-129. Bowman does not find extensive Coptic Christian literature until about A.D. 300 (p. 129). This probably indicates that Christianity was confined to the Jews and Greeks in the early period, though it is not inconceivable that a distinctive nonliterary native Egyptian Christianity did exist earlier. Without literary remains, evidence for the existence of such a group would be slim. Roberts, *Manuscript, Society, and Belief,* 65-9, argues for a late mission of the gnostics to the Coptic peoples. (An earlier Coptic church of *catholic* character would not affect my thesis.)

16. At least for Samaria there was a long-standing separation between its population and the Jews. The Christian church in Samaria may have found it neither possible nor desirable to join with a Jerusalem-controlled church that, at times at least, reflected the more conservative side of first-century Judaism.

B. Bauer's Selection

Bauer investigated several areas in his study of orthodoxy and heresy. In my examination of this question here, which I present in dialogue with Bauer's work, I have limited my investigation to the area of western Asia Minor. This calls for explanation.

First, I will state briefly a number of general objections to the selection of areas made by Bauer for his investigation of the questions of orthodoxy and heresy. Then, in some detail, I will offer more specific reasons for my contention that several of the areas cannot provide the kind of data we need in order to confront the primary questions seriously. Finally, I will argue that no area is even remotely comparable to Ephesus and western Asia Minor as potentially fruitful areas to which to address the questions of the orthodoxy/heresy debate.

Two criteria are required before an area can be considered of fundamental importance to the question of orthodoxy and heresy. First, it must have extensive literature associated with its early period; second, that literature must have the question of heresy as one of its primary concerns. Our focus on the literary material is inescapable, for we have no other access but a documentary one to the church in its earliest period. And, disturbing for the historian, the documentary evidence, at its best, has significant gaps. Of some areas, there remains nothing from the earliest period. Even where documents exist for the early period, the question of orthodoxy and heresy is often not addressed, or not addressed in a useful way. Given this state of affairs, the attractive area upon which to conduct

---

Wayne Meeks, "Galilee and Judea in the Fourth Gospel," *JBL* 85 (1966): 169, believes there may be some substance to the 1936 thesis of Ernst Lohmeyer, *Galiläa und Jerusalem,* that Galilee was, along with Jerusalem, the centre for early Christianity. Meeks links the Galilean and Samaritan communities together into a Christian community that might explain what he calls the "Johannine puzzle" (p. 169). Cf. Martin Hengel, *Acts and the History of Earliest Christianity,* trans. John Bowden (London: SCM/Philadelphia: Fortress, 1979), 76, who notes that neither Paul nor Luke indicates that Galilee played any significant role.

17. Roman Christianity is not Latin Christianity until late. Tertullian was the first Latin writer of note, and Carthage, perhaps, was the real centre of Latin Christianity, a position argued by Helmut Koester, "The Intention and Scope of Trajectories," in Robinson and Koester, *Trajectories through Early Christianity* (Philadelphia: Fortress, 1971), 275-6.

our investigation will be that area for which documentary evidence is not only extensive but also relevant to the question of orthodoxy and heresy.

Bauer's selection is not satisfactory in light of these criteria. For one thing, the two areas Bauer discussed in greatest detail (Egypt and Edessa) were not, even on a fairly generous reading of the evidence, primary centres of the early church, and even if they had been, early literature from these areas is too scarce to provide anything more than muted testimony to the character of the earliest Christianity there.[18] This lack of unambiguous witness to the character of Christianity in these areas should caution against supposedly certain and comprehensive reconstructions of Christianity there. If there is a growing consensus, for example, that early Christianity in Egypt was gnostic and in Edessa heretical of an uncertain character, it is cause for some lament, for such a consensus comes about by a too ready acceptance of a reconstruction as certain when the evidence can promise nothing more than something considerably speculative. I would thus caution against high expectations that an investigation of either Egypt or Edessa will offer significant insights into the character of earliest Christianity. Perhaps in time we shall have less debatable evidence with which to do our reconstructions. At present, however, we must look for less obscure areas to which to address our questions, or, should we decide to concentrate our investigation on Edessa or Egypt, we ought to admit openly that a reliable reconstruction of earliest Christianity in these areas is yet for the future.

Besides Egypt and Edessa, several other centres are judged by scholars to commend themselves as areas for potential insight into the character of primitive Christianity. They are the cities of Jerusalem, Antioch, Ephesus, Corinth and Rome. Of these five cities, Bauer discussed four. He did not discuss Jerusalem, and for

---

18. Bauer himself found almost no material from Edessa, and he recognized the situation was not much different for Egypt. He began his chapter on the church in Egypt with a quote from Harnack, in which Harnack called attention to the "most serious gap in our knowledge of primitive church history," that is, "our almost total ignorance of the history of Christianity in Alexandria and Egypt...until about the year 180..." (49/ET:44).

this he was faulted by Georg Strecker, the editor of the second German edition of Bauer's work. Strecker thought that Jerusalem (or Jewish Christianity) was the most convincing example in support of Bauer's thesis, and he wondered why Bauer had not realized this.[19]

With regard to the key cities Bauer did discuss, fundamental problems are present. Of Antioch, Bauer's investigation is considerably more disjointed than his work on any other major area.[20] Of Rome, Bauer's work has been faulted for being one-sided and extreme.[21] Bauer's discussion of Corinth depends on a peculiar, though not necessarily undefensible, reading of an ambiguous document known as *1 Clement.* Only for western Asia Minor is the case different. For this area, Bauer's work is less disjointed than it was for Antioch; it is less one-sided and extreme than it was for Rome; and Bauer has provided us with two detailed chapters (one chapter, admittedly, covers an area from Antioch to

---

19. Georg Strecker, "On the Problem of Jewish Christianity," in Bauer, *Orthodoxy and Heresy in Earliest Christianity,* 242/ET:241.

20. Bauer uses the letters of Ignatius as evidence for the situation in the church at Antioch (65-71/ET:61-67). Bauer's proof that the majority in Antioch were heretical is not based on a rigorous analysis of the situation in Antioch; rather, it is based on his theory that the group that presses for a monarchical office will be in the minority (66-7/ET:62-3). That puts the orthodox Ignatius, as promoter of the monarchical office, in the minority position. But as I will demonstrate in chapter five of this work, such a theory as that proposed by Bauer is not credible. If I am correct on that point, that will leave Bauer's reconstruction of the situation in Antioch without support. The other scant references by Bauer to the situation in Antioch does not change that situation (see in particular 112-4/ET:108-110). Bauer's claim that a significant gnostic movement could be found in Antioch prior to Ignatius needs the sober observations of someone like John P. Meier, who, in *Antioch and Rome: New Testament Cradles of Catholic Christianity,* by Raymond E. Brown and John P. Meier (New York/Ramsey: Paulist Press, 1983), 45, n. 104, appealed to the lack of interest in gnosticism by the author of the Gospel of Matthew to argue that the rise of gnosticism should be dated around A.D. 100, not earlier. Meier can then account for Ignatius's clear concern to refute a gnostic message. Although I do not agree with all of Meier's reconstruction, I find his point about Matthew convincing enough to contend that gnosticism is the new man on the block, and is much more likely to be a troublesome minority at the time of Ignatius than the dominating majority some scholars contend it was.

21. Arnold Ehrhardt, a sympathetic and generally agreeable critic of Bauer's work, disagrees with Bauer's reconstruction of early Christianity in Rome· "Christianity Before the Apostles' Creed," *HTR* 55 (1962): 108-119.

Greece, but the substantial part is relevant to the situation in western Asia Minor). Fortunately, it is this area that appears to provide the most fertile ground for our primary question. As such, it opens the way for dialogue with Bauer.

We have before us, then, a number of areas that have been investigated, and continue to be investigated, in the attempt to better understand the character of primitive Christianity. In a study such as mine, one could either attempt to examine each of these several centres, or one could select the centre most likely to yield the surest results and exclude the other areas from detailed investigation. I have chosen the latter route, concentrating my investigation on the area of Ephesus and western Asia Minor for two reasons. First, of the various areas, only the Ephesus area seems to offer the extensive kind of material we need for our study. (I say this fully aware of the trend in some recent studies to concentrate particularly on Antioch and Rome, sometimes at the expense of Ephesus.[22]) Second, with that trend to concentrate on Antioch and Rome, the significant contribution to the development of Christianity that has been provided by western Asia Minor is often forgotten. This is perhaps especially so in regard to the substantial contribution of Ephesus in working out clear boundaries between adequate and suspect belief. My examination of Ephesus and western Asia Minor is intended to commend this area as one yet deserving of considerable attention.

My choice of the area is, primarily, a practical one—the issues I wish to consider are more likely to be resolved from an examination of Ephesus than of any of the other significant centres of Christianity. An additional but secondary gain from this study will be that a neglected centre of the early church will be given some recognition for its significant contributions to what has been generally known as "orthodoxy."

The importance of Ephesus will become clear as this study proceeds. At this point, however, it is necessary to discuss in detail the problems that make the other centres less attractive for a resolution of our question. My purpose here is not to provide a comprehensive review of early Christianity in the various areas of

---

22. See chapter 3 §I.B.

the Christian mission; I wish only to show that the available witness to the form of Christianity in these areas is either mute, or that the reconstructions of early Christianity in these areas are unconvincing. Nothing more than that is attempted.

III. Edessa

A. Bauer's Position

Of the various areas examined by Bauer, the case for Edessa was provided with the most sustained argument: almost forty percent of the pages devoted to an examination of particular areas dealt with Edessa. Unfortunately, of all the areas Bauer considered, his investigation of Edessa was based on the least literary evidence, spanning three hundred years of obscurity unmatched by any other area.[23] Although most scholars have rejected the details of Bauer's conclusion about the origin of Christianity in Edessa, surprisingly, even the most resolute critics of Bauer's thesis seem prepared to recognize the nonorthodox character of earliest Christianity in that area, disagreeing with Bauer only in regard to what precisely that unorthodox form of Christianity was.[24]

---

23. Along with the works that will be discussed in this section, for a brief introduction to the church in Edessa, see W. Stewart McCullough, *A Short History of Syriac Christianity to the Rise of Islam*, (Chico, CA: Scholars Press, 1982), 3-35. H.J.W. Drijvers, *Cults and Beliefs at Edessa* (Leiden: E.J. Brill, 1980), 193, says that the earliest history of the church in Edessa is practically unknown. Not until Bardesanes can much be said with confidence. H.E.W. Turner, *The Pattern of Christian Truth: A Study in the Relations between Orthodoxy and Heresy in the Early Church*, Bampton Lectures 1954 (London: A.R. Mowbray & Co., 1954), 41, says of the early history of the church in Edessa: "we know nothing and can conjecture little more."

24. Most scholars disagree with Bauer only in rejecting Marcionism as the earliest form of Christianity in Edessa. R.A. Markus, review of *Orthodoxy and Heresy in Earliest Christianity*, by Walter Bauer, *New Blackfriars* 54 (1973): 284, said that Bauer's "account of early Christianity particularly in Edessa and Egypt has had a rough passage." I think that it deserves rough passage; I am not sure that it has had it. Granted, Bauer's reconstruction has been qualified by others, but the general view seems to be that earliest Christianity in Edessa was heretical, or if not clearly heretical, at least suspiciously so. Even Bauer's staunchest critic, H.E.W. Turner, *Christian Truth*, 45, admitted that the Christianity around Edessa was more heretical than were the churches around the Mediterranean. Helmut Koester, with whose work I shall often be in dialogue here, also qualifies Bauer's

Bauer argued that the earliest form of Christianity in Edessa was that of Marcionism (27/ET:22). He based his conclusion on two things. First, he could not find convincing evidence for a pre-Marcionite Christianity in Edessa. (Bauer found it easy enough to dismiss as legendary the later traditions "preserved" by the orthodox church of the fourth century that Thaddaeus had arrived in Edessa with orthodox Christianity in the thirties of the first century.[25])

---

reconstruction of Edessa, but his own reconstruction is clearly born from Bauer's approach to the question of orthodoxy and heresy, and it provides for early Edessa a form of Christianity hardly more orthodox than that of Bauer's reconstruction (see § III.B of this chapter, "Koester's Position.") So too with Arnold Ehrhardt, "Christianity before the Apostles' Creed," *HTR* 55 (1962): 94-95. Although he dismisses details of Bauer's reconstruction (specifically Marcionism as the earliest form of Christianity in Edessa), he is clearly under the spell of Bauer's thesis–whatever that does to his claim to be still under the spell of F.C. Burkitt's work on Eastern Christianity (p. 94). Jaroslav Pelikan, "The Two Sees of Peter: Reflections on the Pace of Normative Self-Definition East and West," in *JCSD* 1: 71-2, accepts the heretical character of earliest Christianity in Edessa, though he seems to place a Bardesanean form of Valentinian gnosticism prior to Marcionism in Edessa. That raises two questions: first, how gnostic was Bardesanes; and two, does Valentinian gnosticism seek an orthodox community with which to dialogue, just as the Marcionites seem to have? More caution to Bauer's general reconstruction of Christianity in Edessa is expressed by L.W. Barnard, "The Origins and Emergence of the Church in Edessa during the First Two Centuries A.D.," *VC* 22 (1968): 175. Barnard, after careful study of early Christianity in Edessa, concluded that, in spite of the Christianity there being "strongly influenced by an early Jewish-Christian Gospel tradition," it does not, however, "revolutionize the history of the early Church." So, too, Stephen Gero "With Walter Bauer on the Tigris: Encratite Orthodoxy and Libertine Heresy in Syro-Mesopotamian Christianity," in *Nag Hammadi, Gnosticism, and Early Christianity*, ed. Charles W. Hedrick and Robert Hodgson, Jr. (Peabody: Hendrickson, 1986), 289-92.

25. Bauer, in *Orthodoxy and Heresy,* gave almost all of chapter one to a dismissal of the orthodox traditions of the Edessan area. Certainly the Abgar legend is suspicious enough, as is some of the other traditions from the area. It is not my intention here to examine in detail Bauer's reconstruction of early Christianity in Edessa. I will discuss what I judge to be a major flaw in his conclusion that Marcionism was the first form of Christianity in the area. I leave to others an examination of the Edessan area and a critique of Bauer's work on this point. The most substantial is that of Turner, *Christian Truth,* 40-46. L.W. Barnard, "Origins of Church in Edessa," *VC* 22 (1968): 161-175, also challenges Bauer's reconstruction. Han J.W. Drijvers has offered the most detailed recent discussion of Christianity in Edessa. See: "Jews and Christians at Edessa," *JJS* 36 (1985): 88-102; "Facts and Problems in Early Syriac-Speaking Christianity," *SC* 2 (1982): 157-175; and *Cults and Beliefs at Edessa.* On Edessa, see also J.B. Segal, "When did Christianity come to Edessa?" in *Middle East Studies and Libraries: A Felicitation Volume for Professor J.D. Pearson,* ed. B.C. Bloomfield (London:

Second, Bauer was impressed with the application of the name "Christian" to the Marcionites, while the orthodox community, much to their dislike, was called "Palutian." According to Bauer, had the orthodox been the earliest, they would have lain claim to the name "Christian" for themselves; in that they are not called by the name "Christian" but wished to be, some other group must have beaten them to Edessa, identifying themselves there as "Christian" before the orthodox had arrived.[26]

But Bauer's thesis for Edessa does have its problems, in spite of the justifiable dismissal of the orthodox traditions. The main problem is this: if we say that the earliest form of Christianity in Edessa was Marcionism, we are forced to account for at least a century during which Edessa had no Christian witness, for though Marcionism appears to have spread with surprising speed,[27] it seems unlikely that it would have reached Edessa before A.D. 150, since Marcion was not excommunicated in Rome until A.D. 144.[28] Is it possible to argue that no Christian church was established in Edessa before this?

This raises a further question. Was Edessa likely to have been isolated for so long from the Christian mission, which was spreading rapidly throughout the Roman empire? The evidence is conflicting. First, in support of Bauer's thesis: Edessa did not permanently become part of the Roman empire until A.D. 216.[29] This might have kept the area around Edessa more isolated from

---

Mansell, 1980), 179-191.

26. Bauer, *Orthodoxy and Heresy,* 26-29/ET:21-24. Turner, *Christian Truth,* 43, noted a textual problem with the name "Palut." This does not solve the problem; it merely complicates it even more, though that is not to dismiss Turner's observation.

27. Justin, *First Apology,* XXVI, LVIII, speaks of Marcion as someone who has gained a disturbing number of converts. This would have been about A.D. 165.

28. It is possible to question the traditional dating scheme for Marcion, as was done by R. Joseph Hoffmann, *Marcion: On the Restitution of Christianity. An Essay on the Development of Radical Paulinist Theology in the Second Century,* AAR Academy Series 46 (Chico, CA.: Scholars Press, 1984), 44-74. Hoffmann found no reason to date the beginning of the activity of Marcion later than A.D. 110 or 120. For a response to Hoffmann, see G. May, "Ein neues Markionbild?" *TheolRund* 51 (1986): 404-13.

29. Edessa had fallen briefly to Trajan in A.D. 114.

Christian missionaries than would have been the case had Edessa
been a part of the Roman empire earlier. J.B. Segal has argued for
the isolation of Edessa from early Christian influences,[30] as had
F.C. Burkitt some years earlier.[31]

But against Bauer's thesis and against the contention that Edessa
was isolated, the following points deserve consideration. Although
Edessa was not part of the Roman empire at the beginning of the
Christian church, it was, as a city on a major trade route in a
bordering state, not isolated from the Roman empire—a point that
has been made repeatedly by Han Drijvers.[32] Further, a substantial
Jewish community existed there,[33] and it is unlikely that this
community would not have had good links to Antioch. (Antioch
was the largest Jewish centre in the area and was only about two
hundred and fifty miles away, compared to Jerusalem, which was
about three times that distance). Even good links to Jerusalem
would have been possible. If the Jews of Edessa had links to the
Jewish communities of Antioch, and perhaps of Jerusalem, it is
hardly likely that they were not introduced to Christianity during a
century of close, if not friendly, contact between Jews and
Christians in most of the major cities of the Roman world.

But whatever the case for Edessan contact with Christianity prior
to the middle of the second century, the case for Marcionite
Christianity as the original form of Christianity in Edessa must be
dismissed. In fact, if there was a rapid growth of Marcionism in
this area, that may, in itself, demand the presence of a more catholic
form of Christianity in Edessa before the arrival of Marcionism.
The problem with positing Marcionism as the *original* form of
Christianity in an area (whether Edessa or any other place) is that we

---

30. Segal, "When did Christianity come to Edessa?" 181. Drijvers, *Cults at
Edessa,* 14, offers the date of 214 for the fall of Edessa.

31. Han J.W. Drijvers accuses F.C. Burkitt's work, *Urchristentum im Orient,*
of promoting the idea that the linguistic difference provided a real cultural barrier
for the area around Edessa ["East of Antioch: Forces and Structures in the
Development of Early Syriac Theology," in *East of Antioch: Studies in Early
Syriac Christianity* (London: Variorum Reprints, 1984), 1].

32. Drijvers, "Facts and Problems," 174. Drijvers calls Edessa the main centre
of Greek culture in Syriac disguise. Also Drijvers, "East of Antioch," 1-3

33. Drijvers, "Jews and Christians at Edessa," 89-90 discusses the evidence for
a large Jewish community in Edessa.

have no evidence that the Marcionite church offered a relevant and convincing religious option to the pagan population.[34] The crucial question thus becomes: to what audience is the Marcionite message likely to have appealed?

All our evidence indicates that Marcion's activities were directed not at the conversion of pagans but at a reformation of the catholic church in terms of a radical Paulinism.[35] It has even been argued that Marcion's move to Rome and his large monetary gift to the church at Rome was a deliberate attempt to gain acceptance for his position in the catholic church of the capital.[36] And the fact that he lost in Rome apparently did not alter his goal, for Marcion did not turn from a Christian audience to a pagan one even then.[37] In fact,

---

34. See E.C. Blackman, *Marcion and His Influence* (London: SPCK, 1948), 13. See too Roberts, *Manuscript, Society, and Belief,* 51, who contends that gnosticism is provoked by and provokes itself a contrary movement. Cf. Drijvers, "Jews and Christians," 96, who says that Marcionites are mainly gentile in origin, though he offers no convincing reason for concluding that.

35. On the Pauline character of the Marcionite teaching, see R. Joseph Hoffmann, *Marcion: On the Restitution of Christianity. An Essay on the Development of Radical Paulinist Theology in the Second Century,* American Academy of Religion Academy Series (Chico: Scholars Press, 1984).

36. Cf. Blackman, *Marcion,* 2.

37. Marcionism was successful in Edessa, where Bardesanes wrote an attack on the Marcionite position towards the end of the second century (*E.H.* 4.30.1). Our interest is in the kind of audience that would have been open to the Marcionite message in Edessa. Drijvers, "Jews and Christians at Edessa," 96, has argued that Judaism was unlikely to have been the main source of converts in Edessa. Just the opposite, says Drijvers; Judaism attracted Christians *away from* the church. But Drijvers reasoning is not compelling. Although the evidence for the attraction of Christians to Jewish rites and to the synagogue is late, it is not unlikely that from the earliest time, Judaism was a lure to many Christians. (Note Ignatius's vigorous attempt to minimize Jewish influences in the churches of western Asia Minor—indication enough that some Christians were being attracted to Jewish elements.) Such attraction and interest does show at least points of contact between the Christians and Jews, and the question must be raised as to the nature of this contact. If the Christian community in Edessa had from its origin clear links to Judaism, the attraction of Christians to this related but forbidden Judaism would be intelligible. That is not to say that Drijvers' reconstruction is not possible. An original Gentile church could have become increasingly attracted to a Judaism that had been foreign to it in its beginning. But if we are to argue that, we need to speculate about what it was in the history of the church in Edessa that brought about this new direction. Drijvers, "Jews and Christians at Edessa," 96-99, attempted to argue that a minority group within the spectrum of Christianity in Edessa made positive links to Judaism and used those links to strengthen their position. But left unexplained is how this minority group succeeded in becoming

everything about Marcionism points not only to its roots in catholic Christianity but, as well, to its continuing sustained dialogue with that catholic Christianity. For one thing, its church structure was one adopted from the catholics.[38] More important, its proselytizing interest was directed towards the membership of the catholic communities. That is made clear both by the efforts of catholic writers to refute Marcionism and by the novel writings of the Marcionite church. The choice of Scripture[39] and the creation of a new document, *The Antitheses*,[40] place the Marcionite church clearly in polemical dialogue with the catholic community and suggest that the debate of the Marcionite church long continued to be with the catholic community, not with pagans. It was from this community that Marcionism could most readily gain converts, for its message and emphases seem intelligible and attractive only to a Christian community with conscious, though perhaps disturbing, roots in Judaism. It is in this context that the concerns of a man like Tertullian (and even like Bardesanes) make sense:[41] the catholic

---

the dominant form of Christianity in the area if all the other Christian groups (who were by far the majority) lacked roots in Judaism, and some, besides lacking roots (as Drijvers has argued for the Marcionites), were focused in their opposition to Judaism. Thus I contend that a gentile origin for the Christian movement in Edessa is less convincing than a Jewish origin in light of the final victory of the Jewish-coloured group. Further along this line, see my argument in this section against Bauer's thesis on the Marcionite origin of Christianity in Edessa.

38. Blackman, *Marcion*, 1.

39. Its canon is a shortened "catholic" canon, and that statement stands even if the impulse towards the fixing of the canon came from Marcionism rather than from the catholics. See Irenaeus, *A.H.* I.27.2.

40. *The Antitheses*, a work that attempts to show the invalidity of the claim that the Old Testament has a positive role to play in the community of Christians, has not survived—in fact, none of Marcion's writings have survived. But Tertullian does provide extensive quotations from *The Antitheses* in his work titled *Against Marcion*.

41. Both Tertullian and Bardesanes wrote books against Marcion. It will not do to argue that these people are only on the fringe of orthodoxy, and thus cannot count as witnesses to the concerns of the orthodox community. Although Tertullian does later join the Montanists, when he wrote his work against Marcion, he spoke as one of the orthodox community. And Bardesanes (however much his gifts may have earned for his orthodoxy shades of suspicion) seems to speak as a member of the orthodox community, in spite of what some of his ancient critics might have said (see Bauer, *Orthodoxy and Heresy*, 29-35/ET:24-30; Barnard, "Origins of Church in Edessa," 170-1; and Turner, *Christian Truth*, 90-3).

community was threatened by a Marcionite church intent to win its members from the ranks of the catholic community.

We may say that in order to sustain itself, Marcionism required a Christian audience rooted in its Jewish heritage. It had no dialogue with the pagan population. Indeed, unless an audience had already been forced to wrestle with Christianity's struggle to incorporate Judaism into its structure against the opposition and counter-claims of Judaism, the Marcionite message would have been unintelligible. That the Marcionite message would have had substantial attraction to a non-Christian audience seems unlikely, given how completely the message of the Marcionite church was geared to those whose perspective was already Christian. Quite simply, the Marcionite message had too many Christian assumptions at its core for its primary audience not to have been the larger Christian community. If, then, early Marcionism neither looked for nor found an audience other than an already Christian one, the success of Marcionism in Edessa would seem to serve (against Bauer) as evidence *for*, rather than against, an earlier catholic-like Christianity there.

Bauer's reconstruction for Edessa fails. The two fundamental elements of that theory clash, and Bauer has not reconciled them: first, Marcionism as the original form of Christianity in Edessa; second, Marcionism as a successful form of Christianity in Edessa. These two elements perhaps could be reconciled if we were to suppose that Marcionism tailored its message considerably from what we know of it so that it could address its pagan audience intelligibly. An unmodified Marcionite message simply would not have been intelligible to anyone without some basic Christian (and, yes, even Jewish) assumptions. Unless, then, we argue for a significant change in the character of Marcionism, it will not be possible to explain the success of Marcionism among an audience to whom the known emphases of Marcionism would have made no sense or had any relevance.

But if we opt for a substantial change in the proclamation of Marcionism in order to explain a hypothetical success of Marcionism among pagans, we will be forced to date the arrival of Marcionism in Edessa considerably later. In the earliest stages of Marcionism, all its energies would doubtlessly have been directed at the catholic community, to whom its message was at least intelligible, if not also attractive. Only when the first significant gains within the Christian community were slowed might we expect a turn to other fields. This would place the arrival of Marcionism in Edessa even later than the 150s, a date itself problematic enough for the initial arrival of Christianity in a city with a significant Jewish population and not very distant from the great city of Antioch.

To what, then, will the successful Marcionite church in Edessa bear witness? Not to an absence of prior forms of Christianity in the area, but to the presence of some form of Christianity—a Christianity that probably had conscious roots in Judaism: in other words, a Christianity perhaps not unlike the catholic Christianity widespread in the second century.[42]

2. Koester's Position

Helmut Koester, though agreeing with Bauer that orthodoxy was not the first form of Christianity in Edessa or in the larger Osrhöene area, contended that Bauer was mistaken in his claim that Marcionism was the first form of Christianity there. According to Koester, the evidence pointed, rather, to a nonorthodox "Thomas tradition" as the original form of Christianity.[43] I wish to look at Koester's argument in detail—if not to dismiss it, certainly to call attention to the difficulty in settling the question of the original form of Christianity in an area like Edessa. In so doing, I recognize that I will be pointing to problems rather than to solutions. Sometimes that must be done.

The key point in Koester's argument for the priority of the

---

42. Some have argued that the Christianity in Edessa was even more Jewish-coloured than catholic Christianity was, perhaps reflecting the thought of the Palestinian churches (see discussion in Barnard, "Origins of Church in Edessa"). That view is probable, though the theory that a more catholic form of Christianity (perhaps brought from Antioch) is likely too. Segal, "When Did Christianity Come to Edessa?" 190, argues for two distinct missions to Edessa.

43. Helmut Koester, "*Gnomai Diaphoroi:* The Origin and Nature of Diversification in the History of Early Christianity," *HTR* 58(1965): 279-318. Gero, "With Bauer on the Tigris," 291, hesitantly accepts Koester's work, commenting that the Thomas tradition is possibly relevant (though not undisputably so) to the situation in Edessa.

Thomas tradition in the Osrhoëne is his contention that the *Gospel of Thomas* was *native* to that area. Koester pointed out that in the *Gospel of Thomas* the name Judas has been joined to that of Thomas as kind of a compounded name for one of the disciples. The significant point for Koester was that there was no person known by this compounded name outside of documents from the Osrhoëne, where the tradition was widespread (in *Thomas, the Athlete*; in the *Acts of Thomas*; in the Abgar legend; and in sy^c of John 14.22).[44] Thus, according to Koester, the *Gospel of Thomas*, in using the compounded name, has an unmistakable Osrhoëne stamp.

Koester's second point is a minor one, not worthy of detailed discussion, except for the fact that it is one of only three points Koester put forward to prove that the *Gospel of Thomas* originated in the Osrhoëne. In this minor second point, Koester noted that the *Gospel of Thomas* was used by the Manichaeans and was even one of their canonical books. From this he argued that the locale for the contact of the Manichaeans with the *Gospel of Thomas* would have been Edessa rather than a more westerly place like Egypt.[45] That is to say, from point-of-contact, Koester assumes point-of-origin.

The third point that Koester put forward to prove the Osrhoëne origin of the *Gospel of Thomas* was that this gospel was used by the author of the *Acts of Thomas,* which is clearly from the Osrhoëne and can be dated to the early third century A.D. The dependence of the *Acts of Thomas* (which can be dated) on the *Gospel of Thomas* (which date we seek) allows us to date the *Gospel of Thomas* to the end of the second century in the area of the Osrhoëne.[46]

These three points link the *Gospel of Thomas* solidly with the Osrhoëne. That can hardly be disputed. But we must ask what kind of link we have here. For Koester, the solid link of the *Gospel of Thomas* with the Osrhoëne proves that the Gospel was *native* to this area. The flaw in Koester's argument is that the solid link of the *Gospel of Thomas* with the Osrhoëne proves only that the Gospel was *known* in the area.

---

44. Koester, "*Gnomai Diaphoroi,*" 2:291-292.
45. *Ibid.,* 2:292.
46. *Ibid.,* 2:292.

Consider Koester's three points. We can immediately grant that Koester is correct in his observation that there is a distinctive Thomas tradition in the Osrhöene and that the *Gospel of Thomas* was a source for the Osrhöene *Acts of Thomas* and was part of the canon of the Manichaeans, a group that developed in this area. But none of these arguments offers a convincing reason for making Edessa rather than Egypt (or a number of other places) the locale for the composition of the *Gospel of Thomas*.[47] It is not the *composition* of the *Gospel of Thomas* in Edessa that is needed in order to account for the special Thomas tradition in various documents from the Osrhöene; it is merely the *presence* of the *Gospel of Thomas* in Edessa that is needed.[48] And that gospel need not have been present until late in the second century. All of the other documents that reflect this special Thomas tradition are later; some of them much later.

It cannot be argued that, had the *Gospel of Thomas* been composed in Egypt, a special Thomas tradition would have been found there, just as it was in Edessa. We do know that the *Gospel of Thomas* was used in Egypt and left no marks of the special Thomas tradition in other literature from the area. If its *presence* in Egypt did not produce a body of material clearly influenced by it, it cannot be argued that its *composition* in Egypt would have produced such a body of material. The production of such a body of dependent literature depends chiefly, if not solely, on its reception. The scholar need not assume that literature composed locally would have a more ready reception in its area of composition than literature

---

47. At best, we might conclude that the Christianity reflected in the *Gospel of Thomas* is an encratism, but that kind of Christianity seems to have been no less at home in Egypt than in Edessa in the second century. See Henri-Charles Puech, "Gnostic Gospels and Related Documents," in Hennecke, *New Testament Apocrypha*, 2:306.

48. Drijvers, "Facts and Problems," 172-3, has a different view on the matter. He places the composition of the *Gospel of Thomas* in the Edessa area, but he dates its composition much later than Koester does. He believes that the Judas/Thomas tradition is not rooted in the *Gospel of Thomas* but in Tatian's *Diatessaron* (p. 159). The *Gospel of Thomas* is possibly dependent on Tatian's work, and if Drijvers is correct on that point, the Gospel could not be used to indicate the character of the first form of Christianity in the area. Drijvers' discussion on the *Gospel of Thomas* provides a good balance to Koester's treatment.

composed elsewhere might have. There are too many other factors involved in the popularity of a document to make its local composition a key factor for its popularity in an area.

Were it merely argued, in support of a position like Koester's, that literature *native* to a particular area might better reflect the concerns of the area and thus be more attractive locally, that much might be admitted, provided it is not made into some general principle to which appeal might be made to determine the place of composition of a document. But if one is to *prove* that a document was composed in the Osrhöene, one cannot do so simply by demonstrating that the document made an impact in the area. That, I contend, is the core of Koester's argument for the Osrhöene com-position of the *Gospel of Thomas*.[49] And that is not satisfactory.

Further in regard to Koester's argument: Koester had contended that Edessa was the point of contact of the *Gospel of Thomas* with the Manichaeans. Probable enough: Mani's movement did originate in the east. But how does that support Koester's thesis that the *Gospel of Thomas* originated in the Osrhöene? Even supposing that Mani did come into contact with the *Gospel of Thomas* in the Osrhöene, that tells us nothing about the origin of the *Gospel of Thomas*, which was Koester's reason in the first place for raising the connection of the *Gospel of Thomas* with the Manichaeans. All that the canonical status of the *Gospel of Thomas* among the Manichaeans indicates is that the Gospel was *known* in the Osrhöene by the middle of the third century. It indicates nothing about the locale of origin of the *Gospel of Thomas* nor does it indicate the date of the composition of the Gospel. The weakness—indeed, the irrelevance—of this point in Koester's argument does not serve well to make Koester's hypothesis of the Osrhöene origin of the *Gospel of Thomas* compelling.

It was crucial that Koester establish the Osrhöene origin of the

---

49. Granted, Koester, *"Gnomai Diaphoroi,"* 291 n. 25, does mention that H.-Ch. Puech and W.C. van Unnik too have argued for the Edessan origin of the Gospel of Thomas. But van Unnik, *Newly Discovered Gnostic Writings*, Studies in Biblical Theology 30 (London: SCM Press, 1960), 49-50, in spite of using the same kind of arguments that Koester has used to place the composition of the *Gospel of Thomas* in the Edessa area, argues for a later date for its composition.

Gospel of Thomas, for that was the first step in his argument used to establish that a "Thomas" kind of Christianity was the original form of Christianity in the Osrhöene. But Koester made a questionable move at this point. Having supposed that the Osrhöene origin was firmly established, Koester then noted that the *Gospel of Thomas* was *known* in Egypt in the second half of the second century. This would require, according to Koester, that the Gospel have been written prior to that, and since Koester has already concluded that the *Gospel of Thomas* was *composed* in far-off Edessa, he can propose an interval of a number of years for that Gospel to have made its way from Edessa to Egypt. His conclusion is that the Gospel must have been composed by the middle of the second century or earlier, a date not undisputed.[50] After arguing for this early date of composition, Koester abruptly concludes: "This proves that the Thomas tradition was the oldest form of Christianity in Edessa, antedating the beginning of both Marcionite and orthodox Christianity in that area."[51]

But it was only by requiring that the *Gospel of Thomas* be *composed* in the Osrhöene that Koester could argue that this was the original form of Christianity in Edessa: having established the *presence* of the *Gospel of Thomas* in Egypt in the latter half of the second century, Koester could argue for an even earlier date for the composition of that gospel in far-off Edessa. The problem is that Koester had no solid grounds for contending that the gospel was composed in the Osrhöene, and in a later work, Koester seems to give some grounds for a challenge to his own earlier conclusion.[52]

---

50. Koester, *"Gnomai Diaphoroi,"* 293. An extensive discussion regarding the date for the *Gospel of Thomas* is provided in James M. Robinson, "On Bridging the Gulf from Q to the *Gospel of Thomas* (or Vice Versa)," in *Nag Hammadi, Gnosticism, and Early Christianity*, ed. Charles W. Hedrick and Robert Hodgson, Jr. (Peabody: Hendrickson, 1986), 127-175.

51. Koester, *"Gnomai Diaphoroi,"* 293. Koester could make that statement because he believed that orthodox Christianity did not arrive much before A.D. 200 (p. 291), and for Marcionism, a date before 150 would be difficult to defend. [The date for the beginning of the Marcionite movement has usually been placed in the 140s. Irenaeus (*A.H.* I.27.1) places Marcion after Cerdo, who, according to Irenaeus, had come to Rome in the episcopate of Hyginus (c.137-45).]

52. A discussion of Koester's forthcoming work on the *Gospel of Thomas* is discussed in Robinson, "From Q to the *Gospel of Thomas*," 145. Koester concludes in his new work that the *Gospel of Thomas* was written in Palestine or

Even if we were to grant that the *Gospel of Thomas* was composed in Edessa, and that it reflected the general character of Christianity in the area, we would still be at a loss regarding the nature of *early* Christianity in the area. It is generally recognized that the *Gospel of Thomas* has gone through a number of editions. In the form we now have it, the *Gospel of Thomas* would not necessarily reflect, then, the perspectives of the first community in which it was used.[53] In fact, many scholars question the gnostic character of the Gospel, arguing that it simply reflects a Jewish encratism.[54] But even granting that the tone seems to suggest at least an encratic community as the source of this document,[55] we would still not be able to determine whether this encratism was of a sufficient degree to exclude it from the circle of credible orthodoxy in its earliest forms, for consideration must be given to the creative relationship of a community on the material it preserves. We have become familiar enough with this process in our study of the canonical gospels, and similar insights must be brought to bear on the *Gospel of Thomas* too. It is not only the synoptic material that has been shaped in the hands of its preserving community. Surely the *Gospel of Thomas* has been sujbect to the same forces. Thus the question arises: how much of the encratic character of the *Gospel of Thomas* is the colouring of the community in which the Thomas material was preserved? And from this a further question: could the preserving community not have become more encratic over time, so shaping an innocuous document into something that could comfortably fit only on the perimeter of orthodoxy?[56] Such are the

---

Syria between A.D. 70 and 100. But several scholars date the *Gospel of Thomas* to the end of the second century (pp. 257-9). Cf. Birger A. Pearson, "Earliest Christianity in Egypt: Some Observations," in *The Roots of Egyptian Christianity*, 150 n. 99.

53. Puech, *NTA*, II.305-6; Robinson, "From Q to the *Gospel of Thomas*," 160-64).

54. G. Quispel "Gnosticism and the New Testament," *VC* 19 (1965): 65-85. Also see Koester, *"Gnomai Diaphoroi,"* 301-5. Koester speaks of the "seed of Gnosticism" that this material has (p. 302).

55. Puech, *NTA*, II.306. Also see n. 42 above.

56. Puech, *NTA*, II.306. Puech says: "Perhaps there is ground for associating this first version [of the *Gospel of Thomas*] with a group which professed that rather bizarre Christianity, strongly tinged with Encratism, which was widespread in Syria and Egypt in the 2nd century." Perhaps. But such a conclusion about the

questions that must be considered when we attempt to reconstruct the character of earliest Christianity in an area like Edessa, where our literary evidence is extremely meagre for the earliest period, and other kinds of evidence nonexistent.

My reservations about Koester's reconstruction does not mean that I assert that earliest Christianity in the Osrhöene was unquestionably orthodox. Our information for the orthodox in Edessa is notably difficult to evaluate. The Abgar Legend and other orthodox traditions of Edessa are generally viewed with suspicion (mainly due to Bauer's attack), though there are some scholars who still are comfortable in using this legend in a reconstruction of early Christianity in Edessa.[57] Against such scholars, I find myself in agreement with Bauer that the orthodox traditions are wisely treated with caution here.

But that should not make the *Gospel of Thomas* more attractive as a source in our reconstruction. All that can be said with any certainty about the *Gospel of Thomas* is that, about the end of the second century, it was known in the Osrhöene and had impact on some of the material composed in the area afterwards. Nothing compelling regarding the character of earliest Christianity in Edessa has been established by Koester's argument based on his analysis of the *Gospel of Thomas*.

The question of the character of Christianity in Edessa is still an open one, and one that I do not attempt to resolve. My concern here is not to demonstrate which particular form of Christianity was first to arrive in Edessa; rather, it is to show that our information is too ambiguous or mute to allow us confident reconstructions of Christianity in this area. In contrast to this situation, I hope to show

---

"first version" would seem to demand at least as rigorous an analysis of the impact of a developing community as has been imposed on the canonical gospels. The skepticism that prevents us from confidence with the canonical material should not be exchanged for credulity when we approach noncanonical material, which would have been subject to similar community forces.

57. For a recent discussion, see Drijvers, "Facts and Problems." Drijvers thinks that some of the orthodox material is a direct response to the Manichaeans (pp. 166-9). Barnard, "Origins of Church in Edessa," illustrates a more positive use of the orthodox traditions.

the superiority of the materials we have for a reconstruction of Christianity in western Asia Minor.

IV. Egypt

A. Bauer's Reconstruction

Egypt is similar to Edessa in the muteness of the evidence for the earliest period. As C. H. Roberts said: "The obscurity that veils the early history of the Church in Egypt and that does not lift until the beginning of the third century constitutes a conspicuous challenge to the historian of primitive Christianity."[58]

But Bauer believed that a credible reconstruction could be accomplished with the materials available. According to Bauer, the evidence indicated that catholic Christianity was not represented in Egypt until Bishop Demetrius at the beginning of the third century, though a trajectory away from gnosticism began with Clement. Prior to that, Christianity existed in two forms, both of them heretical from the perspective of catholic Christianity. One group, the gentile, Bauer identified from a document called the *Gospel of the Egyptians;* the other, the Jewish, from a document called the *Gospel of the Hebrews.*[59] According to Bauer, the lack of early evidence for Christianity in Egypt was not be be taken as a lack of an early presence of Christianity in Egypt but only as a lack of an

---

58. Roberts, *Manuscript, Society, and Belief,* 1. The obscurity of the early period is universally recognized. Bauer, *Orthodoxy and Heresy,* 49/ET:44, too, admitted that little was known about early Christianity in Egypt. And also Koester, *Introduction,* 219, who has much to say about early Christianity in Egypt, admits that "there is no direct evidence for the beginnings of Christianity in Egypt." Koester cautions: "The historian must therefore attempt to draw conclusion from various pieces of later evidence. This is difficult and even hazardous..." (p. 219). The most recent work on this subject is the volume by The Institute for Antiquity and Christianity, *The Roots of Egyptian Christianity,* Studies in Antiquity and Christianity, ed. Birger A. Pearson and James E. Goehring (Philadelphia: Fortress, 1986). Note also B.H. Streeter, *The Primitive Church* (London: Macmillan, 1929), 233, who says that "the early history of the Church of Alexandria is darkness itself." As to the difficulty of making use of the early Christian literature associated with Egypt, see A.F.J. Klijn, "Jewish Christianity in Egypt," in *The Roots of Egyptian Christianity,* 161-75.

59. See the extended discussion in Bauer, *Orthodoxy and Heresy,* chapter 2.

early presence of *orthodox* Christianity in Egypt. The dearth of
literature for early Egyptian Christianity did not indicate that such
literature never existed but only that, with the arrival and subsequent
success of orthodox Christianity in Egypt, the nonorthodox literature was either actively suppressed or passively suppressed by not
being given the recognition that would have promoted its preservation.

Most scholars have granted that Bauer has made his point for
Egypt.[60] Even Turner, generally a staunch critic of Bauer's thesis,
agrees that early Christianity in Egypt reflects a prominent position
for Gnosticism. Admitting that the outstanding figures of the
second century appear to be gnostics and that the orthodox are
known to have used gnostic works, Turner concludes that the
gnostics were, on the whole, more brilliant than those who
represented other Christian perspectives.[61]

B. Koester's Reconstruction

Koester is clearly a disciple of Bauer in his reconstruction of
early Christianity in Egypt.[62] As the most dedicated and consistent
promoter of the Bauer Thesis, Koester himself attempted to
strengthen Bauer's thesis of the heretical and, more precisely,
gnostic character of early Christianity in Egypt. I shall give some
attention now to the particulars of Koester's support for Bauer's
reconstruction, after which I will turn to a recent substantial
response to Bauer on Egypt.

Koester's reason for supposing that early Christianity in Egypt
was gnostic is that he was convinced that the Gospel of John was

---

60. Birger A. Pearson, "Earliest Christianity," 132, notes that Bauer's thesis
that the earliest type of Christianity in Egypt was "heretical" (specifically
"gnostic") is widely held.
61. Turner, *Christian Truth*, 47-49. Hans Dieter Betz, "Orthodoxy and Heresy
in Primitive Christianity: Some critical remarks on Georg Strecker's republication
of Walter Bauer's *Rechtgläubigkeit und Ketzerei im ältesten Christentum*,"
Interpretation, 19 (1965): 306, agrees that there was a strong gnostic Christianity
in Egypt but rejects as an overstatement a comment that early Christianity in
Egypt was only gnostic.
62. Koester, *Introduction*, 2:220. Pearson, "Earliest Christianity," 132-3 n.
4, points out that Koester has introduced an important modification in the Bauer
Thesis in his latest work.

the most popular of all the gospels in Egypt in the second century.[63] That, in itself, would prove nothing. But Koester continues: "Later witnesses prove that John was a favourite book among Egyptian gnostics."[64] The argument depends on the following logic. Premise one: the Gospel of John was popular among the Egyptian gnostics. Premise two: the Gospel of John was the most popular gospel in second-century Egypt. Conclusion: the first Christians of Egypt were gnostics. One is made uncomfortable both by the unconvincing logic and by how little material there is even to be misused in a reconstruction of early Egyptian Christianity.

A closer look hardly helps Koester's argument. The evidence used to argue for the popularity of the Gospel of John in Egypt was a mere two scraps of papyri[65]—hardly overwhelming under the best of circumstances. The fragments [one from the Gospel of John (p^{52}); the other from the *Unknown Gospel* of *Papyrus Egerton 2*[66]] are the two earliest pieces of Christian writings to be found in Egypt.[67]

And what of these two fragments? The one fragment of the *Unknown Gospel* may disprove more than it proves for Koester. The existence of that fragment may demonstrate the popularity of some *Unknown Gospel* (as Koester argued), but much more likely it demonstrates (against Koester) the accidental nature of manuscript discoveries. Even though Koester admitted in this context that one had to keep the accidental nature of manuscripts discoveries in mind, the ease with which Koester uses these two fragments to determine the popularity of documents makes one wonder whether the sur-

---

63. Koester, *Introduction*, 2:222.

64. *Ibid.*, 2:222.

65. My term "scraps" is intentionally negative, though nonetheless accurately descriptive. Koester used the phrase "manuscript finds." His term is more positive and equally descriptive. But whatever term is used, the fragmentary nature of the evidence must be recognized.

66. The importance of this fragment for establishing the popularity of the Gospel of John in Egypt is, according to Koester (*Introduction*, 2:222), that the unknown gospel may have supplied source material for the Gospel of John.

67. Koester, *Introduction*, 2:222-3, also drew attention to two other fragments of the Gospel of John and to three fragments from the *Gospel of Thomas*, one of which could be dated earlier than 200. But these latter papyri are of no significance, for fragments of Matthew and Luke, as well, exist for the same period (early third century), a point that Koester himself admitted.

viving papyri have not been weighted too heavily by Koester, especially as it is from these two scraps of papyri that Koester draws what he considers a likely conclusion that "Christians who not much later were called 'gnostics' were the first Christian preachers to appear in Egypt."[68]

Not only does Koester's logic weigh too heavily on the scanty fragments of surviving manuscripts, Koester's argument is unconvincing because it disregards other evidence that could contribute to our knowledge of what literature was popular among the Christians of Egypt. Koester recognizes that the writings of Clement of Alexandria show that both Matthew and Luke were used in Alexandria before the end of the second century.[69] But Koester should have admitted more than that: Clement's writings show, as well, that the extant manuscripts of the second century (of which Matthew and Luke are not represented) fail to reflect the full spectrum of the documents that were in use in the Christian communities. Koester's argument is thus shown to be defective at this point, for it requires that the manuscript evidence truly reflect the popularity of the preserved literature. Nothing compels us to that conclusion.

A much more cautious reconstruction of the popular literature of the second-century church in Egypt has been provided by James McCue.[70] McCue, who called Bauer's work "one of the great undigested pieces of twentieth century scholarship,"[71] attempted to determine whether one particular form of gnosticism, Valentinianism, supported Bauer's thesis that gnosticism was older than catholic Christianity in Egypt. His conclusions, with cautious qualifications, are that the orthodox community functions in the Valentinian self-understanding, and functions repeatedly as the larger group in terms of which the Valentinians define themselves.[72] Further, in the middle of the second century, the Valentinians used the orthodox New Testament "in a manner that is best accounted for

---

68. Koester, *Introduction*, 2:222-3.
69. *Ibid.*, 2:223.
70. McCue, "Walter Bauer and the Valentinians," 118-130.
71. *Ibid.*, 118.
72. *Ibid.*, 120.

by supposing that Valentinianism developed within a mid-second century orthodox matrix."[73] These conclusions stand in obvious opposition to Koester's conclusions, and they have the benefit of offering a more cautious and convincing theory of the literature of the early church in Egypt. Strangely, Koester admitted that the gnostic schools that developed out of Valentinianism reveal some connection to the catholic church (even if that connection is a polemical one) and reveal, as well, dependence on the canonical gospels and the Pauline letters.[74] Yet Koester says no more about this, and for some reason dismisses the role of the canonical gospels and the letters of Paul in the gnostic systems with the comment that "we cannot discuss this further in this context..."[75] Why we cannot, he does not say. Considering the observations of McCue on this matter, Koester's dismissal of this subject is troubling.

Another feature of Koester's support of the Bauer Thesis in Egypt is an appeal to the Nag Hammadi texts.[76] Koester's contention is that Syrian gnostic writings must have reached Egypt no later than the *beginning* of the second century. But, again, the logic of Koester's argument is suspect. Koester points out similarities between the thought of the second-century schools of Valentinian gnosticism and certain writings of the Nag Hammadi library (the date and origin of which little can be said).[77] Although Koester's observation is worthy of note, there is a crucial problem in his argument. He uses certain of the Nag Hammadi texts for his reconstruction of the development of Gnosticism in Egypt *prior* to the middle of the second century, contending that these Nag Hammadi writings are sources for the thought of the Valentinian schools.[78] But surely before constructing earliest Egyptian

---

73. McCue, "Walter Bauer and the Valentinians," 120.
74. Koester, *Introduction*, 2:232-233.
75. *Ibid.*, 2:233.
76. *Ibid.*, 2:225-229.
77. A discussion of the "disposal" of the library is provided by Armand Veilleux, "Monasticism and Gnosis in Egypt," in *The Roots of Egyptian Christianity*, 289-291, and a date in the last half of the fourth century appears reasonable. But that tells us little about the date of the composition of the autographs.
78. Koester, *Introduction*, 2.225, of course, has qualified his statements with words like "might be" and "could have been," but these qualifications are

Christianity on the basis of the Nag Hammadi writings, Koester must first face the difficulty (or impossibility) of showing that the Nag Hammadi writings were, in fact, the sources of the Valentinian schools. This is too critical a juncture in Koester's reconstruction for it to rest solely on assumption.

It is not my intention here to analyze Koester's whole argument. I think I have identified crucial points in that argument and have shown them to be weak. I wish only to show that Koester has added no convincing support to the Bauer Thesis. In fact, the same is true for other reconstructions that attempt to posit gnosticism as the earliest form of Christianity in Egypt. The scarcity of the materials from Egypt results in suspicious gaps in the logic of these various reconstructions. This reinforces my conviction that the problems of the orthodoxy/heresy debate are unlikely to be solved in the sands of Egypt.

C. The Reconstruction of C.H. Roberts

The most recent attempt to make sense of the mute first century of Christianity in Egypt is that presented by C.H. Roberts.[79] It is Roberts' conclusion that the thesis of the gnostic character of earliest Christianity in Egypt can be, and should be, challenged. Birger Pearson agrees, and contends that Bauer's theory "is cogently called into question, if not definitely overturned" by Roberts' work.[80]

Roberts approaches the problem of early Christianity in Egypt from a number of perspectives. First, there is the manuscript evidence, or rather, the lack of it. Although numerous gnostic texts have been found in Egypt (the Nag Hammadi find being by far the most significant), most of the gnostic manuscripts were copied in the fourth or fifth centuries.[81] In fact, only one gnostic papyrus has been found prior to the beginning of the third century. In light of this, Roberts ponders:

---

considerably weakened by Koester's conclusion, in which he claims that "it necessarily follows."

79. Colin H. Roberts, *Manuscript, Society, and Belief in Early Christian Egypt*, The Schweich Lectures of the British Academy for 1977 (London: Oxford University Press, 1979).

80. Pearson, "Earliest Christianity," 132.

81. Roberts, *Manuscript, Society, and Belief*, 51.

> Where are the Gnostic papyri of the first two centuries? Unless the movement was strictly confined to Alexandria and the Delta from which no papyri survive, we should expect some manuscript evidence, however slight, to be forthcoming from the papyri. There is one text only, and that ambivalent, from the second century...the silence of the first hundred years certainly calls for an explanation; but it is not Bauer's.
>
> And once the evidence of the papyri is available, indisputably Gnostic texts are conspicuous by their rarity. Of the fourteen Christian texts that I would date before A.D. 200 there is only one, the first fragment of the *Gospel of Thomas* from Oxyrhynchus, which may reasonably be regarded as Gnostic.[82]

There is, too, the problem of the identification of Egypt as the place of writing of some of this gnostic literature. Roberts wondered whether some of the gnostic material is assigned an Egyptian origin for no other reason than some controlling assumption that Egyptian Christianity was gnostic, a method that runs the risk of circular argument.[83]

One might counter: even if the manuscript evidence is not as supportive as one would like it to be, is there not evidence that the outstanding figures of early Christianity in Egypt were of a heretical bent? Even Turner, a rigorous critic of Bauer, was forced to admit as much, was he not?[84]

Again, we must be careful how we read the evidence. While admitting, along with Roberts, that the "only two historical figures of consequence...before the later second century are both Gnostics,"[85] this evidence must be weighed in light of two other observations. One is the possibility that these men may have had their roots in a tradition more orthodox than what is expressed in their developed positions.[86] The second is that "undue weight

---

82. Roberts, *Manuscript, Society, and Belief*, 51-2.

83. *Ibid.*, 53-4.

84. Turner, *Christian Truth*, 49, says that the gnostic leaders "far outshone their more orthodox contemporaries in brilliance."

85. Roberts, *Manuscript, Society, and Belief*, 50. Valentinus and Basilides.

86. The observations of both Roberts, *Manuscript, Society, and Belief*, 50-51, and McCue, "Walter Bauer and the Valentinians," 118-130, are important here. Valentinus seems to have had his roots in the orthodox tradition. This would make sense of the report that he had hoped to gain for himself the bishop's chair

should not be attached to two individual teachers however important," as Roberts rightly cautions us.[87] How mistaken we would be in reconstructing the character of common Christianity for any age were we to take as our guide the most innovative and progressive theologian of that age. Novel theologians are as untrustworthy an indicator of the average believer or average clergy as we could possibly find. It is a cause of some concern to see that reconstructions of primitive Christianity fail to take this relatively undebatable point into account.

The historical situation of first and second-century Egypt introduces another complication into a reconstruction of primitive Christianity in Egypt. It has always struck scholars as surprising that no evidence for first-century Christianity can be found for Alexandria and Egypt. One would have thought that Alexandria would have been among the first—if not the first—non-Palestinian city to have had a Christian community. Alexandria was perhaps the third largest city in the Roman empire in the first century; its Jewish community was almost certainly the largest of any in the Roman empire, perhaps outdoing Jerusalem itself several times over; and of all the significant cities of the empire, Alexandria was the closest to Jerusalem. How is it then that, in spite of these things, we have no evidence for a Christian community in Alexandria in the first and early second century?

Roberts thinks that he can offer clues about early Christianity in Egypt, even though concrete evidence for Christianity there is lacking. It is only at this point that I express some reservations about Roberts' work. My reservations stem from a caution that prevents me from speculation when the evidence is as meagre as it is for a place like Egypt.

It was Roberts' contention that the early Christian community in Alexandria was likely closely tied to Judaism.[88] The hypothesis has the advantage of explaining the lack of evidence for early Christianity in Egypt, given the almost certain fact that it did exist, for if the

---

in Rome.

87. Roberts, *Manuscript, Society, and Belief,* 51.

88. *Ibid.,* 55-59. Also see Henry A. Green, "The Social-Economic Background of Christianity in Egypt," in *The Roots of Egyptian Christianity,* 100-113.

Christian community was so closely tied to the Jewish community, it might appear as merely Jewish, rather than distinctively Christian, given the kind of evidence we have for that period. But Roberts' hypothesis is simply that: a hypothesis. The character (and perhaps even the existence) of early Christianity in Egypt simply cannot be determined, for we have no evidence with which to work. We can only say that we believe that Alexandria did have a Christian community in the first century, defending that position simply by pointing out that it is more difficult to believe that it did not have a Christian community than that it did. But we have no solid evidence for either position.

I would agree with Roberts that it would be reasonable to assume that this Christianity would have had a Jewish colouring, but again we have no evidence to which to appeal for support. One might even argue against this particular part of Roberts' presentation that, given what would seem to be an environment for the church in Antioch similar to that in Alexandria, we have in Antioch an example of an early Christian community that, though in the midst of a large Jewish population, is not clearly shaped by the local Jewish environment. Whatever we make of the conflict between Peter and Paul in Antioch, the pull in the direction of Judaism does not come from Antioch but from Jerusalem, and once that influence is removed, a less Jewish position apparently returns—if Ignatius is any example of what happens to the Christian church in Antioch.[89] And Ephesus is an example of another city in which a large Jewish

---

89. There is a theory that Paul was defeated in Antioch. Whatever the support for this theory for the last years of Paul's ministry, the theory is weakened by the high office held by Ignatius, a Paulinist, at the beginning of the second century. Ignatius, as bishop of the church at Antioch, reflects a familiarity with Pauline theology, and his anti-Judaizing stance is as Pauline as anything Paul himself ever expressed. If Paul's party lost in Antioch in the late forties to James, it soon recovered to become influential and dominant. Placing the composition of the Gospel of Matthew in Antioch in the eighties does not weigh the scales in favour of a dominant pro-Jewish element in late first-century Antiochene Christianity, for again the theological position of Ignatius complicates the picture considerably. At most we can say that Christianity in Antioch had become sensitive to Judaism, as is illustrated by the tone of Matthew's Gospel and by the possibility of attraction to Judaism by some members in Ignatius's church, but we cannot determine whether these tones and tendencies come from a pro-Pauline or pro-Jewish church. Also see §VIII of this chapter.

population does not mould the early Christian community into a consciously Jewish group.

Of course, one might argue that in both Antioch and Ephesus, the church was founded by Hellenistic Jews, and thus these cities should not be the standard by which Alexandria is measured. True. But, on the other hand, we cannot simply assume that Alexandria was unlike Ephesus or Antioch. We might ask where we have an area outside of Palestine for which we can assume a conservative form of Christianity to have been the original community? Alexandria is not necessarily the best candidate, for it must have been a somewhat attractive centre for the persecuted Hellenists of the early church. In addition, the form of Judaism itself in Alexandria may have been more open to, and tolerant of, the liberal perspective of the early Hellenistic Christians. We simply cannot be certain.

Some caution, too, must be exercised in determining the character of earliest Christianity in Egypt from its later forms. Roberts has pointed to the historical situation in which the Jewish community of Egypt suffered repression. In the Jewish War of A.D. 70, perhaps as many as 50,000 Jews in Alexandria were killed, and in the revolt under Trajan, heavy fighting occurred throughout Egypt, with tremendous Jewish losses. Roberts thinks that, given this situation, the early Christians (who appeared to the outsider as a Jewish sect) would not have been able to attract gentiles into the church.[90] If Roberts is correct about the increased tensions between Jew and Greek in Alexandria in the late first and early second centuries, then a Jewish-coloured Christianity often proposed for Egypt may actually hide an initial successful thrust to the Gentiles of the kind we have in Antioch and Ephesus. But here again we are hampered by the ambiguity and muteness of the evidence.

From another perspective, the Jewish difficulties in Egypt may account for the attractiveness of the gnostic message, in which the Jewish heritage was radically reshaped or discarded. Wisdom may have dictated that the Christian community draw a sharper line

---

90. Roberts, *Manuscript, Society, and Belief,* 56, 58. Hengel, *History of Earliest Christianity,* 107 thinks that as a result of the Jewish rebellion of A.D. 116-7, the Jewish-Christian community would have disappeared.

between itself and Judaism, a task that could not be fully carried out because the roots in Judaism were judged to be in some way essential. Perhaps it is at this point that Gnosticism could have provided an intelligent, or at least an attractive, option. Again, that century in Egypt is simply too mute for us to decide anything with confidence.

V. Corinth

A. The Scarcity of Evidence

Paul's correspondence with the church at Corinth provides some insight into the character of Christianity in Corinth. The church there has won for itself, not undeservably, fame as Paul's most problem-filled church. But the glimpse we have of life there is of the church in its first two or three years, and caution must be exercised in using the portrait of the church reflected in Paul's letters to provide a view of that church over the decades that followed. What we have for Corinth is a detailed glimpse of the brief infancy period of the church there. We have nothing to support the contention that significant changes did—or did not—take place as the church matured.

Not until four decades later do we have any other literature addressed to the church at Corinth.[91] It was in the last decade of the first century, according to most scholars, that the church at Rome sent a letter to the church at Corinth. This letter, known as *1 Clement*, was the key to Bauer's reconstruction of the early history of

---

91. A.I.C. Heron, "The Interpretation of I Clement in Walter Bauer's *Rechtgläubigkeit und Ketzerei im ältesten Christentum*," *Ekklesiastikos Pharos* 55 (1973): 530-31, says: "I Corinthians does indeed witness to the existence of various factions in the congregation there at the time of Paul; but Bauer's suggestions that these factions combined in the way he describes, and that the resultant tensions ultimately produced the crisis with which Clement is concerned, are both, though not improbable in themselves, undeniably speculative. By Clement's day, more than a generation has passed since the time of Paul, and we possess no evidence for the intervening period: this leaves room for an infinite number of possible developments, each as likely as the others."

the church at Corinth. As such, it is investigated in detail in the following section.

B. Bauer's Reconstruction

Bauer believed, on the basis of *1 Clement,* that heretical movements (i.e., gnostics) had gained the upper hand in Corinth and had deposed the more orthodox leadership.[92] It is my contention that *1 Clement* provides us with only a glimpse of a conflict within the church at Corinth and that that glimpse is not a sufficient base from which to offer any reconstruction of detailed certainty. All we know about the situation is that sides were drawn, and a group had succeeded in having at least some of the older men removed from positions of authority. We do know, too, that the leaders in Rome threw their support behind the older men who had been removed from office.[93]

Bauer thought he could fill out the picture offered by *1 Clement* concerning the church in Corinth in the nineties by examining the correspondence from the Apostle Paul some forty years earlier (103-5/ET:100-101). In this material (1 Corinthians and 2 Corinthians), Paul is seen struggling against a church in which parties apparently had been formed, and there is enough information about one of the parties to allow for the hypothesis that some sort of proto-gnosticism was involved.[94] It is here that Bauer found the beginnings of a gnostic movement that some forty years later had gained control of the church in Corinth (which was how he had interpreted the situation of the Corinthian church reflected in *1 Clement*).

---

92. Bauer, *Orthodoxy and Heresy,* 99-107/ET:95-103. Bauer's discussion of the situation in Corinth is in the context of his discussion of Roman Christianity, especially Roman Christianity viewed as the chief promoter of orthodoxy throughout the Mediterranean area.

93. In the opening of the letter (I.1), the church at Rome clearly shows whose side it is taking, and it is the side distinguished by the presence of older men (XLIV).

94. See E. Earle Ellis, "Paul and His Opponents: Trends in the Research," in *Christianity, Judaism and Other Greco-Roman Cults: Studies for Morton Smith at Sixty,* ed. J. Neusner (Leiden: E.J. Brill, 1975), 2:264-98.

C. Critique of Bauer's Reconstruction

Those who dispute Bauer's reading of the situation have pointed out that there is nothing in *1 Clement* itself that would indicate a theological issue was at the heart of the conflict, and certainly nothing that would indicate that Gnosticism was an issue.[95] Really all that is necessary is some personality clash or political power struggle to account for the conflict, and the terms used in *1 Clement* to describe the dispute need imply nothing more than this. It is only by appealing to the situation some forty years earlier that the hypothesis of a theological dispute for the nineties becomes attractive.

Although the letter of *1 Clement* is more ambiguous than we might wish regarding the particulars of the conflict in Corinth, enough can be ascertained about that conflict that would call Bauer's reconstruction into question. Two points are particularly weighty. First, the newly victorious group had apparently lacked power previously. They seemed not to have shared in the leadership of the community but were associated with the community merely as members of the laity. Second, a significant element in this group were young.

First with regard to the previous lack of power of this group. It was Bauer's thesis that the church's power structure was collegial. Such a structure would have consisted of members from a variety of theological positions. Indeed, as we will discuss in detail later (chapter five), Bauer considered the rise of the monarchical episcopate to have been caused by the inability of the orthodox to gain more than an ineffective minority voice in this collegial structure of power. In other words, orthodox presbyters could always be (and apparently often were) outvoted by the more numerous nonorthodox presbyters.

Strangely, however, we see no sign of such a situation in

---

95. See Turner, *Christian Truth*, 70-1. Turner draws attention to the learned conclusion of Lightfoot at this point. Lightfoot saw the quarrel as personal or political (*Apostolic Fathers*, I.1.58). See, too, Heron, "I Clement," 517-545. If there is a theological issue in the conflict in Corinth, that does not really help Bauer's thesis. Betz, "Orthodoxy and Heresy," 307-8, finds it astonishing that Bauer did not consider Paul's fight in Corinth as an instance of his own thesis.

Corinth, even though this is the city where we would most confidently look for it, given that church's birth in an atmosphere of competition and theological diversity. But, according to *1 Clement*, the structure of power is not one in which this rival group had previously shared. Numerous verses explicitly exclude these people from the ranks of the presbytery. Especially in a dense section from XXXVII - XLIV, the indication is that the new group had not previously been represented in the structures of power. Note how the author argues. He says that not all are prefects or tribunes or centurions or leaders of fifty (XXXVII.3). He continues: "The great cannot exist without the small, nor the small without the great; there is a certain mixture among all (XXXVII.4). It would be strange for the author to draw these distinctions if the rival party had been actually part of the power structure. Only if the schismatics were part of the "small" (i.e., laity) would such an argument be intelligible here. A few sentences later (XL), the author draws a distinction between those appointed to serve and those of the laity. The layman is bound by the ordinances of the laity; proper officials have already been appointed for the ritual activities (in particular, the Eucharist). Again, this is a strange distinction to make if the rival party had been represented in the structures of power. So, too, the exhortation that each man be bound by his own rank (XLI.1). And the concluding words of this section forcefully reinforces the clear division that the author has already drawn repeatedly. Here we find an explicit defense of the office of bishops and deacons.[96] The author defends this structure by saying that it was approved by the apostles [i.e., was not novel (XLII.2-3)], and then goes on to describe the troubling situation in the clearest words of the entire letter:

> Our Apostles also knew through our Lord Jesus Christ that there would be strife for the title of bishop. For this cause, therefore, since they had received perfect foreknowledge, they appointed those who have been

---

96. We are not at a stage in *1 Clement* where there is a threefold ministry. We seem to have a plurality of "overseers" (or bishops) and of deacons. Presbyters, as a distinct group set off from the bishops and deacons, are not yet visible. In *I Clement* 44, bishop and presbyter are used interchangeably.

already mentioned, and afterwards added the codicil that if they should fall asleep, other approved men should succeed to their ministry. We consider therefore that it is not just to remove from their ministry those who were appointed by them, or later on by other eminent men, with the consent of the whole Church...For our sin is not small, if we eject from the episcopate those who have blamelessly and holily offered its sacrifices...For we see that in spite of their good service you have removed some from the ministry which they fulfilled blamelessly (XLIV).

Clement then places the blame for this attack on the leadership on the shoulders of one or two persons (XLVII.6) and calls these people to submit to the presbytery (LVII). If the troublemakers were part of the presbytery, and part of the controlling element within that presbytery, this makes no sense.

Somewhat less explicit references to a distinction that cuts between office and laity are also found in this letter. The worthless are contrasted to those in honour, and those of no reputation to those who are renowned (§ III.3). Although this kind of contrast is clearly polemical, it nonetheless makes sense in Clement's argument only if the troublemakers had not held the same rank as those deposed. Further, Clement calls for the members to be subject to his neighbour *according to the position granted to him* (XXXVIII. 1). As part of an attempt to correct the situation, this injunction makes no sense unless the opponents were not members of the highest offices of the church. And, at the end (LVII.1), there is a call on the schismatics to submit to the presbytery, a call that makes sense only if the presbytery is not controlled by the rival party. "It is better," the schismatics are told, "to be found small but honourable...than to be preeminent in repute but to be cast out from [God's] hope" (LVII.2). The contrast between the positive "small" and the negative "preeminent" in describing the troublemakers' *change* of status is most intelligible in a situation in which the rival party had forced their way from a minor role into a major role in the church. This would suggest that they did not take over a new position from a prior position of repute in the presbytery. The repeated call for the schismatics to return to the role they once occupied is a call for them to return to a minor position—not to a role in the presbytery. This reconstruction is further supported by the description of the schismatics in the opening of the letter. They are called "worthless," "of no reputation," "foolish," and "young." This is in contrast to those whom they replaced: "those who were in honour," "the renowned," "the prudent," and the "old." This particularly negative description of the rival party is intelligible only if the rival party did not have positions in the presbytery.

Another point to note about the opposition is that it is characterized by pride and by ability.[97] Although the charge of pride is clearly polemical, we need not dismiss it simply because it is polemical. Polemical language can be descriptive. As to their ability, Clement admits that these people are eloquent or gifted in some way.[98] (Of course, as with all serious polemic, the positive is tainted by some discrediting remark.) But we can learn something about the situation even from these polemical comments. We have here people with ability who apparently are members of the laity, not of the official structures of power. They see no reason why they should be excluded from the structures of power, and apparently their gifts are obvious enough that they can gain substantial support in the church for their claim. Who would such a group have been?

A key is given in several of the statements of Clement. The group is described by the adjective "young," (among other things). As we have seen in the opening of the letter (III.3), the young are contrasted to the old in a passage where those without reputation are contrasted to the renowned, the foolish to the prudent, and the worthless to the honoured. All four pairs of contrast are intended to be polemical, but in the case of one pair, it can be effective polemically only if it is descriptive as well. That is the contrast between the young and the aged. Of the other comments, we do not know whether the rival party was foolish, or worthless or even without reputation;[99] it is all a matter of perspective, and the terms

---

97. The statements to this effect are numerous for both. See, for example, *1 Clement* XIII.1; XIV.1; XVI.1; XXI.5; XXX.1; XXXVIII.2; XXXIX.1.

98. *1 Clement* XXX.4-6; XXXVIII.2; LVII.2.

99. There is, perhaps, a descriptive element in this comment: the rival party may have been without reputation—at least, they do not seem to have had a position of authority in the church prior to this time. But that they had no reputation at all is refuted by the fact that they are highly enough regarded to have

are drawn from a standard stock of polemical vocabulary with which the modern reader is hardly less familiar than the ancient. But the term "young" is another matter. It is, admittedly, a potentially polemical term in a culture where age counted. But in that it is descriptive in a way the other terms are not, it is restricted in a way that the other terms are not. The group to which the label "young" is applied must not be well-greyed and stooped if the charged is to have impact.

The importance of this use of "young" to identify the opponents at this early place in the letter is strengthened by the positive comments made about the aged throughout the letter. In the salutation, the writer praises the Corinthian church. A number of positive things are said about them, two of which are joined: "obedient to your rulers, and paying all fitting honour to the older among you (I.3). Further, the church is encouraged to respect those who ruled over them and to honour the aged (XXI.6), and is rebuked for removing those who had served long (XLIV.3). Even the men chosen to carry the letter from Rome to Corinth ["without blame from youth to old age" (LXIII.3)] may serve to give credit to the aged at the disadvantage of the young.

I believe that the discussion of the schism in Corinth can be taken one step past what has become somewhat of an impasse. We can dismiss as unlikely the hypothesis of Bauer that the situation at the end of the first century reflected a takeover of the leadership by gnostics. What rules against Bauer's hypothesis is the age of the people involved in the takeover. They are called "the young." But nothing in that term points particularly to gnostics. In fact, any appeal to Paul's 1 Corinthians to establish the gnostic character of the opposition at the time of Clement will be challenged by the use of the term "the young" to distinguish one of the groups in the dispute at the time of Clement. Indeed, there can be no convincing connection made between "the young" of Clement's day to any of the groups that might have existed in Paul's Corinth. Anyone involved in those parties is hardly to be classified as "the young"

been recently placed in positions of authority in the church, in spite of that action requiring the dismissal of aged men against whom apparently no charge had been laid.

some forty years later in the time of Clement; the members of any group that existed in Paul's Corinth, be they gnostic, or Jewish, or dedicated Paulinists, will be old by the end of the century. All such groups, if they existed at all at the end of the first century, would have consisted of aged men, rooted in the Corinth of Paul, along with men spanning the whole age spectrum who had been attracted to a particular understanding of the Christian message over the previous forty years.

If age, then, is a distinguishing feature of the groups involved in the conflict reflected in *1 Clement* (and that does seem to be the case), then appeal cannot be made to the situation in Corinth some forty years earlier. The age distinction weighs heavily against the hypothesis that we have in *1 Clement* a situation with roots in Paul's Corinth. The only way around this would be to argue that Gnosticism was particularly attractive to the young. But that is merely anchoring one unconvincing hypothesis to a hypothesis even less convincing.

What, then, can we say about the situation in Corinth at the end of the first century? First, it must be admitted that the only information that we have *(1 Clement)* is obscure. Second, the situation in Paul's Corinth *cannot* throw light on the situation in Clement's Corinth; the age distinction between the parties in Clement's Corinth rules that out. One wonders whether what we have in the Corinthian church of the nineties is a normal second or third-generation discontent (XXIII.3). The attempt by certain of the "young" to gain positions of authority could make sense in this context. The crisis does happen roughly at the time when we would expect leaders appointed in Paul's day to be dying simply of old age. What we may be faced with is a situation in which a new criterion is required for the appointment of leaders. A leader appointed by an apostle or his delegate might appear to have a credible appointment, but this kind of validation would be no longer available in the last decade of the first century. This seems to be the problem addressed in XLIV.2. Although the author argues that the apostles intended that, when their own appointees died, other approved men should succeed, this is an ambiguous guideline for a community to follow. What would validate a new candidate's appointment? What should be the mark of approval? Charismatic gifts? The young could claim that. Age? We know that that was not a required qualification in western Asia Minor, where young Damas was bishop of Magnesia, and the author of the Pastorals knew of young leaders.[100] What we most likely have in Clement's Corinth are young men pressing for opportunity in a structure where those who lead have no undisputable validation, due simply to the new historical situation. To add a theological dimension to this dispute is not only unnecessary but misleading. As we have seen, the theological dimension is appealing only by giving undue emphasis to Paul's letters to the Corinthians, for the information from *1 Clement* itself is ambiguous.

What we have, then, for Corinth is a detailed, but selective, report of the church in its infancy period and then, some forty years later, we have a less detailed and considerably more ambiguous momentary glimpse of that church from a person who seems not to have had first-hand acquaintance with the church there. That makes for inventive, untestable, and not necessarily accurate hypotheses.

Whatever the situation, the problem is not clearly enough a theological one, nor is the literary data sufficiently extensive, to make the area of Corinth attractive for working out the questions of the orthodoxy/heresy debate.

VI. Rome

A. The Beginnings

It was the church at Rome that Bauer proposed as the driving force in the formation and the consolidation of the second-century orthodox movement.[101] But several things make Rome an un-

---

100. See pp. 173, 189-190.

101. Bauer, *Orthodoxy and Heresy,* 231/ET:229, says that Rome was "from the very beginning the center and chief source of power for the 'orthodox' movement..." According to Bauer (195/ET:193), "[O]nly in the case of Rome can we state confidently that orthodoxy possessed the upper hand." Pelikan, "The Two Sees of Peter," 1:70-2, shows the clear impact of Bauer's theory on early church historians.

fruitful centre for the study of the character of earliest Christianity.

As with most areas of the early Christian mission, so too with Rome: we know almost nothing of the beginnings of Christianity in that city. The first substantial evidence for Christianity in the area is Paul's letter to the Romans, written probably in the year A.D. 57 or 58.[102]   A church was already established, and had been for some time apparently, for its fame was spread throughout the churches (Rom 1.8). But we know little about this church. We do not know when it was founded or by whom, and we do not know the make-up of its membership. Informed guesses have been made that the expulsion of Jews from Rome by Claudius in A.D. 49 was the result of open conflict between the large Jewish population and a zealous, though perhaps small, Christian community.[103] Another informed guess is that Aquilla and Priscilla were members of this expelled community, and that they met Paul shortly afterwards in Corinth and later became a nucleus from which the first mission in

---

102. J.A.T. Robinson, *Redating the New Testament*, (London: SCM Press, 1976), 352; Brown, *Antioch and Rome*, 108, opts for A.D. 58; and Donald Guthrie, *New Testament Introduction*, 3rd ed. (Downers Grove, Ill.: Inter-Varsity Press, 1975), 396-7, argues that any date from 57 to 59 would fit the evidence.

103. See F.F. Bruce, *The Pauline Circle*, (Grand Rapids: Eerdmans, 1985), 46. See, too, Raymond Brown, "Rome," part 2 of *Antioch and Rome,* 100-102. The theory of an expulsion of Christian Jews from Rome is based on two notes in the ancient literature: one in the Christian literature and one in the secular. In Acts 18.2, Aquilla, a Jew, and his wife, are said to have left Italy due to an order from Claudius expelling all Jews. Paul met with this couple shortly after his arrival in Corinth, and shortly after their arrival too (according to the note in Acts). The guess is that Aquilla and Priscilla were Christians before they arrived in Corinth since nothing is mentioned of their conversion under Paul, though the conversion of other prominent people in the church is mentioned (Acts 18.7-8). This would make reasonable the hypothesis that Aquilla and Priscilla became Christians before leaving Italy. But the Acts account is insufficient here for us to argue that Christian preaching was the main reason for the expulsion from Rome. Since Aquilla was a Jew, a non-Christian Jewish matter could have been the issue. It is at this point in the reconstruction that the comment by Suetonius (*Claudius* 25.4) may be important. Suetonius said that Claudius had "expelled Jews from Rome because of their constant disturbances impelled by Chrestus." The proper name "Chrestus" is thought to be a confusion with the similar name "Christus" (see Brown, *Antioch and Rome,* 100-101). If this is correct, then the expulsion takes on a Christian character and thus becomes our oldest piece of evidence for Christianity in Rome.   Brown is rightfully cautious in his reconstruction, questioning not only the statement in Acts that all Jews were expelled (p. 102), but also the alternative hypothesis that, though not all Jews were expelled, all Christians were (p. 109).

Ephesus was organized.[104] But these suggestions tell us little about the character of Christianity in Rome in the early days. Quite the contrary: the pieces of information that might throw some light on the character of early Christianity in Rome, rather than clarifying the picture, actually complicate it.

Consider the common assumption that Roman Christianity was more Jewish than the Christianity of the Pauline mission.[105] Suppose for the sake of argument we do grant that Roman Christianity in the late fifties of the first century was more deeply coloured by Judaism than was Pauline Christianity of the same time. Some caution must be exercised in using this information to determine the character of the initial form of Christianity in Rome. If, as is widely accepted, the expulsion of Jews under Claudius was caused by a conflict with Christians, we must ponder what kind of Christians these must have been. We know that conflict between Jews and early Christians was possible: Stephen was lynched, and Paul came within bruises of the same fate.[106] But was such opposition the norm? During the first three decades of the church, did not law-abiding Christian Jews manage, for the most part, to live peacefully with their non-Christian neighbours in the heart of conservative Judaism, Jerusalem itself?[107] Even in Antioch, with its large Jewish population, we hear nothing of significant conflict between Jews and Christians at this time. Paul's position was radical enough when he was in Antioch, and the leadership of the

---

104. Bruce, *Pauline Circle*, 46-47; and Brown, *Antioch and Rome*, 100.

105. Brown, *Antioch and Rome*, 109-111, thought that the Jewish character of Roman Christianity was demonstrated by the way in which Paul modified his emphases when writing to that church.

106. Stephen's attack is against both the temple and the Torah, according to the account in Acts (6.13). Paul, of course, is mainly taken up with an attack on Torah. This is natural enough. As one engaged in a mission outside of Jerusalem, Paul finds a more ready target in the Torah; Stephen, as one of the deacons of the Jerusalem church, finds a ready target in the temple and well as in the Torah.

107. That is not to say that life in Jerusalem was comfortable for the Christians, but other than for the initial attacks on the hellenists and the occasional outburst of violence, the Jewish-Christian community seems to have survived in the capital until the time of the Jewish War, when sides became more clearly drawn. For a review of this matter, see Gerd Lüdermann, "The Successors of Pre-70 Jerusalem Christianity: A Critical Evaluation of the Pella-Tradition," in *JCSD* 1:161-173.

church there, though probably more conservative than Paul, almost certainly had its roots in Stephen's Christianity and, indeed, went beyond this, allowing for the admission of Gentiles without requiring circumcision of them. Even Peter and Barnabas's move to a more conservative position did not make circumcision a requirement for gentile converts. Thus Christianity in Antioch, even with the concessions of Peter and Barnabas, was radical enough. Yet we hear of no riots there by Jews against Christians there.

How is it, then, that a Jewish-Christian conflict broke out in Rome if the Christianity there was, at most, a liberal Judaism, without the radicalism of a Stephen or a Paul? Must we not revise our understanding of one of two points? Either the expulsion under Claudius had nothing to do with Christians (and we loose our earliest evidence for Christianity in Rome), or we modify our view of the character of earliest Christianity in Rome, aligning it more with the radical tendencies within the early church than with the conservative tendencies. If we find that Christianity in Rome was considerably more conservative at some later period, we could account for that by the loss of the more radical element during the expulsion. This could make better sense of Aquilla and Priscilla's common concerns with Paul, if, as is often argued, they were part of the expelled community.

Raymond Brown considers another point. He argues that Paul was attempting to avoid offending Jewish sensibilities in his letter to the Romans, and Brown thinks this points to the conservative character of the Christian church in Rome, one with not uncordial ties to the synagogue.[108] And the Acts' account of Paul's imprisonment in Rome seems to suggest a fairly cordial initial relationship of Paul himself with the leaders of the Jewish community.[109] But these ties could not have been cordial from the outset if the expulsion under Claudius was caused by Jewish/Christian riots.

---

108. This is the perspective from which Brown interprets the whole of the letter to the Romans (*Antioch and Rome*, 105-127).

109. Acts 28.17-24. The weight of this account for the present discussion will depend on whether one sees this as a creation of Luke or an actual event in Paul's early days under Roman house arrest. F.F. Bruce, *The Acts of the Apostles*, 2nd ed. (Grand Rapids: Eerdmans, 1952), 477-8, puts forward a case for the general accuracy of Paul's meeting with the leaders of the Jewish community in Rome.

Besides, if we are looking for some explanation for Paul's politeness in his letter to the Romans, could we not account for this by positing an initial radical Christianity in Rome that resulted in intense conflict with the Jews there and an expulsion of the Christians, after which Christianity was reintroduced, or re-organized, by less radical Jewish Christians, who recognized the need to accommodate themselves fully to the non-Christian Jewish community if they were to remain in the capital? The visit that Paul planned may have needed a conciliatory introduction in light of the bitter memories of the past tensions with a radical form of Christianity—memories of which would have been stirred up afresh by the announcement of the coming of a recognized leader of this radicalism. Were this the case, the account in Acts of an initial contact Paul made with the leaders of the non-Christian Jewish community to explain his position would be intelligible.[110]

I have offered this sketch of the Christianity in Rome primarily to show that our information is simply too incomplete or mute to allow us to reconstruct the character of the earliest form of Christianity in Rome. Brown's reconstruction may be correct: earliest Christianity in Rome may have been conservative. But I think a case of equal merit can be made that the character of the earliest Christianity in Rome was considerably more radical. A convincing case is probably not possible for either (mainly due to the lack of data). The option that I have suggested must be left open, however: the conservative character of the Christianity in Rome may reflect not the most primitive form of Christianity in the city but, rather, a loss of an original radical element.

B. The Literature

Although the church at Rome was founded sometime before the early fifties of the first century, we have only scanty information about the condition of the church until well into the second century. Compared to the quantity of literature connected in some way to Ephesus in the first half-century or so of its existence, the literature

---

110. I say it would be "intelligible." I am not arguing that such contact did— or did not occur.

connected to Rome is strikingly meagre. Conceivably, a rigorous examination of the first-century materials relevant to Rome might supply us with valuable information about the state of Christianity there. In this regard, Raymond Brown has recently investigated all the early materials he judged relevant to an investigation of primitive Christianity in Rome.[111] There is Paul's letter to the Romans, there is Hebrews and 1 Peter, and there is *1 Clement*. Brown supplements his lists with some less likely candidates: Paul's letter to the Philippians, the epistle to the Ephesians, Mark's Gospel, Ignatius's epistle to the Romans, the *Shepherd of Hermas,* various legends of Peter and Simon Magus in Rome, and finally, 2 Peter.

The list is somewhat impressive initially. But there are problems with the list. One might wonder how much one can learn about the character of primitive Christianity in Rome from letters written to Rome by persons who had never even visited the churches there, let alone worked in them. Yet that is precisely the case with Paul's letter to the Romans and with Ignatius's letter. These letters will show us considerably more about Paul and Ignatius than about the Romans. In fact, these letters will show us more about the Ephesian church and the Antiochene church than about the church at Rome. Paul's letter was probably written from Macedonia or Achaia, immediately after a long period of ministry in western Asia Minor, with headquarters in Ephesus.[112] What we hear in Paul's letter to the Romans is much more likely to be what the Ephesian Christians heard in their Sunday assemblies than what the Roman Christians were accustomed to hearing.[113] As for Ignatius's letter to the

---

111. Brown, *Antioch and Rome*, Part II.

112. According to Acts 19.21, when Paul left Ephesus, his intention was to go to Jerusalem and then to Rome. But the trip was not to be a direct one, for according to Acts, Paul had first to go through Macedonia and Achaia, although the reason for going is not stated in Acts. But from the letter to the Romans, it is clear that Paul takes a route through Macedonia and Achaia in order to collect the offerings the Gentiles had raised for the poor in Jerusalem (Romans 15.25-28). After going through Macedonia and Achaia, Paul heads for Jerusalem to deliver the collection, planning after a short stay in Jerusalem to go on to new pastures (Spain), taking a route through Rome (15.24-28). But, as we know, Paul had to spend a little more time in Palestine than he had planned (Acts 21.27-27.1).

113. I am obviously not comfortable with the way that Brown, *Antioch and Rome,* 105, describes Paul's letter to the Romans. It is, according to one of Brown's section titles, "A Letter *Shaped* by Roman Christianity" [emphasis mine].

Romans, much the same can be said. It is Ignatius who is reflected in that letter; not the Roman Christians. And this Ignatius wrote his letter to the Romans only weeks after being escorted under guard from Antioch, where he was the leader of the church. Of the two groups of Christians (those at Antioch and those at Rome), it would be those at Antioch who would have been the more familiar with the message of Ignatius's letter to the Romans. It would seem, then, that these letters may contribute only minimally to our understanding of the character of early Christianity in Rome.

And what of the other material examined by Brown? Few would deny that 1 Peter was written in Rome.[114] But a host of questions confront us about this work. Besides the much-debated questions of authorship and date, there is the question most important to our concerns here—the question of locale. In regard to locale, we can at least say that the author's interest does not seem to be with the Christians of Rome, but with those of Pontus, Galatia, Cappadocia, Asia and Bithynia. Is the author only a visitor in Rome, whose connections are mainly with Asia Minor? And what do we make of the Pauline colouring of the thought of the epistle? Is this really representative of the thought of the Roman church? These questions are serious enough to caution against reading 1 Peter as an expression of Roman Christianity.

As for the remainder of the literature, the testimony of each is mute or uncertain for the reconstruction of earliest Christianity in Rome.

C. The Problem with Heresy

Whatever our judgment about the value of this literature for reconstructing the character of Christianity in the early church in Rome, it seems that we must admit that for the questions of the orthodoxy/heresy debate, little is likely to be found. The earliest

---

Brown offers a list of scholars who agree that Paul's letter to the Romans is concerned about the situation in Rome and those who disagree (p. 106 n. 217). Concern for the situation in the Roman church on the part of Paul will not alone make that work an ideal one from which to determine the shape of Roman Christianity though.

114. See discussion in Guthrie, *Introduction,* 801-3.

picture of the church in Rome is one of the church against its persecutors (e.g., the fire at Rome under Nero[115] and the concerns expressed in the letter known as 1 Peter[116]); internal church conflicts are not addressed. That does not necessarily mean, as Bauer assumed, that Christianity in Rome was relatively uniform and free of heresy. It simply means that the evidence we have for the earliest period of the Roman church relates to problems apparently considered more serious to the survival of the church than whatever doctrinal disputes may have been present. We do know that by the middle of the second century a host of heretics had found their way to Rome.[117] Undoubtedly, the Roman reaction to these heretics is of considerable significance in the history of the conflict between orthodoxy and heresy.

For the early period, however, the literature is scarce, and more of concern to the substance of our discussion here, none of it confronts the issue of orthodoxy and heresy in the way that the literature of western Asia Minor does. For that reason, my emphasis will be on Ephesus rather than on Rome.

VII. Jerusalem

A. The Beginnings

Jerusalem has its appeal as a centre in which something might be learned about the character of primitive Christianity, especially regarding any early attempt to discriminate between sound belief and suspect belief. Jerusalem was the mother-church, and we do know of a dispute that occurred there early (the dispute between the "Hebrews" and the "Hellenists").[118] We also know that a theological difference may have been at the root of this conflict, though the contention by the author of Acts that the dispute had a practical

---

115. Tacitus, *Annals* 15.44. See Brown, *Antioch and Rome*, 98-9.

116. The letter mentions nothing about heresy. The repeated theme is that of suffering (1.6-7; 2.12, 19-21; 3.14-17; 4.1, 12-19; 5.10).

117. See Ehrhardt, "Apostles' Creed," 110-11. There is even a tradition that the gnostic Valentinus had reasonable hopes of gaining the position of Bishop of Rome (Tertullian, *De praescr.* 30).

118. Acts 6.1-6. See Hengel, *History of Earliest Christianity*, 71-80.

side [the Hellenists' widows were neglected (Acts 6.1)] is not to be dismissed.[119]

Yet, though this problem in Jerusalem may be of significance in a discussion of orthodoxy and heresy, we really know so little about the issue and its resolution that most of what we could say would be speculation.[120] The difference between the two groups may have been considerable, but the literature is generally obscure on the point, and the dispute thus can provide only muted testimony in our investigation of the conflict between orthodoxy and heresy. Today, the Tübingen scheme and its various modifications, which exaggerated the split between conservative and liberal elements within the Palestinian community, is being replaced by many scholars with a scheme that places Paul and Peter and James in considerable agreement, while allowing that fringe radicals and reactionaries may have represented minor, but vocal, options.[121]

Even if we could resolve the problem of determining the scope or even the central issue of the dispute in the Jerusalem community, it is almost certain that the issue in Jerusalem has little connection with the issues of the classical heresies that generally are thought of

---

119. The account in Acts emphasizes the practical side of the conflict to the exclusion of the theological side. There seems to have been a theological side to the conflict, for a short time later when the Jewish authorities took action against the Christians, it appears that only the Hellenists were forced to flee. See F.F. Bruce, *New Testament History* (Garden City: Doubleday, 1971), 226; see too James D.G. Dunn, *Unity and Diversity in the New Testament* (Philadelphia: Westminster, 1977), 268, who titles his section on the Hellenists' dispute about food distribution "The First Confessional Schism in Church History."

120. Some scholars, to be sure, have attempted to trace the history of the hellenists after their departure from Jerusalem [a departure which, according to the author of Acts, was due to external persecution rather than to internal church hostilities in the Jerusalem community (Acts 8.1-3)]. According to the impression left by the author of Acts, the internal church tensions had been resolved by the time of the problems involving the Hellenists and the Jewish authorities (6.8). See discussion in Leonhard Goppelt, *Apostolic and Post-Apostolic Times*, trans. Robert A. Guelich (London: A. and C. Black, 1970), 61-8. Also, I. Howard Marshall, "Palestinian and Hellenistic Christianity: Some Critical Comments," *NTS* 19 (1972-3): 271-87.

121. For recent discussions on this issue, see Ben F. Meyer, *The Early Christians: Their World Mission and Self-Discovery*, Good News Studies 16 (Wilmington: Michael Glazier, 1986), and Paul J. Achtemeier, *The Quest for Unity in the New Testament Church: A Study in Paul and Acts* (Philadelphia: Fortress, 1987).

when we discuss orthodoxy and heresy in the early church. That is not to say, in contradiction of Strecker, the editor of the second German edition of Bauer's work, that the conflict in Jerusalem could not be the earliest and perhaps best example of Bauer's hypothesis. But a number of problems do confront that view.

Although we know that distinct Jewish-Christian groups did exist[122] (the Ebionites are the classic example), it is not clear that the later groups accurately reflect the earlier tensions in the Jerusalem community related to the admission of gentiles into the church. Surely the series of striking set-backs and defeats experienced by Judaism in the second half of the first century must have had a profound effect on these Jewish-Christian groups—with Jerusalem devastated by the Romans and the temple destroyed. We know from the book of Acts that as late as the late fifties the temple still played an important role in the lives of Jewish Christians, and nothing suggests a radical change in that attitude in the sixties. A further stress on Christian Jews would have been the stunning success of the Christian mission to the Gentiles, as compared to the mission to the Jews. This reduction of Jewish Christianity to the status of a minority element in the church must have had some impact on the shape and direction of Jewish Christianity.

The structure of later Jewish-Christian groups would likely reflect an attempt by these Jews to preserve as much of their threatened culture as possible. That concern would not have been as conscious a concern in the early years. Even the schism at Antioch (whatever its nature) was not an Ebionite phenomenon. That is not to dismiss outright the hypothesis that the later Jewish-Christian groups like the Ebionites might have represented the most original form of the Christian message. It is simply to point out that the fundamental factors in the shaping of the later Jewish-Christian groups are sufficiently changed from those affecting the original Jewish-Christian communities of Palestine to make such a hypothesis suspect and in need of rigorous support.[123]

---

122 See Koester, *Introduction,* 2:198-207.

123. *Ibid.,* 2:199, says that we know nothing about Jewish-Christian communities outside Palestine and Galatia. A few pages later (p. 203), he says that there is no sign of a self-reliant and independent Jewish-Christian tradition in early

B. The Literature

The lack of written material from the Jerusalem community poses a problem for an investigation of the issues of the orthodoxy/ heresy debate. Although isolated attempts have been made to place particular documents in the Jerusalem area, little has been plausibly established. Other than for Paul's letters, which clearly were written neither from nor to Jerusalem, scholars date almost every other document of the early church to some time after the destruction of Jerusalem. In regard to literature, then, Jerusalem is strikingly barren compared to Ephesus.[124]

VIII. Antioch

A. The Beginnings

Antioch is little different.[125] We know of a dispute in the early period; a theological issue seems to be at stake (though it was the practical aspect that was emphasized—both by Paul and by the writer of Acts).[126] The conflict seems to result in some kind of separation, though neither a temporary nor a permanent division of the Christian community need have occurred. For a time, admit-

---

Christianity; the later Jewish-Christian groups are "not due to any continuing, separate tradition which had originated in the very beginning of Christian history." See too J. Munck, "Jewish Christianity in Post-Apostolic Times," *NTS* 6 (1960): 103-16. Cf. Dunn, *Unity and Diversity,* 244-5, who argues the opposite: "Heretical Jewish Christianity could claim a direct line of continuity with the most primitive form of Christianity. It could certainly claim to be more in accord with the most primitive faith than Paul, say."

124. Those who argue for the apostolic authorship of the epistles of James and Jude might find Jerusalem a plausible place for composition. Even so, this does not call into question my observation that Jerusalem is an impoverished source of information for the early Christian movement.

125. A recent examination of Christianity in Antioch has been provided by Wayne A. Meeks and Robert L. Wilken, *Jews and Christians in Antioch in the First Four Centuries of the Common Era* (Missoula: Scholars Press, 1978).

126. The status of the gentile converts was the theological issue; the break in table fellowship between Jewish and gentile converts was the practical issue. According to Paul (Gal 2.12-3), Peter and Barnabas withdrew from table fellowship with the gentile believers. The author of Acts records a break between Paul and Barnabas, which he explains in terms of a personality clash between Paul and the young nephew of Barnabas, John Mark (Acts 15.36-40).

tedly, Antioch seems to have ceased to be a primary base for Paul's ministry, leading many scholars to speak of Paul's defeat at Antioch.[127] John P. Meier has even argued that not only was Paul defeated at Antioch (as many scholars have argued), but that Paul turned from Antioch to Jerusalem.[128] Meier's conclusion was based mainly on the accounts of Paul's visits to Palestine recorded in Acts (hardly the firmest base of support).[129] One might just as credibly contend that Jerusalem simply continued to function for Paul as it always had (as the mother church to which all owed special allegiance); what changed may have been merely the base for operations (from Antioch to the more westerly centres of Corinth and Ephesus), and this change may have reflected practical considerations rather than polemical or theological ones. The evidence is simply too incomplete to serve as a basis for more than conjecture.

B. The Literature

As Jerusalem was, Antioch too is barren of relevant literature for the concerns of the orthodoxy/heresy debate.[130] Unlike Ephesus,

---

127. Meier, *Antioch and Rome*, 24, 39. Koester, *"Gnomai Diaphoroi,"* 286, thinks that Paul was wrong, and that he lost, though his influence continued on in Antioch; also, Koester, *Introduction*, 2:167. Hengel, *History of Earliest Christianity*, 98, thinks that Peter took over from Paul in Antioch. Also see Bengt Holmberg, *Paul and Power: The Structure of Authority in the Primitive Church as Reflected in the Pauline Epistles* (Philadelphia: Fortress, 1980), 32-5.

128. Meier, *Antioch and Rome*, 39-40. Also Hengel, *History of Earliest Christianity*, 123-4.

129. According to Acts, Paul returned to Antioch only one other time (Acts 18.22-3). On the other hand, the "Jerusalem collection" (organized by Paul for the poor in Jerusalem) seems to serve as evidence that Paul had established (or was taking steps to establish) better relations with Jerusalem. But these two observations cannot be forced together in any coherent framework of separation from Antioch and realignment with Jerusalem, for according to the account in Galatians, Paul's anger with Peter and others in Antioch stems from their bowing to pressures from a more conservative element in the leadership at Jerusalem (Gal. 2.12). The more coherent reconstruction is one that, in light of the collection, qualifies the seriousness (or the permanence) of the break with Antioch. Paul's reconciliation with Jerusalem would seem to require a reconciliation with Antioch as well, since the situation in Jerusalem reflects the sharper differences.

130. Meier, *Antioch and Rome*, 27, is disappointed with the major work by G. Downey on Antioch because it has a "gaping hole" for the period from A.D. 70-100 [Downey, *A History of Antioch in Syria from Seleucus to the Arab Conquest* (Princeton: Princeton University Press, 1961)]. But the only information that

which has many documents both early and relevant to the question of heresy, Antioch has almost no literature that can be assigned to it with any certainty, and even what might be, with some generosity, assigned to it, lacks the kind of interest in the problems of orthodoxy and heresy that is central to numerous documents associated with western Asia Minor.

Meier, in his attempt to describe the character of primitive Christianity in Antioch, examined mainly the Gospel of Matthew, chapter two of Galatians and chapters eleven to fifteen of Acts, the letters of Ignatius, and the *Didache*. But Matthew's Gospel contributes little to our understanding of orthodoxy and heresy; its concerns relate to the distinction between Jew and Christian; nothing is offered about substantial internal Christian divisions. The material from Galatians and Acts does address an internal Christian conflict, but, as I have already noted, we know too little about the matter to use this material fruitfully in a study of orthodoxy and heresy in Antioch. The Ignatian material, at first sight, appears promising to our question; clearly the language of the orthodoxy/heresy debate is dramatically employed, and well-marked dis-

---

Meier has to fill in that "gaping hole" is the Gospel of Matthew, and though Matthew may well be witness to a second generation of Christianity in Antioch, if anything, rather than filling the hole, it widens it. Matthew has a Jewish character than neither Paul (first generation) nor Ignatius (third generation) has, and we are left to wonder just what role Matthew plays in a tradition running from a Pauline Paul to a Pauline Ignatius. Matthew seems more like the "monkey in the middle" than an intermediate stage in the Pauline development. If we argue that two kinds of Christianity existed in Antioch (a Pauline type and a conservative-to-moderate Jewish type), and that Matthew was a part of the latter, do we then, in light of Ignatius's position in the early second century, turn with equal fondness to speak of a Matthean defeat in Antioch as scholars have spoken of a Pauline defeat? I think Meier shows a cautious balance when he says that one should not try to harmonize Pauline and Matthean thought on the one hand nor, on the other, to "facilely" posit opposition (p. 62). But that does not make our period any less obscure, and one might wonder whether Meier has not, in fact, brought Paul and Matthew closer together than what the evidence permits. Meier seems a little more uncomfortable in bringing Matthew and Ignatius together (p. 74), as perhaps he should be. Koester, *"Gnomai Diaphoroi,"* 287-8, thinks that Matthew stands in opposition to the Pauline tendencies of Ignatius. Cf. Christine Trevett, "Approaching Matthew from the Second Century: The Under-used Ignatian Correspondence," *JSNT* 20 (1984): 59-67. My impression is that if the Gospel of Matthew does not in fact obscure our understanding of second-generation Christianity in Antioch, it does little to enlighten it.

tinctions are set up between what beliefs are judged to be wholesome and what are judged to be corrupt.[131] But a debate rages as to whether the letters of Ignatius reflect the situation in Antioch,[132] and we are far from any agreement regarding the situation in the church at Antioch at the time of Ignatius from our study of other documents.[133] It does come as some surprise to find such a Paulinist as Ignatius in charge of the church there, given the tendencies of modern scholarship to speak of Paul's defeat in Antioch.[134] And surprising, too, are the opponents with whom Ignatius engages. They do not reflect the supposedly victorious position of Peter or James; they are, whatever their Jewish colouring, clearly docetic.[135] We know nothing about the source of this belief in Antioch. We are no better off to argue for two groups of opponents in Antioch, one Jewish-Christian and one docetic. We would still not know where the docetic group came from, and for the Jewish group, we would not know what links it had with Peter and James's group, and we would not know what caused them to loose the prominent position they supposedly had in Antioch after Paul left.

Even if we could establish with some certainty what happened in Antioch (and I repeat, at present we cannot), the issues in Antioch are nothing like those that are central to the classical disputes between orthodoxy and heresy. Whether Paul turned from Antioch to Jerusalem, and having turned, made some sort of novel alliance with Jerusalem, his writings do not suggest that he judged the

---

131. See ch. 5, and appendix B.

132. See chapter 5 §II.B.

133. Koester, *"Gnomai Diaphoroi,"* 287, recognizes the continued Pauline influence in Antioch after Paul's departure. The Pauline Ignatius is bishop there in the early second century, though the Pauline position was supposedly repudiated, according to some scholars, after Paul's dispute with Peter. Matthew, if written in Antioch in the late first century, reflects a Jewish consciousness—something that Ignatius as leader a few years later sharply opposes. One might argue that both a Pauline party and a Petrine (or Jerusalem) party continued to exist in Antioch, for there are two bishop lists for Antioch. These lists, however, are likely fictional constructs based on the recognition that both Peter and Paul played a role in the early church in Antioch. Cf. Ehrhardt, "Apostles' Creed," 100-102, who disputes Bauer's reconstruction in which a strong gnostic movement is proposed.

134. See p. 67 n. 89, and p. 88.

135. See Appendix A.

leaders of Antioch as outside of the community of the redeemed. This does not mean, however, that Paul refused to draw the line between the tolerable and the intolerable (contrary to Bauer, 236-7/ET:234-5). Paul can, and does, exclude some believers, but the leaders of Antioch (or of Jerusalem) never are placed in that group. Whatever we may say, then, of Paul's break with the church at Antioch and his organization of a fairly independent mission, Paul does not see the break in terms of a separation between orthodoxy and heresy, though in the case of some Christians, he seems to view separation in precisely those terms. Thus, Paul's dispute in Antioch would not seem to parallel the situation we confront when the classic questions of orthodoxy and heresy are raised.

IX. Conclusion

My intention in this chapter has been to demonstrate that most areas of early Christianity lack extensive and relevant data from which the questions of the orthodoxy/heresy debate could be resolved. That is not to say that we cannot learn anything about the character of earliest Christianity in some of these areas (Edessa, for example, seems more encratic than other areas of the Christian mission). But it appears that our information for these centres is too limited to give to the Bauer Thesis a compelling ring of truth. In fact, where we have an area with extensive relevant data for the questions of the orthodox/heresy debate (i.e., Ephesus), I contend the Bauer Thesis rings hollow. That is the subject of the remainder of this work.

Chapter Three

Ephesus and Western Asia Minor: A Leading Centre of Early Christianity

I. Ephesus in Early Christianity

A. The Importance of Ephesus Recognized

Numerous comments have been made over the years concerning the importance to the developing church of Ephesus and the west Asia Minor area. The most influential attempts to argue for the importance of Ephesus are now somewhat dated. Adolf Harnack spoke of Ephesus as the "third capital of Christianity" and said that "for a while it looked as if Ephesus was actually destined to be the final headquarters of the faith."[1] B.H. Streeter recognized that after A.D. 70, Ephesus, along with Antioch and Rome, were the important Christian centres.[2] G.S. Duncan and E.J. Goodspeed both recognized the importance of Ephesus and promoted that view in some detail.[3] Goodspeed even argued that by A.D. 90, Ephesus

---

1. Adolf Harnack, *The Mission and Expansion of Christianity in the First Three Centuries*, trans. James Moffatt, with intro. by Jaroslav Pelikan (New York: Harper & Brothers, 1962), 76.

2. Burnett Hillman Streeter, *The Primitive Church*, (London: Macmillan, 1929), 258. Streeter recognized that after A.D. 200, Alexandria replaced Ephesus as a leading centre, but that change does not affect his observation concerning the earlier Ephesus, which is what my study here deals with.

3. G.S. Duncan, *St. Paul's Ephesian Ministry* (London: Hodder and Stoughton, 1929). E.J. Goodspeed, *The Meaning of Ephesians* (Chicago: Chicago

was the leading centre and quoted with approval Harnack's comment that Ephesus was the second fulcrum of Christianity after Antioch.[4]

Numerous other scholars have given passing attention to the prominence in the early church of Ephesus and the west Asia Minor area. F.F. Bruce thinks that Asia was, for centuries, the strongest Christian province,[5] and James Moffatt is prepared to say that in the early period it was Asia Minor, not Rome, that was the leading force in the Christian movement.[6] Helmut Koester speaks of the "quick-growing" Christian communities of Asia Minor;[7] J.G. Davies, of Asia Minor as the Christian country "par excellence" at the end of the Apostolic age.[8] Jean Daniélou recognizes that Ephesus was a centre for Christianity in the late first century, and he speaks of western Asia Minor as the centre in which Christianity "shows the most extraordinary vitality."[9] Raymond Brown, in his discussion of the Johannine community (which he placed in the west Asia Minor area) states that, given the presence of Christian groups representing a wide spectrum of Christian interpretation, this area could not have been a "back-water."[10] Bo Reicke observes that, of Christians in the Roman empire at the end of the first century, those in western Asia Minor were "particularly numerous."[11]

Although passing reference has generally been given to the importance of Ephesus and western Asia Minor in histories of the early church, even this passing reference is now frequently

---

University Press, 1933), and Goodspeed, *An Introduction to the New Testament* (Chicago: Chicago University Press, 1937), 211-18.

4. Goodspeed, *Introduction*, 217-8.

5. F.F. Bruce, *New Testament History*, Anchor Books (Garden City: Doubleday, 1971), 303.

6. James Moffatt, *Exp Tim* 45 (1933/4): 475.

7. Helmut Koester, *Introduction to the New Testament* (Philadelphia: Fortress, 1982), 2:251.

8. J.G. Davies, *The Early Christian Church* (London: Weidenfeld & Nicolson, 1965), 86.

9. Jean Daniélou, *The Christian Centuries*, vol. 1, *The First Six Hundred Years*, trans. Vincent Cronin (London: Darton, Longman and Todd, 1964), 40.

10. Raymond E. Brown, *The Community of the Beloved Disciple* (New York: Paulist, 1979), 98.

11. Bo Reicke, "The Inauguration of Catholic Martyrdom according to St. John the Divine," *Augustinianum* 20 (1980): 278.

challenged, or consciously disregarded. W.H.C. Frend's recent work on the early church is a refreshing exception. He says that western Asia Minor was the main centre for Christianity for a century and a half,[12] and he calls Ephesus the "radical point" of the strongest area of the church.[13] But such is not the usual perspective of church historians today.

B. The Importance of Ephesus Disregarded

Several trends in New Testament scholarship reflect the growing neglect of the importance of Ephesus in histories of the primitive church. For one thing, it is now customary to speak of Paul's defeat in Antioch, and to contend that Paul's mission in Asia Minor and the Agean took on a colouring not reflected by the larger church. Koester says that Paul not only lost in Antioch, but charges that Paul was wrong as well.[14] Since Ephesus was the chief city of Paul's most successful mission, the kind of Christianity we find there is somewhat discredited because of Paul's supposed defeat and separation from the mainstream.[15] The second trend is closely related to the first. The supposed defeat of Paul in Antioch is, from another perspective, the victory of Peter. Raymond Brown and John Meier, in their recent work on Antioch and Rome, attempt to show that it was not the Pauline stream that became dominant in Christianity, but the Petrine stream. As Brown and Meier say:

---

12. W.H.C. Frend, *The Rise of Christianity* (Philadelphia: Fortress, 1984), 38.

13. *Ibid.,* 127.

14. Helmut Koester, *"Gnomai Diaphoroi:* The Origin and Nature of Diversification in the History of Early Christianity," *HTR* 58 (1965): 286. Koester does admit continued Pauline influence in Antioch, in spite of Paul's defeat. But not every scholar thinks Paul lost at Antioch. See B. Holmberg, *Paul and Power* (Philadelphia: Fortress, 1980), 34 n. 117.

15. This trend is most clearly reflected in the title of a recent volume by Raymond E. Brown and John P. Meier, *Antioch and Rome: New Testament Cradles of Catholic Christianity* (New York/Ramsey: Paulist, 1983). Antioch and Rome become the cradles of catholic Christianity; Ephesus is slighted, and its significant contribution to the development of orthodoxy is passed over unmentioned. Hans Conzelmann, "Luke's Place in the Development of Early Christianity," in *Studies in Luke-Acts,* ed. L.E. Keck and J.L. Martyn (Nashville/New York: Abingdon, 1966), 302, thinks that Ephesus appears in a "twilight" by the time Acts is written; Jerusalem and Rome are the chief centres for the writer of Acts.

It is often assumed that in the areas of NT Mediterranean Christianity which really came to matter in subsequent western church history (Syria, Asia Minor, Greece, and Italy) Paul's thought 'won out...' [We] are convinced...it was not the Pauline view about the Law and Judaism that prevailed but a moderate view that could be associated with Peter—even though ultimately some of the Pauline strains were domesticated and incorporated into that Petrine strain...We are convinced that the somewhat-right-of-Paul strains of Christianity that emerged at Antioch and Rome in association with Peter were a key factor in the emerging church catholic.[16]

The third trend in recent scholarship is the recognition that Paul was either misunderstood, or simply not regarded at all, by the orthodox church engaged in a violent struggle with Gnosticism in the second century.[17]

Paul's formative influence on the church is often, in light of these trends, taken to be minimal: his impact on the first-century church is proportionately reduced.[18] When this is done, Antioch and Rome (or other cities) appear more attractive than Ephesus as centres for the study of early Christianity.

Frequently, Ephesus is not even mentioned as ever having been one of the chief centres of early Christianity; the centres of importance are listed in the following chronological order: Jerusalem first; Antioch, for a brief time, second; and Rome, by the early second century, the third centre of the church. Kirsopp Lake says that after Antioch, it was Rome that was the most important centre, even in the first century.[19] Jaroslav Pelikan follows the same order: after A.D. 70, he says, it was not Rome and Jerusalem but Rome

---

16. Brown and Meier, *Antioch and Rome,* vii-viii.

17. See Martinus C. de Boer, "Images of Paul in the Post-Apostolic Period," *CBQ* 42 (1980): 359-80. See also C.K. Barrett, "Pauline Controversies in the Post-Pauline Period," *NTS* 20 (1974): 229-245.

18. As noted in the quote of Brown, above. Note, too, Bauer's repeated charge that, even in Ephesus, the memory of Paul was quickly lost (87-91/ET:83-7).

19. Kirsopp Lake, *Landmarks in the History of Early Christianity* (London: Macmillan, 1920), 102. Lake does hold that Ephesus has an important role to play in the history of early Christianity, and he sets Ephesus against Rome. Rome takes over from Antioch a Jewish form of Christianity; Ephesus is more radical.

and Syria that were the chief centres of the church.[20] Although Pelikan is here emphasizing the shift from Jerusalem to Syria, he assumes the importance of Rome and Antioch but disregards western Asia Minor.

One might well ask: where is Ephesus? Is it such a minor centre in early Christianity that it cannot hope to compete with the centres of Jerusalem, Antioch and Rome? Or, can it perhaps demand for itself a place as *the* primary centre of Christianity in the late first and early second centuries, between the recognized centres of Antioch and Rome?

C. Indicators of the Importance of Ephesus

1. The Canon

The canon, itself, points to the importance of Asia Minor in the primitive church. As we will see below (§I.D), numerous writings of the canon reflect an Asia Minor context; in fact, no other area is even remotely as well represented in the canon. We would exaggerate the point were we to call the canon an "Asia Minor" canon, but it would be only a slight exaggeration. If any area has a special claim to the canon, it is clearly western Asia Minor.

The plausibility of the theory of a collection of Paul's letters in Ephesus[21] (and perhaps of the Johannine and Gospel collections too),[22] and of the impulse towards defining the canon, particularly against the influence of Marcion,[23] point to Asia Minor as anything

---

20 Jaroslav Pelikan, "The Two Sees of Peter: Reflections on the Pace of Normative Self-Definition East and West," in *JCSD* 1:59.

21. For the most recent theory, see Farmer, "The Collection of Paul's Letters," in William R. Farmer and Denis M. Farkasfalvy, *The Formation of the New Testament Canon* (New York/Ramsey/Toronto: Paulist, 1983), 77-81. Also see C.F.D. Moule, The Birth of the New Testament, 3rd ed. (San Francisco: Harper & Row, 1982), 258-265, who discusses the possibility that the collection of Paul's letters was the work of one individual and that the letter to the Ephesians was a covering letter. See also E.E. Lemcio, "Ephesus and the New Testament Canon, " *BJRL* 69 (1986): 210-234.

22. See Farmer, *The Formation of the New Testament Canon*, 71-3

23. See the general discussion in Farmer and Farkasfalvy. That Marcion was active, for a time, in western Asia Minor might be reflected in the tradition concerning the confrontation between Marcion and Polycarp, the bishop of Smyrna [see discussion in R. Joseph Hoffmann, *Marcion: On the Restitution of Christianity: An Essay on the Development of Radical Paulinist Theology in the*

but an isolated theological backwater.

2. A Centre of Emigration from Palestine

According to a tradition recorded by Eusebius, a number of prominent Palestinian Christians immigrated to western Asia Minor (*E.H.* 3.31.2.ff; 5.24.2ff). Some scholars have argued for a significant immigration to Asia Minor about the time of the destruction of Jerusalem, and even if a significant immigration cannot be established beyond doubt, it seems likely that many others besides prominent leaders would have made a similar move to the area.[24] Whether these Christians immigrated there because the church was well established in this region, or for some other reason, the immigration would, in any case, strengthen the prestige of the church in the area, given that some of the immigrants were prominent church leaders.

3. Prominent Church Leaders

Paul is not the only first-generation Christian of some note to be associated with western Asia Minor. The Apostle John and the mother of Jesus are associated with the area too, as are Philip and his daughters.[25] Another apostolic witness, an Aristion, is mentioned by Papias (*E.H.* 3.39.4). Possibly some memory of Timothy's presence there is reflected in 1 Timothy.[26] And even

---

Second Century, (Chico: Scholars Press, 1984), 37-9].

24. We cannot be sure whether a large number of immigrants came to western Asia Minor. We know the names of only the more prominent, but that list surely does not count the full number who would have moved from Palestine around the time of the destructive war under Vespasian and Titus. Bauer, *Orthodoxy and Heresy*, 89-90/ET:85-6, offers a brief discussion. He rejects the theories of Holl and Schwartz, who see a more organized immigration into the west Asia Minor area. Bruce, *New Testament History*, 376-7, notes the immigration and the resulting conservative tendency, though he believes that most of the immigrants were Hellenists.

25. Eusebius, *E.H.* 3.31.2; 3.39.5-9; 5.24.2. The tradition of Mary's residence in Ephesus is later and may reflect nothing more than the passion tradition in which Jesus assigns to "the beloved disciple" the responsibility for the care of his mother (John 19.26-7).

26. As the area of Paul's most successful mission, Ephesus might well have come under the leadership of Timothy after the death of Paul. Unfortunately, we have no reliable historical data for Timothy's activities after Paul's activity in the area, though the memory of Timothy is not lost. In the late first century,

Peter is associated with the area.[27] Around the turn of the century, there may have been a John known by the name, "The Elder."[28] And, of course, there is Papias, the bishop of Hierapolis, and Polycarp, the bishop of Smyrna.

How reliable the traditions concerning the earlier figures are is a matter of dispute.[29] Most of the reports come from Eusebius. Eusebius says he is dependent for his information on a letter from Polycrates, bishop of Ephesus when Victor was bishop of Rome (c. A.D. 191). Polycrates was attempting to deny to Victor the kind of power Victor was assuming over Ephesus and western Asia Minor in regard to the Easter controversy, and as a counterclaim against this extension of power, Polycrates claimed that Ephesus had a great company of credible bearers of apostolic tradition (*E.H.* 3.31.2; 5.24.2). In this context, Polycrates would not have consciously passed over apostolic witnesses associated with western Asia Minor. That his list is as restrained as it is (at least for apostolic witnesses)[30] speaks well for it accuracy, or at least for a fairly established tradition about these apostolic figures when Polycrates wrote. In other words, he is no creator of the tradition.

Timothy figures prominently in Acts and in the post-Pauline material [1 and 2 Timothy, Colossians (if pseudonymous), and 2 Thessalonians]. Timothy's connection to Ephesus seems to be reflected in the Acts material. There, Timothy is associated with Paul during the Macedonian, Corinthian, Ephesian circuit (Acts 16-20). This complements the frequent mention of Timothy in the authentic Pauline letters written during the time of Paul's association with Ephesus (Romans, 1 and 2 Corinthians, Philippians). According to these letters, Timothy is either with Paul or in his service. And if Hebrews was written to Ephesus, Timothy's association with Ephesus is even further strengthened. Timothy is expected, according to the author of Hebrews, to visit there after his release from prison (Heb 13.23).

27. Reflected in 1 and 2 Peter (see n. 48 below), and mentioned in Eusebius (*E.H.* 3.1), but Eusebius is clearly dependent on the epistle of 1 Peter for his information.

28. Mentioned by Papias; cited by Eusebius (*E.H.* 3.39.4).

29. There is a possible reference here to Philip the evangelist and Philip the Apostle (*E.H.* 3.39.4-9). See Hugh Jackson Lawlor and John Ernest Leonard Oulton, *Eusebius, Bishop of Caesarea: the Ecclesiastical History and the Martyrs of Palestine* (1928), 2:114-5; reprint. London: S.P.C.K., 1954).

30. *E.H.* 5.24.8. Polycrates listed twelve nonapostolic witnesses and said that, were he to list them all, they would number to the "many multitudes."

4. Church Structure

Ephesus and western Asia Minor are important, too, for the contribution they made toward the development of a monarchical church structure, which came to be universally accepted in the Christian church.[31] Certainly as early as the first decade of the second century, if indeed not a decade earlier, a monarchical office is present in a number of western Asia Minor cities, and in the letters of Ignatius directed to that area a sustained defence of that office is presented.[32]

Whatever the reasons that may be given for the origin of this new structure of authority, it is a structure that the catholic communities in other areas soon consider and adopt.

5. Self-Consciousness

It is in the western Asia Minor area that the clearest early attempts were made to distinguish between adequate and inadequate belief. I have already mentioned canon and church structure, both of which play a key role in drawing lines between the orthodox and the heretic. More important, the very consciousness itself that such lines could be drawn seems to appear first in western Asia Minor.[33] To that issue, the major part of this present work is directed.

It would be useful to note here, though, that there is in western Asia Minor a strong appreciation for the role of tradition. Even in the writings of Ignatius, the second-century church is linked to the

---

31. Streeter, *The Primitive Church,* 142, sees Asia as a leader in the developments in church order.

32. See Appendix B.

33. A good summary of the contributions made by western Asia Minor to Christian orthodoxy is found in Frederick W. Norris, "Ignatius, Polycarp, and I Clement: Walter Bauer Reconsidered," *VC* 30 (1976): 38-9. Norris points to the institution of monepiscopacy, to the theological justification for the bishop's role in the church, to distinctions between "orthodoxy" and "heresy," and to the canon. He thinks that Antioch plays a role along with Asia Minor in these developments, and grants to the Syrian area one other contribution to orthodoxy: that is, liturgical texts. H.E.W. Turner, *The Pattern of Christian Truth: A Study in the Relations between Orthodoxy and Heresy in the Early Church,* Bampton Lectures 1954 (London: A.R. Mowbray, 1954), 74, recognizes that the orthodoxy of Asia Minor was no mere "sounding board" of Roman orthodoxy; rather, it represented native growth—"collateral, not derivative."

apostolic foundations of the first-century church.[34] A consciousness of this link was one element in the self-understanding of the churches of western Asia Minor, and a sense of a link with the past is at the heart of the frequent appeal to the "rule of faith."[35]

D. The Literature

Although the area of Ephesus and western Asia Minor appears to have been a significant centre of early Christianity, that alone cannot be the reason I turn to it in my discussion of the primitive church. I have already been critical of many attempts to reconstruct the character of the primitive church, even though such studies have been based on various areas which were, without question, primary centres of early Christianity. I have been particularly critical when those reconstructions have been done with scanty literary remains. In such cases, I have charged that the attractiveness of the results owed more to the author's inventiveness and daring than to the completeness of the record, for the record itself would allow nothing more than markedly more sober and restrained hypotheses. Unless, then, the literature of Ephesus and western Asia Minor can offer considerably more in terms of quantity and relevance than that offered by the other areas, I will have no basis upon which to proceed. But, then, that is my point. This area *is* distinctive in terms of its literature from all other important centres of early Christianity.

The documentary evidence for Christianity in western Asia Minor is so extensive that it is almost astounding.[36] In fact, no other area can begin to compare in quantity of written material for

---

34. See chapter one, §I.B.3.

35. See Gérard Vallée, "Theological and Non-Theological Motives in Irenaeus's Refutation of the Gnostics," in *JCSD* 1:256-7 n. 24.

36. To quote Koester, *"Gnomai Diaphoroi,"* 306, "For the earliest history of theological controversy in parts of Asia Minor, Macedonia, and Achaia, our sources are more plentiful. A considerable part of the writings which were later incorporated into the New Testament canon was written in this region, particularly on the west coast of Asia Minor. Much of this literature is the direct result of the battles waged between the various groups of Christian missionaries throughout the second half of the first century." But note Arnold Ehrhardt, "Christianity Before the Apostles' Creed," *HTR* 55 (1962): 102-3 n. 42. questions the Asianic origins of some of the documents traditionally assigned to this area.

the earliest period of the church. But what is even more compelling about the literary wealth of western Asia Minor is that much of it—indeed, most of it—addresses the question of orthodoxy and heresy—sometimes indirectly, but more often than not, bluntly. In fact, almost all of the classic attacks against heresy in the early period come from the western Asia Minor area.

Within the sixty years from the founding of the church in Ephesus to the martyrdom of Ignatius, the bishop of Antioch, who left an extensive correspondence with the churches in western Asia Minor, document after document raises some question about the problem of heresy. To begin with the latest literature: of the seven letters written by Ignatius, five were addressed to churches in western Asia Minor; one was addressed to Polycarp of Smyrna, a bishop of one of these churches. In each letter, Ignatius confronts the problem of heresy head-on.[37] The same issue is at stake in the letter of Polycarp to the Philippians, written only a few days later.[38] The slightly earlier Apocalypse, in its introductory "seven letters" to west Asia Minor churches, focuses on suspect teachings in these churches.[39] The Pastoral epistles, with connections to Ephesus and Crete are somewhat more difficult to date, but they are almost certainly earlier than the letters of Ignatius.[40] These letters reflect a

---

37. For a full discussion, see Appendix B.

38. According to PolPhil 13.2, Polycarp has not yet learned what had happened to Ignatius, and it seems that Polycarp is not even sure that Ignatius would have been executed by this time. Note, too, the matters of concern to Polycarp (PolPhil 13). These matters are most reasonably related to a time not long after Ignatius had passed through. Cf. P.N. Harrison's theory: *Polycarp's Two Epistles to the Philippians* (Cambridge: Cambridge University Press, 1936).

39. It is difficult to determine the precise nature of the heresy or heretics, but some group known as the Nicolaitans is definitely a problem (Rev. 2.6; 15, and possibly 20). Whether this group is to be associated with later heretical groups is another matter, and I take that question up in chapter five §VII.

40. The Pastoral letters must be dated, it seems, earlier than the Ignatian material, because the Pastoral letters, written to the same general area of the Ignatian letters, do not reflect a church structure as developed as that reflected in the Ignatian letters, where a bishop is clearly set off from a subordinate presbytery. Some have, admittedly, argued that a monarchical-like office does exist in the Pastorals. For a review of this issue, see A.T. Hanson, *The Pastoral Epistles*, NCBC (London: Marshall, Morgan & Scott/Grand Rapids: Eerdmans, 1982), 32-34. In this context, the cautions of Norbert Brox should be considered [*Die Pastoralbriefe*, Regensburger Neues Testament 7.2 (Regensburg: Friedrich

similar concern and call for some discrimination between adequate and inadequate belief.[41] So, too, the Johannine material, especially the letters: we find here perhaps the sharpest lines drawn between acceptable and suspect belief of any of the writings of the canon.[42] (It is a matter of some dispute whether the Johannine material reflects the situation in western Asia Minor, though a credible argument can be made that it does.[43]) The author of the Book of Acts provides further evidence of the problem with heresy in the churches of western Asia Minor, and of the importance of that area. Although numerous churches are mentioned in the work, Ephesus plays a key role in the story in a number of ways.[44] Of particular importance to our discussion here is Paul's final speech to the elders of Ephesus. Its theme is the prediction of the rise of heresy in the church after Paul's death (Acts 20.17-38). The letter to the Colossians, too, reflects a problem with suspect views in a church about a hundred miles to the east of Ephesus, and the letter addressed to the

---

Pustet, 1969), 148-9].

41. Again, as with inadequate beliefs attacked in other documents, it is difficult to determine the precise nature of the belief attacked by the author of the Pastorals. Most believe there is only one heretical element. See de Boer, "Images of Paul," 371.

42. "Anti-christs" (1 John 2.18-9) and "lairs" (1 John 2.4, 22) are two of the terms the author uses to describe those who have broken with the community.

43. Raymond Brown and J.A.T. Robinson, both of whom have made recent significant contributions to Johannine studies, place the Johannine community in western Asia Minor: Brown, *The Gospel According to John*, AB 29 (Garden City: Doubleday, 1966/London: Geoffery Chapman, 1971), ciii-civ; Robinson, *Redating the New Testament* (London: SCM, 1976), 307. Brown comments briefly on Alexandria and Antioch (or Syria) as possible places for the composition of the Fourth Gospel, but its home by the end of the first century is clearly in western Asia Minor.

44. The account in Acts begins at 18.18. This account contains a mixed bag of incidents (the disciples of John, the inadequately taught Apollos, the healings and exorcisms, the book-burning and subsequent riot). The author of Acts believes Ephesus to have been the centre from which all Asia heard the gospel (19.10), and it is to the Ephesian elders that the author has Paul address his great speech against heresy (20.28-31). As for the conflict that caused Paul to be arrested, the author of Acts attributes it to a riot stirred up by some Jews from Asia (21.27), and in all probability the author has Ephesian Jews in mind, for the Jews who started the riot knew one of Paul's companions, a Trophimus, who was a resident of Ephesus (21.29). Given the theologically significant role played by Jerusalem and Rome in the story, the author's frequent mention also of Ephesus at key points is all the more striking.

Ephesians reflects some of the same concerns.[45]

Several other early documents may reflect the concerns of the churches in the area, though in none of the following documents is the problem of heresy accented. Some, if not all, of the prison epistles are thought to have been written from Ephesus.[46] Chapter 16 of Romans is believed by many scholars to have been originally a separate letter to Ephesus, though the case is not completely con–vincing.[47] 1 Peter includes the province of Asia in its address, and 2 Peter professes to be to the same area.[48] Further, there is Paul's

---

45. Colossians, as a whole, seems to be directed against a particular false teaching. The letter to the Ephesians is not so clearly directed against a particular false teaching, though it is clear that false teaching is a problem (Eph 4.14). Concerning the question of the destination of the letter to the Ephesians, I contend that, if not originally addressed exclusively to the church at Ephesus, Ephesus would likely have at least been included in any wider address.

46. Koester, *Introduction*, 2:104, argues that Philippians, Philemon and 2 Corinthians 10-13 were written during an imprisonment in Ephesus, and he thinks it possible that most of Paul's letters were written from Ephesus (2:116).

47. For a review of the discussion, see Kümmel, *Introduction*, 314-20; Koester, *Introduction*, 2:139, thinks it is possible that Romans 16 was originally addressed to the church at Ephesus. See Harry A. Gamble, Jr., *The Textual History of the Letter to the Romans: A Study in Textual and Literary Criticism* (Grand Rapids: Eerdmans, 1977), for a challenge to that theory.

48. The author writes his letter to Christians in Pontus, Galatia, Cappadocia, Asia and Bithynia (1 Peter 1.1). This basically includes all of Asia Minor. Note that the Roman province of Asia was only one of several provinces comprising what we call Asia Minor. When reference is made to western Asia Minor, the area intended is roughly the Roman province of Asia, or the western quarter of modern Turkey. Bauer, *Orthodoxy and Heresy*, (85-6/ET:81-2) attempted to make a case for heretical majorities throughout the Asia Minor provinces of Lycia, Pamphylia and Cilicia, on the grounds that the author of 1 Peter omits these provinces but includes the rest of Asia Minor. Although we do not know why the provinces were not addressed, it is possible that they were assumed to be included in the address. It is doubtful that whole areas went so completely into heresy. The three provinces omitted are all crowded together along the southern coast of Asia Minor, and even if omitted intentionally because of the presence of some strong heretical element there, these provinces would represent only a small part of Asia Minor. We do know that at the time of Ignatius, the area was not closed to orthodoxy. Philo, a deacon, is from Cilicia (IPhil 11.1), and neighbouring churches sent representatives to Antioch after the problem there had been settled (IPhil 10.2). These neighbouring places would have almost certainly included the two most easterly provinces omitted in the address of 1 Peter. Further, given even a few orthodox communities in the excluded provinces, surely an author would have extended welcomed greetings to these communities if he had intended to address all of Asia Minor. Bo Reicke, *The Epistles of James, Peter and Jude*, Anchor Bible 37 (Garden City: Doubleday, 1964), 72, thinks that the provinces

own witness to the success of his mission in Asia Minor, recorded in a letter written from Ephesus to the church at Corinth.[49] Some scholars have placed the Epistle to the Hebrews in this area, as well.[50] Koester argued that, of the Synoptic Gospels, only Matthew is not tied to the western Asia Minor church situation.[51] The Gospel of John, he thinks, could also be from this area, though he believes that Syria is the most likely setting for its composition.[52] All things considered, only two of the twenty-seven documents of the New Testament are without some connection to western Asia Minor,[53] though some of the connections are, admittedly, not entirely compelling.[54]

---

addressed by the author of 1 Peter were under the sphere of Rome; the provinces omitted, under the sphere of Antioch. My only reservation about Reicke's theory is that I think it more likely that Ephesus has the role that Reicke has granted to Rome. As for 2 Peter, although it has no specific address, the note in 3.1 suggests that the letter was intended for the same general area as was 1 Peter.

49. 1 Cor 16.8. It is clear that Paul considers his ministry at Ephesus to be particularly successful. The Marcionite prologue of Colossians suggests that Paul wrote not only 1 Corinthians from Ephesus, but 2 Corinthians as well.

50. John J. Gunther, *St. Paul's Opponents and Their Background: A Study of Apocalyptic and Jewish Sectarian Teachings* (Leiden: Brill, 1973), 77; Robert Jewett, *Paul, Messenger and Exile. A Study in the Chronology of His Life and Letters* (Valley Forge: Judson, 1972), 151-60.

51. Koester, *"Gnomai Diaphoroi,"* 313-5.

52. Koester, *Introduction*, 2:7.

53. Koester, *"Gnomai Diaphoroi,"* 306, recognizes both the quality and quantity of the literature associated with western Asia Minor. Even if Bruce is correct that, of Paul's letters, only 1 Corinthians is without question written from Ephesus, that does not detract from the literary wealth of the Ephesian area (*New Testament History*, 330). Regardless what Paul wrote from Ephesus, it is nonetheless the Paul of Ephesus who writes the various letters of the Pauline corpus. Surely for Ephesus to have been the home for a time of the prime mover of Christianity in western Asia Minor is nothing to depreciate, especially when other areas cannot claim even a tenuous literary connection to any author of note as their founder or main guide. Unless Paul can change his theological perspective as readily a scribe his quill, then the theology reflected in letters written by Paul in the fifties surely must have some bearing on the kind of theology introduced into western Asia Minor, the area of Paul's main mission during this decade. Of all the literature of the New Testament, only two documents lack any connection to western Asia Minor. They are Matthew and James (and, if 2 Thessalonians is pseudonymous, that as well).

54. Consider Jude, for example. Although it has no specific address and no indication of the place of composition, it may nonetheless be tentatively tied to western Asia Minor, for it appears that it was used by the author of 2 Peter, an author who had links with western Asia Minor (see fn. 45 above). Tenuous connection? Admittedly. But it is better than many areas can claim.

With such a quantity of literature, we have the potential, at least, for finding answers to our questions about the character of early Christianity, especially as it may reflect a consciousness of orthodoxy and heresy. In fact, the material from western Asia Minor offers considerably more controls than we are likely to find for any other area. Within a seventy-five mile radius, ten churches are addressed, and generally these churches are in the most important cities.[55] A number of these churches are addressed by more than one church leader, and for the church at Ephesus we have several church leaders who address the situation there.[56] Further, several of the churches are addressed by the same church leader.[57] Obviously, such a situation as we have here is preferable to a situation in which we have one solitary voice addressing a single church, at one moment in a half-century history, as would be the case for the primitive church in almost any other area.[58]

More significantly, as I have already noted, most of the material associated with western Asia Minor takes the problem of heresy

---

55. Ephesus, Smyrna, Sardis, Pergamum, Thyatira, Philadelphia, Magnesia, Tralles, Laodicea, Colossae, and we have explicit reference to others: Hierapolis and Troas.

56. Smyrna is addressed by the Apocalyptist and by Ignatius, as is Philadelphia. Laodicea is addressed by the Apocalyptist and possibly, by the author of Colossians (Col 4.16), and even though that letter is now lost, we could guess the theological perspective of that letter by reading the letter to the Colossians, which the church at Laodicea was intended to read anyway. And, of course, Ephesus is addressed by a number of early churchmen: by the Paulinist who wrote the Pastorals (1 Tim 1.3); by the author of the letter to the Ephesians (unless this was a form letter, but even then, Ephesus must have been one of the cities meant to receive a copy); by the Apocalyptist; by Ignatius; and perhaps by the author of Hebrews (see n. 50 above). And the Johannine material may have been addressed to Ephesus as well.

57. The Apocalyptist addresses seven churches; Ignatius addresses five.

58. Consider the recent work by Raymond Brown and John Meier, *Antioch and Rome: New Testament Cradles of Catholic Christianity*. For Antioch, Meier uses Matthew, the Didache, Ignatius, some of Acts and Galatians ch. 2. Most of this material is of little service in the discussion of orthodoxy and heresy. Brown finds slightly more material for Rome (Paul's letter to the Romans, 1 and 2 Peter, Hebrews, *1 Clement,* Paul to the Philippians, Ephesians, Gospel of Mark, Ignatius *to the Romans, The Shepherd of Hermes,* and the Legends of Peter and Simon Magus at Rome). The list is long, but were we to eliminate from it the late, the irrelevant, and the strained connections to Rome, it could hope for no credible comparison to the material firmly associated with western Asia Minor—material that takes the question of heresy seriously.

seriously; indeed, it is the primary concern of much of the material. We have, thus, both in quantity of material and in the content of that material, a situation for western Asia Minor unmatched by any other area to which we may address the questions of the orthodoxy/heresy debate.

E. Population

As we noted at the beginning of this chapter, it has frequently been recognized that western Asia Minor was the most successful area in the early church's missionary expansion. The question of the size of the Christian population is difficult to resolve, and the calculations vary considerably.[59] Suffice it here to say that the Christians in western Asia Minor must have numbered, even on the least generous reading of the evidence, into the several thousands by the beginning of the second century.[60] We are not able to determine from these figures just how visible the Christian movement would have been to the society at large. But we can say that whatever the situation was for the church of western Asia Minor in the eyes of the society, in the eyes of the church itself, the assemblies of western Asia Minor at the end of the first century would have been important for their size and for the apostolic traditions associated with them.

---

59. Robert M. Grant, *Early Christianity and Society* (San Francisco: Harper & Row, 1977), 5, says that the question of the size of the Christian population cannot be regarded as "close to a solution." J.B. Lightfoot, *The Apostolic Fathers* (London: Macmillan, 1889-1890; Grand Rapids: Baker, 1981), II.1.458, contended that there were hundreds of thousands of Christians at the time of Hadrian. Bo Reicke, *The New Testament Era: The World of the Bible from 500 B.C. to A.D. 100*, trans. David E. Green (Philadelphia: Fortress, 1968), 302-3 thinks that there would have been some forty thousand Christians in the empire by A.D. 67, and some eighty thousand in Asia Minor alone by the turn of the century. Such figures may be excessive. See the caution expressed by Robin Lane Fox, *Pagans and Christians* (New York: Alfred A. Knopf, 1987), 315: after an initial core of believers had been won, Fox believes that the church's cautious policy in evangelization and its generally low profile in the society would have prevented quick growth.

60. Taking even unrealistically low figures of fifteen converts each year in a city the size of Ephesus, we should expect to find at least five hundred Christians there at the end of the first century. Several other cities would have had a Christian population of similar size. See Grant, *Early Christianity*, 1-12, for a discussion of the general question of the size of the Christian population and an examination of comments of various ancient authors.

For the special position of Ephesus, Ignatius's comments are particularly noteworthy. He speaks of the church's "much beloved name" and of it being a church "blessed with greatness" (IEph intro). Later in that letter, he speaks of the church as "famous from eternity" (8.1). These notes of praise stand out in light of the absence of comparable comments in the letters to the other churches.

A century later, a comment by Origen may reflect the continuing importance of Ephesus. Origen notes that one of his opponents had written a document alleged to be a report of a disputation between the two. The debate had never taken place. Origen was aware that copies of this document had appeared in Rome, Antioch and Ephesus.[61] Although Ephesus could have been mentioned by Origen simply because it happened to have had a copy of the document in question, it is likely that it figures in Origen's statement because of its prominence as a leading centre of the church.

II. The Gentile Character of the Area

A. Population

Calculating the population of ancient cities is a task beset with difficulties. The population of Ephesus, for example, has been placed at a low of 150,000 to a high of 500,000.[62] This is a wide

---

61 Cited in Bauer, *Orthodoxy and Heresy,* 169/ET:166.

62. Fox, *Pagans and Christians*, 46, offers the low figure of 150,000. Richard Duncan-Jones, *The Economy of the Roman Empire: Quantitative Studies* (Cambridge: Cambridge University Press, 1974), 261, thinks that there were about 180,000 people in Ephesus (though possibly that figure does not include the slaves: p. 273). David Magie, *Roman Rule in Asia Minor to the End of the Third Century after Christ* (Princeton: Princeton University Press, 1950), 146, thinks the population was about 200,000. Nigel Sitwell, *The Roman Roads of Europe* (New York: St. Martin's, 1981), 192, estimates the population at 250,000. These figures are possibly more realistic than those of a half million or so, offered by Xavier Léon-Dufour, "Ephesus," in *Dictionary of the New Testament*, trans. Terrence Prendergast (San Francisco: Harper & Row, 1980), 178. Duncan-Jones argues cautiously, recognizing that half of the population of the area would have been rural, and thus should be considered residents in nearby cities only in a broad sense (p. 260). The countryside was generally considered under the control of the nearby city, where many of the landowners would have lived [see Robin Osborne, *Classical Landscape with Figures: The Ancient Greek City and its Countryside*

range and should caution against dogmatic assertions about the size of the cities of interest to this study. Fortunately, even such a range as this is not a serious limitation for the kinds of questions important to most works on the general demographic context of the young church. A sense of the relative size of cities is generally adequate, and this is usually within our reach.

Regarding Ephesus, for example, we can say that, comparatively speaking, of all the cities in the Roman empire, only Rome, Alexandria, and Antioch were larger. Thus, even without an exact population figure, we are able to gain some impression of the greatness of Ephesus: the status of fourth largest city in the empire is no mean position for a city outnumbered only by the capital of the empire itself and by the former capitals of the Ptolemaic and Seleucid empires.[63] The impact of that comparison is not significantly lessened by taking a figure of a quarter of a million rather than a half million for the population of the city.

Actually, it is not so much Ephesus that is important but, rather, all of western Asia Minor. Several other cities in the area may have been almost as large as Ephesus.[64] This, however, does not so much lessen the significance of Ephesus as it emphasizes the importance of the entire province of Asia Minor—the most populous and the richest of all the Roman provinces.[65] And for the purposes of this study, it is important to note that both the population and the wealth of the province would have been proportionately greater in

---

(London: George Philip, 1987)].

63. Alexandria, the capital of the Ptolemaic empire; Antioch, the capital of the Seleucid.

64. Several cities seem to have been almost as large as Ephesus. Magie, *Roman Rule*, 146, stated that Smyrna and Pergamum were about the same size as Ephesus. They may well have been, for it seems that they competed vigorously with Ephesus for the title of "First of Asia." See W.M. Ramsay, *The Letters to the Seven Churches of Asia* (London: Hodder and Stoughton, 1904), 175. See, too, Hemer, *The Letters to the Seven Churches,* 82-84. The cities of Cyzicus, Halicarnassus, Rhodes and Miletus were also huge cities (Sitwell, *Roman Roads,* 192).

65. Sitwell, *Roman Roads,* 192; Wayne A. Meeks, *The First Urban Christians: The Social World of the Apostle Paul* (New Haven and London: Yale University Press, 1983), 43-4.

the western area,[66] where Ephesus and a number of other cities with Christian churches were situated.

B. The Status of Ephesus

The exact political status of Ephesus is difficult to determine. A number of modern writers refer to it as the capital of the province,[67] but this does not seem to be accurate. Pergamum, the former capital of the kingdom of Attalus III, had retained its position as capital of the area after being bequeathed to Rome by its last king,[68] and it may have continued with that titular role (as Rome's first possession in the area) even after it was overshadowed by some of the Greek cities to the south—Ephesus and Smyrna, in particular. Ephesus did gain the right of *cataplous*, which required each senatorial governor to land there when he began his year in office.[69] Ephesus was also the residence of the proconsul of Asia.[70] Moreover, as the leading seaport, Ephesus had considerable importance apart from these special recognitions, and it is not surprising to find that the road markers for the Roman road system in Asia were marked in terms of their distance from Ephesus.[71]

Part of the reason for the confusion in the debate over the status of Ephesus is that, more than likely, the Roman government played a political game, allowing several cities to compete for primacy, each

---

66. Sitwell, *Roman Roads*, 192-3.

67. Goppelt, *Apostolic and Post-Apostolic Times*, 91; Sitwell, *Roman Roads*, 193; M. Stern, "The Jewish Diaspora," in *The Jewish People in the First Century*, vol. 1, ed. S. Safrai and M. Stern (Assen: Van Gorcum, 1974), 144, 152; and Reicke, "Catholic Martyrdom," 181. Léon-Dufour, *Dictionary*, in the article on Ephesus, called Ephesus the capital of Asia, but qualified that statement by adding that Pergamum was capital as well (p. 178).

68. H.T.F. Duckworth, "The Roman Provincial System," in *The Beginning of Christianity*, ed. F.J. Foakes Jackson and Kirsopp Lake (London: Macmillan, 1920), 1:201, stated that Pergamum was the capital; this position for Pergamum is recognized by G.B. Caird, *A Commentary on the Revelation of St. John the Divine*, HNTC (New York and Evanston: Harper & Row, 1966), 29, 37; by J. M. Ford, *Revelation*, AB 38 (Garden City: Doubleday, 1975), 388; and F.F. Bruce, *Paul: Apostle of the Heart Set Free* (Grand Rapids: Eerdmans, 1977), 288.

69. W.M. Ramsay, *The Church in the Roman Empire Before A.D. 170* (New York and London: G.P. Putman's Sons, 1912), 318.

70. Ford, *Revelation*, 388.

71. Léon-Dufour, "Ephesus," 39.

thinking that they, for some reason, held highest honour.[72] But whether the capital in name or merely in appearance, Ephesus was recognized as a leading city of the province, and of the Empire as well. And that is all we need recognize for the purposes of this study.

C. The Religious Character

When we think of the religious character of western Asia Minor, the temple of Diana at Ephesus and the grandiose Altar of Zeus or the Temple of Asklepios, both at Pergamum, probably come to mind. These are not, however, the most important religious features for a study of Christianity in the area. More important for understanding the religious tensions of the developing church are two factors, neither of them particularly Asian or Greek. One is the growth of the imperial cult; the other is the hostility of a strong diaspora Judaism.

The imperial cult was becoming a prominent feature of the religion of the cities of western Asia Minor at roughly the same time that Christianity was being introduced. Domitian, emperor from A.D. 81-99, had a temple built to his honour in Ephesus, and Hadrian, in the interest of his own honour, had one built for himself a couple of decades later. To the north, in Pergamum, a temple to Trajan was constructed.[73]

Much earlier, temples to the goddess Roma had been built. The imperial government had favoured such temples as a token of the loyalty of subject peoples to Rome, and the people gladly welcomed these temples, often even competing with neighbouring cities for the right to build.[74] Smyrna, Ephesus's seaport competitor to the north, had, as early as 195 B.C., constructed a temple to the goddess Roma, and partly because of that, continued to be a centre for the imperial cult, though not the exclusive centre.[75]

---

72. For a recent cautious analysis of the evidence, see Hemer, *The Letters to the Seven Churches*, 82-4.

73. See Duckworth, "Roman Provincial System," 1:201-17.

74. Tacitus, *Annals* IV.53-6. Eleven cities are said to have competed for the right to build the first temple in Asia Minor.

75. Duckworth, "Roman Provincial System," 205; Lightfoot, *The Apostolic*

It should not be thought strange that the Greek-speaking peoples of Asia Minor would have so willingly accommodated within their own cities the worship of the goddess of the city of Latin Rome. Rome had done much to bring stability to the Mediterranean area, most effectively, perhaps, by routing the pirates who threatened the shipping.[76] From the middle of the first century B.C., key shipping ports entered an era of prosperity. This was especially so for Ephesus and Smyrna, both lying at the end of important land routes to the east.

The Christian movement, in its refusal to give even token honour to the emperor in these temples, was taking a path that would bring suspicion not only from the imperial government itself but from these conquered peoples who recognized Rome as a source of their prosperity.

III. The Jewish Character of the Area

A. Population

It is sometimes forgotten that a considerable number of Jews lived in Ephesus and in western Asia Minor. That point is never forgotten for Alexandria or Antioch, or even for Rome.[77] It must not be forgotten for Ephesus either.

We have already seen that Ephesus was one of the leading cities of the Roman Empire. It was a city of considerable importance for the Jews, too. There is evidence of the emigration of a large number of Jews from Babylon about 200 B.C., as well as from other areas over many centuries. Many of these Jews settled in Ephesus and in other of the Ionian cities.[78] Philo said that there was not a city in

---

Fathers, II.1.467-8. But Ford, *Revelation,* 399, thought that Pergamum held that position.

76. Sitwell, *Roman Roads,* 185-6.

77. Eduard Lohse, *The New Testament Environment,* trans. John E. Steely (Nashville: Abingdon, 1976), 147; Brown, *Antioch and Rome,* 1.

78. See E. Mary Smallwood, *The Jews Under Roman Rule: From Pompey to Diocletian,* Studies in Judaism in Late Antiquity (Leiden: Brill, 1976), 121; and Victor Tcherikover, *Hellenistic Civilization and the Jews,* trans. S. Applebaum (New York: Atheneum, 1970), 287-8.

Asia or Syria in which Jews did not live (*Leg*. 245), and given Juster's examination, where he found evidence for a Jewish element in some seventy-one cities of Asia Minor,[79] Philo's statement hardly appears suspicious.

It is difficult to determine the size of the Jewish population of the area or of particular cities, but if we are content to speak in terms of relative size or to work with qualified calculations, we can gain some impression of the visibility of the Jewish element in the society of western Asia Minor. My attempt is merely to show that the Jews made up a significant part of the empire and that, in numerous cities of the empire, the early church would have felt itself growing within a Jewish context perhaps as much as within a gentile context.

The most widely accepted calculation of the Jewish population of the Roman empire is somewhere between six and seven million.[80] The figure seems to have at its source the statement of the thirteenth-century Bar Hebraeus, who said that some seven million Jews lived in the empire during the reign of Claudius.[81] Victor Tcherikover questioned the figure,[82] and a number of other scholars have placed the figure lower: Lohse at four and one half million,[83] and Harnack even lower.[84] All scholars, however, whether accepting a low or a high figure, recognize that many more Jews lived in the diaspora than lived in Palestine. Léon-Dufour, for example, thinks that there were about fifteen times as many Jews outside of Palestine as within Palestine; Lohse would reduce that figure by half.[85]

Whatever the case, the Jews seem to have made up about five to

---

79. Jean Juster, *Les Juifs dans l'empire romain: Leur Condition juridique, économique, et sociale*, 2 vols. (Paris: Guethner, 1914), 1:188-90. Smallwood, *Jews Under Roman Rule*, 121, says that Jews settled "thickly and early" in western Asia Minor.

80. Meeks, *Urban Christians*, 34, set the number between five and six million in the diaspora; Léon-Dufour, *Dictionary*, 36, seven to eight million in the Roman empire; see too F.J. Foakes Jackson and Kirsopp Lake, "The Dispersion," in *The Beginnings of Christianity*, 1:159; Smallwood, *Jews Under Roman Rule*, 374.

81. Cited in Tcherikover, *Hellenistic Civilization*, 292.

82. Tcherikover, *Hellenistic Civilization*, 292.

83. Lohse, *New Testament Environment*, 122.

84. Harnack, *Mission and Expansion*, 8-9.

85. Léon Dufour, *Dictionary*, 46; Lohse, *New Testament Environment*, 122.

ten percent of the population of the empire,[86] an estimate that seems realistic enough given certain statements from pagan writers.[87] And with the Jews living mainly in the cities,[88] Jews may have num‑bered as much as fifteen percent of the population of some cities.[89] This would have been a significant minority by any calculation.

I am, of course, interested particularly in the situation of Asia Minor and certain of its chief cities. Although it seems that the largest part of the diaspora was to the east, and especially to Syria, and that Egypt itself had a considerable number of Jews,[90] evidence suggests that the Jewish population of Asia Minor was itself large.

Guesses of the Jewish population of Ephesus, for example, would be merely guesses, but if Ephesus attracted slightly more Jews than other centres (as seems to have been the case),[91] Jews could easily have made up ten percent of the city's population, and according to Wayne Meeks, as much as fifteen percent.[92] Given figures of one fifth to one half million for the population of Ephesus, the Jewish community could have numbered as high as 75,000, taking Meeks' figure of fifteen percent. That may be unrealistically high, yet even if we were to take the lowest figures all round (five percent of the population Jewish; total population of Ephesus, 150,000), the Jews in Ephesus would have numbered about 7,500—hardly an insignificant number.

The figures we have offered hardly help us considerably. We probably should discard the higher figure: it uses the calculation of a

---

86. Lohse, *New Testament Environment,* 36, eight to ten percent; Reicke, *The New Testament Era,* 284, six to nine percent, including proselytes (citing M. Simon, *Verus Israel*).

87. A useful collection is that by Menahem Stern, *Greek and Latin Authors on Jews and Judaism* (Jerusalem: The Israel Academy of Science and Humanities, 1974); vol. 1, *From Herodotus to Plutarch.*

88. Tcherikover, *Hellenistic Civilization,* 294.

89. If one half or more of the general population was rural (Duncan-Jones, *Economy of the Roman Empire,* 260), and if Jews were mainly urban, the Jews would be proportionally greater in the cities. And considering that particular cities would have been more attractive than others, the Jews could have easily made up fifteen percent of the population of some cities.

90. Tcherikover, *Hellenistic Civilization,* 289.

91. Smallwood, *Jews Under Roman Rule,* 127 n. 24.

92. Meeks, *Urban Christians,* 34.

half million people for Ephesus, and at best this figure would have included the rural population as well, which according to Duncan-Jones would have been at least fifty percent of the entire population.[93] But the lower figure is equally suspect. Jews doubtlessly made up more than five percent of the population of a city like Ephesus. For one thing, as has already been mentioned, the Jews of the diaspora were generally urban. For another, the cities of western Asia Minor seem to have been particularly attractive to Jews,[94] and this would have led to an even higher percentage of Jews in such cities. It would not be arbitrary, then, to propose a figure of 20,000 or more Jews in a city like Ephesus.

Laodicea offers a different kind of evidence for the size of the Jewish population of the area. Flaccus, proconsul of Asia, had seized the temple tax in 62-61 B.C. (Cicero, *Pro. Flaccus* 66-9). According to Reinach, the amount seized suggests that Laodicea must have had about 7500 adult Jewish males.[95] Others have argued from the total amount of this seized temple tax that there would have been some 50,000 adult males in the province of Asia.[96] According to Tcherikover, the average family had five members,[97] and from this we might cautiously estimate the Jewish population of Asia Minor to have been somewhat less than one quarter of a million in the middle of the first century B.C.[98]

---

93. Duncan-Jones, *Economy of the Roman Empire*, 260.

94. The Jews settled in large numbers in the Greek cities of Alexandria and Antioch. The Greek cities in western Asia Minor were not much farther from Palestine. For a summary of the evidence for Jews in Asia, see M. Stern, "The Jewish Diaspora," 143-7.

95. Cited in Ford, *Revelation*, 420.

96. Meeks, *Urban Christians*, 206 n. 151, estimates that there were 50,000 adult males in Asia Minor at the time of Flaccus. Meeks calculates that from figures presented in Smallwood, *Jews Under Roman Rule*, 126. But A.J. Marshall, "Flaccus and the Jews of Asia," *Phoenix* 29 (1975): 146-7, cautioned against the use of these figures in calculating the Jewish population. The population could have been considerably greater if the amount seized by Flaccus represented only what was collected in four cities rather than the entire province; the population could have been considerably smaller if the amount seized represented the temple tax for the entire province, with additional donations of gold for the temple.

97. Tcherikover, *Hellenistic Civilization*, 293.

98. If each of the 50,000 males had three children, the total Jewish population would have been about one quarter of a million. But that figure must be lowered to account for the overlap in family units: the parents of a young family unit are

But this figure would likely have increased considerably by the latter part of the first century A.D., some one hundred and fifty years later. After the fall of Jerusalem, Asia Minor seems to have become a favourite area of immigration from Palestine.[99] Those cities with a large Jewish population, and with special rights for Jews, are likely to have seen a considerable increase in the number of Jews in their cities.

B. The Status of Jews in the Greek Cities

Much ink has been spilled in the attempt to determine the precise status of Jews in the Greek cities of the Roman empire.[100] The Greek cities, in which significant numbers of Jews had made their home, had been the leading centres throughout the Mediterranean world prior to the rise of the Roman empire. With the success of the campaigns of Alexander the Great, Greeks had moved into the conquered areas and had established impressive (and distinctively Greek) cities. Alexandria and Antioch, capitals of the Ptolemaic and Seleucid empires respectively, are two classic examples. Of a different history were the Greek cities on the west coast of present-day Turkey. These cities had been founded by Greek colonists a millennium earlier.

When the Greek kingdoms fell to the Romans, the Romans had to decide upon an expedient method of government. For the most part, the Greek cities were allowed considerable autonomy in local

---

themselves the children of an older family unit.

99. There seems to have been an immigration by some Palestinian Christians to western Asia Minor in the late first century (§I.C.2 of this chapter). And Josephus, *Antiquities* XIV.223-64, writing about the same time, calls attention to a series of Roman decrees protecting the rights of the Jews. Many cities of western Asia Minor had been addressed by specific decrees, and Ephesus figures prominently.

100. Duckworth, "Roman Provincial System," 1:186, thought Jews had citizenship rights in most cities. This view is no longer widely held; see Tcherikover, *Hellenistic Civilization*, 309-32. Also, Smallwood, *Jews Under Roman Rule*, in particular, chapter six "The Diaspora and Jewish Religious Liberty." See too Shim'on Applebaum, "The Legal Status of the Jewish Communities in the Diaspora," in *The Jewish People in the First Century*, eds. Samuel Safrai and Menahem Stern, 1:420-63. Compendia Rerum Iudaicarum and Novum Testamentum, 1. (Assen: Van Gorcum; Philadelphia: Fortress, 1974). Individual Jews, of course, could have gained citizenship in certain cities, and some were even elected to public office. See Josephus, *Ant.* XIV.234, 240.

affairs.[101] Of importance in the Greek mind was the right of citizenship in the *polis*—a right established by heredity, not merely by birth or residence within the confines of a particular city.[102] Only citizens were allowed to participate in the political affairs of the city, and for cities with their power stripped down to this sphere, citizenship was a right closely guarded.[103]

A conflict developed when the Jews began to claim equal rights with the non-Jewish citizens of these cities. Their claim was not without some foundation. The Romans had looked on the Jews with favour from the time of Julius Caesar because of the aid they had given him against the Greeks. And after Palestine itself came under Roman control, Herod and his family maintained generally cordial relations with the Roman emperor. As a result, the Jews were given special rights. This made the Jews seem in some ways more like allies than like conquered peoples, and the Romans were generous in the rights they extended to the Jews. It is the exact nature of these rights that is a matter of considerable dispute. In particular, the issue is whether these rights included citizenship in the Greek *polis*.

The matter is complex. I have chosen not to deal with it in any detail, except to say that much of the discussion has possibly been misdirected. The question of the precise rights of the Jews may have been ambiguous even for the courts of the first century, and our search for a clearer resolution to this ambiguity may do injustice to the conflict between two sets of rights that had, built-in, areas of overlap. For the purposes of our discussion, all we need recognize is that Jews had considerable rights in the empire—and even within the somewhat autonomous Greek cities. The recognition that these rights could be (and were) pushed into the claim of right of

---

101. A.H.M. Jones, *The Cities of the Eastern Roman Empire* (Oxford: Oxford University Press, 1937), 60-95.

102. See chapter 2, "The Law of Status," in J.A. Cook, *Law and Life of Rome, 90 B.C.-A.D. 212* (Ithaca: Cornell University Press, 1967), 36-67. Citizenship in the *polis* was a Greek idea, not a Roman one (p. 37).

103. This is illustrated by the intense effort made by the citizens of various Greek cities to restrict the rights of Jews. See Tcherikover, *Hellenistic Civilization*, 309 32, for a full discussion.

citizenship would, in itself, go far to providing an informative portrait of the extensive privileges of the Jews in the Roman diaspora. Whether the Jews, technically speaking, had citizenship in the Greek *polis* is a question that, even if answered in the negative, does not reduce the Jews of the diaspora to a disenfranchised, alien people. The evidence is too extensive for the prominence of Jews in the empire, and the evidence is particularly good for western Asia Minor, where the Sardis synagogue stands as the most striking example of the privileged status of the Jews.[104]

C. Religious Syncretism or Religious Purity?

It has been argued that the Judaism of the Roman diaspora was less pure than that of Palestine and Babylon.[105] It would not be surprising to find evidence of syncretism among the Jews, given the considerable number of Jews in the area, but a few choice seats reserved for Jews in the theatre at Miletus cannot censor the whole of Judaism in the area.[106] The more serious evidence of syncretism has been the subject of extensive investigation by A.T. Kraabel, who has argued for a purer form of Judaism in western Asia Minor than had come to be accepted in recent scholarship.[107] The issue is still unresolved.

IV. The Christian Character of the Area

The Christian character of western Asia Minor is, of course, the primary issue of this thesis and is dealt with in detail in the chapters

---

104. See S. Applebaum, "The Social and Economic Status of the Jews in the Diaspora," in *The Jewish People in the First Century,* 2:701-27; and Meeks, *Urban Christians,* 44-5.

105. Sherman E. Johnson, "Christianity in Sardis," in *Early Christian Origins: Studies in honor of Harold R. Willoughby,* ed. Allen Wikgen (Chicago: Quadrangle Books, 1961), 81-90.

106. Stern, "The Jewish Diaspora," 1:152.

107. Alf Thomas Kraabel, "Judaism in Western Asia Minor under the Roman Empire, with a Preliminary Study of the Jewish Community at Sardis, Lydia" (Th.D. diss., Harvard University, 1968), and "Paganism and Judaism: The Sardis Evidence," in *Paganisme, Judaïsme, Christianisme: Influences et affrontements dans le monde antique,* ed. A Benoit *et al* (Paris: Boccard, 1978), 13-33.

that follow. Two features of the church in western Asia Minor should, however, be noted before we begin.

A. The Influence from Judaism

New Testament scholars continue to argue the degree to which Judaism affected the developing church.[108] Most of the early Christian literature from western Asia Minor shows that the church did not escape Judaism simply by moving away from Jerusalem. In our Christian materials, we find repeated acceptance of some Jewish ideas; repeated rejection of others.

The influence of Judaism should not surprise us. We have already seen that Judaism was a significant force in the society of western Asia Minor, and it is difficult to see how the early Christian community, growing out of Judaism and with considerable baggage from Judaism, could have successfully isolated itself from the Jewish element in western Asia Minor. Later, when the church had grown markedly stronger, Judaism proved attractive enough to draw Christians.[109] The early Christian materials from western Asia Minor suggest the situation was similar in the earliest days.[110]

B. The Social Structure for Corporate Worship

We have seen that, given even minimal success of the Christian mission in western Asia Minor, the area would have had several thousands of Christians by the early second century. This is

---

108. W.H.C. Frend, *The Early Church* (London: Hodder and Stoughton, 1965; Philadelphia: Fortress, 1982), 35-6, said that the main problem facing the church in the sixty years after the fall of Jerusalem was its relationship to Judaism, a point true for Asia Minor too. See, too, de Boer, "Images of Paul," 377 n.65; also Jacob Jervell, "The Mighty Minority," *ST* 34 (1980): 13-38.

109. Robert L. Wilken, "The Christians as the Romans (and Greeks) Saw Them," in *JCSD* 1:123, says that the church was involved in dialogue with Judaism until the fourth century. William G. Braude, "The Church Fathers and the Synagogue," *Judaism* 9 (1960): 113, calls attention to the problems faced by Jerome and Chrysostom. Some Christians seem to have regarded the synagogue as more holy than the church, and Jewish birth could be an asset for selection to high office in the church.

110. In particular, the groups in Magnesia and Philadelphia opposed by Ignatius (See Appendix A). The Pastoral letters (Titus 1.10-15) may reflect a similar problem, and the author of the Apocalypse condemns something that he calls "The Synagogue of Satan" (Rev 2.9; 3.9).

significant, for it provides some grounds upon which to reconstruct the organization of the church at the city level—a point that until recently was not given attention.

As a result of extensive work in the last few years, we can say with some certainty that the early churches were generally only small assemblies of about thirty persons who met regularly for their corporate worship in the homes of one of the members.[111] These small units we call house churches. We know of no regular, larger meetings. This forces us to conclude that, by the turn of the first century in a city like Ephesus, there could have been (and perhaps must have been) dozens or even scores of these house churches. That conclusion provides a rather concrete framework upon which to consider a range of questions dealing with everything from diverse theological communities to the nature of schism and in particular to the need for an office like the monarchical episcopate.[112]

V.   Conclusion

It is always difficult to address our questions to a past culture when that culture is known to us only through scattered remains. That difficulty is reduced, however, when those remains are literary;

---

111. The most comprehensive treatment is in Hans-Josef Klauck, *Hausgemeinde und Hauskirche in frühen Christentum* (Stuttgart: Verlag Katholisches Bibelwerk, 1981). Other works of importance are: Abraham J. Malherbe, *Social Aspects of Early Christianity*, 2d ed. (Philadelphia: Fortress, 1983); Robert Banks, *Paul's Idea of Community: The Early House Churches in their Historical Setting* (Grand Rapids: Eerdmans, 1980); Peter Stuhlmacher, *Der Brief an Philemon* (Zürich: Einsiedeln, 1975), 70-75; N. Afanasieff, "L'assemblée eucharistique unique dans l'église ancienne," *Kleronomia* 6 (1974): 1-36; Stanley Kent Stowers, "Social Status, Public Speaking and Private Teaching: The Circumstances of Paul's Preaching Activity," *NovT* 26 (1984): 59-82; Joan M. Petersen, "House-Churches in Rome," *VC* 23 (1969): 264-272; E.A. Judge, *The Social Pattern of Christian Groups in the First Century* (London: Tyndale, 1960); Floyd Filson, "The Significance of the Early House Churches," *JBL* 58 (1939): 109-12; and Meeks, *Urban Christians,* chapter 3.

112. Malherbe, *Social Aspects,* 70, says that little is known about the relationship among the various small house-church units. But, as Malherbe points out, whatever the relationship, the units did not view themselves as separate churches. What, we might ask, prevented that? A recognized head (whether an individual or a body) over all the churches in a city is the most likely answer.

it is strikingly reduced when that literature is as interested in our questions as we are. For the questions of orthodoxy and heresy, the material from western Asia Minor goes a considerable way to meeting our needs. We have relatively extensive material from the area. Most of the material takes our questions seriously. And finally, since the area we have judged most attractive for our questions is an area of considerable importance both to pagan and Jew too, various additional relevant data to our questions become available to us. It is to this area that we now turn to test the adequacy of the Bauer Thesis for the questions of orthodoxy and heresy in primitive Christianity.

Chapter Four

Identifying Heretical Tendencies
in Western Asia Minor

I. Introduction

A. Bauer's Reconstruction

Walter Bauer offered what has become the classic exposition of those tendencies in the Christian tradition that are generally known as "heresy,"[1] and it is to particular aspects of that work that we turn in this chapter and the following. In examining Bauer's work, I will concentrate on his discussion of the western Asia Minor area. In chapter three, I defended my choice of that area, and of Ephesus, its chief city, and I expect general agreement on the following point: of the primary centres of early Christianity, Ephesus is as important as any and is of sufficient importance for the questions of the orthodoxy/heresy debate to be addressed to it with profit.

---

1. Walter Bauer, *Orthodoxy and Heresy in Earliest Christianity*, ed. Robert A. Kraft and Gerhard Krodel (Philadelphia: Fortress, 1971). In this work, Bauer concerns himself with those interpretations of the Christian message that were excluded from the developing orthodoxy. His work does not deal with the entire spectrum of diversity within early Christianity, for the diversity that is incorporated into the catholic movement becomes, in Bauer's work, merely part of a monolithic orthodoxy. Bauer's work, then, is not so much a reconstruction of earliest Christianity as it is a reconstruction of a particular aspect of earliest Christianity—the heretical or the non-catholic aspect. Some of Bauer's followers have focused on the diversity within the catholic movement: in particular, note James D.G. Dunn, *Unity and Diversity in the New Testament: An Inquiry Into the Character of Earliest Christianity,* (Philadelphia: Westminster, 1977).

Bauer broke the history of early Christianity in western Asia Minor into several stages, though those stages were not always clearly laid out by him. The first stage was the Pauline: this would have begun with Paul's missionary activity in Ephesus in the early fifties.[2] Unfortunately, Bauer did not deal with this stage in any detail (86/ET:82), nor did he deal with the possibility of a Christian mission in Ephesus before Paul,[3] a point that might have loaned support to his contention that the early period was theologically diverse. The little that Bauer has to say about Paul's founding mission in western Asia Minor (other than for admitting it as fact) stands in sharp contrast to Bauer's insistent and frequent claim that the memory of Paul as the founder of the church was lost by the late first century (87/ET:83-4; 88-9/ET:84-5; 91/ET:87).[4]

After Paul, there is Apollos to consider. Bauer did not deal with a movement around Apollos in western Asia Minor, though he did indicate that Apollos might reflect a non-Pauline movement in

---

2. Paul's mission in Ephesus is usually dated in the early fifties, and the years from A.D. 52-55 seem the most probable. That is arrived at by placing the ministry of Paul in Ephesus just after his ministry in Corinth. Paul's ministry in Corinth is the only part of Paul's chronology that can be fixed to a definite date. A passage in Acts mentions a Gallio, proconsul of Achaia, in Corinth when Paul was there (Acts 18.12-17). An inscription from Delphi places this Gallio in Corinth in A.D. 51 or 52, thus Paul can be dated to Corinth around this time. According to Acts 19.1, Paul leaves Corinth for Ephesus. That particular tradition is credible on two grounds. For one thing, it corresponds to the note in one of Paul's letters to the Corinthians (1 Cor 16.7-9), which places the ministry in Ephesus *after* the ministry in Corinth. More important, the Corinth-first/Ephesus-second order is not the order that one would have expected for Paul's mission. Ephesus lies closer than Corinth does to the base of Paul's missionary activity in Antioch, and an inventive historian would have placed the mission in Ephesus before that in Corinth, unless he had reason to believe that the *expected* progression of the mission was inaccurate. This, then, says something about the sources used by the author of Acts. He knew that the ministry in Corinth took place prior to that in Ephesus; further, he recognized that the order was unusual and attempted to explain it by including a report that Paul was specifically directed by the Spirit away from the province of Asia (and Bithynia) to Macedonia (Acts 16.6-10). Chapters 16 and 17 of Acts reports a series of extremely brief missions to a number of cities (Philippi, Thessalonica, Beroea, and Athens). Not until Paul arrives in Corinth does he settle down (Acts 18.1).

3. Jean Daniélou, *The Christian Centuries*, vol. 1, *The First Six Hundred Years*, (with Henri Marrou), trans. Vincent Cronin (London: Darton, Longman and Todd, 1964), 41-42.

4. See discussion in §IV of this chapter.

Corinth (105/ET:101), as many have argued.[5] But Bauer's work does not suffer from its lack of attention to Apollos. As Helmut Koester has argued, Paul and Apollos were not opposed to each other.[6] Koester's position appears credible, given that evidence is too ambiguous to support a conflict between Paul and Apollos—and probably contradicts it outright.[7]

The next stage is one crucial for Bauer's reconstruction, but one for which he surprisingly supplies no information. Bauer's thesis seems to require a very successful gnostic movement early in western Asia Minor (a point I discuss later). But the existence of such a movement is one of assumption rather than one of proof, for Bauer simply passes over this stage. After the initial discussion of the Pauline mission, the next stage presented by Bauer was the change brought about by the immigration of a number of prominent Palestinian Christians to Asia Minor about the time of the fall of Jerusalem. This new Jewish element was supposedly welcomed by an ecclesiastically oriented Pauline group that was engaged in a struggle with a more powerful gnosticizing Pauline element (91/ET:87).[8] But the powerful gnosticizing group appears, quite

5. Frederick W. Norris, "Asia Minor Before Ignatius: Walter Bauer Reconsidered," in *Studia Evangelica* 7 (Berlin: Akademie-Verlag, 1982), 366-9, thinks that Bauer could have helped his thesis by giving some attention to this.

6. Helmut Koester, *"Gnomai Diaphoroi:* The Origin and Nature of Diversification in the History of Early Christianity," *HTR* 58 (1965): 311.

7. Paul credits Apollos with watering the plant of the church (1 Cor 3.6). Possibly by saying in the same context that he, Paul, was the one who planted what Apollos had watered, Paul intended to place himself above Apollos, but such a reading of the passage does some injustice to the dialectic Paul set up. For Paul, it was not his ministry contrasted to that of Apollos, but the ministry of the human agent contrasted to that of the divine agent. Further, Paul presents Apollos and himself as examples from whom the Corinthians could learn how to conduct themselves (1 Cor 4.6), and the particular point that concerns Paul is competition among Christians—one Christian being puffed up against another (1 Cor 4.6-7). Competition between Paul and Apollos would have made these leaders unlikely candidates for role models in a group torn by competition. Finally, Paul indicates at the close of the letter that he had wanted Apollos to return to Corinth—an unlikely wish had Paul been attempting to reduce the influence of Apollos there. That, of course, does not mean that groups had not formed around the teachings or personalities of particular leaders. It does mean, however, that if such groups were formed in Corinth, it is unlikely that Apollos can be charged as instigator of, or participant in, a movement in competition against Paul.

8. Bauer was not specific about the strength of the gnosticizing Pauline movement, but his argument that the anti-gnostic Paulinists needed to form an

uncomfortably (though conveniently) for Bauer's theory, almost out of thin air, for we are told nothing about the background of this group at all, and we learn about its existence almost by accident when it is introduced as the protagonist to account for the particular conservative alliance that Bauer wishes to propose.

Bauer goes on: the union of the Palestinian immigrants with the anti-gnostic Pauline element resulted in a Christianity that adopted certain Jewish traits (apocalyptic elements, synagogal structures, and respect for the Sabbath and for the Passover) but dropped the more problematic requirements of circumcision and of observance of the ceremonial law for gentile Christians (91-2/ET:87-8).[9] Even with the alliance, the anti-gnostic group is still in the minority, according to Bauer. But the alliance does mark, for Bauer, the significant turning point for Christianity in this area, for from this point on "the line of demarcation...no longer runs between Jewish and gentile Christianity, but rather, between orthodoxy and heresy" (91/ET:87).

Bauer then argued for a stage in which the minority "orthodox" element attempted to gain control of the church. This reconstruction is surprising and problematic. Bauer's claim is that, even after the alliance with the new Palestinian group, the anti-gnostic forces were still in the minority. The gnostic movement must have been in-

---

alliance with Jewish Christians and his argument that the monarchical office, backed by the orthodox, was typical of the power shifts favoured by minorities, would indicate that Bauer viewed the heretics as the stronger. There are, too, explicit statements by Bauer that the orthodox have the majority in very few of the churches (67, 73, 81/ET:63, 69, 77), and in those churches where the orthodox were in the majority, it seems that Bauer viewed the situation as one that had just recently changed to the advantage of the orthodox. In regard to Bauer's arguments here, Frederick W. Norris, "Ignatius, Polycarp, and I Clement: Walter Bauer Reconsidered," *VC* 30 (1976): 24, challenged Bauer: either prove that Ephesus, Magnesia, Tralles and Philadelphia had heretical majorities prior to Ignatius, or demonstrate that they did not have truly monarchical bishops. Bauer thought he had proved both.

9. Koester differs from Bauer here in that, while Koester agrees that an apocalyptic emphasis appeared in Asia Minor after the fall of Jerusalem, he accounts for that by the possible influence of Qumran (*"Gnomai Diaphoroi,"* 315-6), whereas Bauer, writing before the discovery of the Dead Sea Scrolls, spoke more generally of a Jewish influence (of which apocalyptic was but one element) and saw the source of this influence in the immigration of prominent Palestinian Christians to Asia Minor (91-2/ET:87-8).

credibly powerful at this time—only a brief decade or two after Paul's mission in the area, for even with the new orthodox alliance against them, the gnostic group is still the stronger.[10] The weaker orthodox group then engaged in a power play, according to Bauer. The power play was initially prompted by the unwillingness of the anti-gnostic orthodox group to have power rest in the hands of the common assembly in which they were in the minority. An attempt was supposedly made by this minority to concentrate power in the hands of one man, a monarchical bishop, whom they hoped would represent the minority (i.e., anti-gnostic) viewpoint (66/ET:62). This was, according to Bauer, the situation in western Asia Minor when Ignatius passed through, and thus accounts for the energy exerted by Ignatius in favour of a monarchical office for the churches in the area—churches that until this time had been largely controlled by the gnostics.[11]

Even though the orthodox and heretical camps shared common services of worship for some time in western Asia Minor, already by the time of Ignatius, the schism had resulted in separate meetings in some areas, according to Bauer. These meetings appear to be outside the rubric of the main church, which by this time was coming increasingly under the control of the ecclesiastically oriented group.[12] These few unauthorized assemblies led to a sharper division between the "orthodox" and the "heretic" until finally the break between the two became complete and permanent. It was

---

10. If the anti-gnostic Paulinists are still in the minority even after they are joined by the Palestinian immigrants, imagine their status in the community prior to the alliance with the newcomers.

11. Bauer was not perfectly clear here. He did not say what led some of the Paulinists in the direction of Gnosticism, and he did not indicate how large this gnosticizing group was, except to say that in a number of areas it was the majority view in the nineties (82/ET:78). Some scholars have argued that Paul's churches almost as a whole went into Gnosticism after Paul's death: for example, Ernst Haenchen, *The Acts of the Apostles: A Commentary*, trans. Bernard Noble and Gerald Shinn (Philadelphia: Westminster/Oxford: Blackwell, 1971), 596-7. But this is not what Bauer had argued. Bauer thought that at least an element in the Pauline movement rejected the trend towards Gnosticism and worked to defeat it (91-3/ET:87-9).

12. Separate assemblies seem to have been formed in at least Magnesia and Philadelphia, and likely in Smyrna (see extensive discussion in chapter 5 §V; see too Appendix B).

Ignatius, according to Bauer, who, by promoting a kind of unity that would seriously challenge the right of certain beliefs to a place within the church, forced the issue to a head.[13]

Bauer's conclusion is that the heretics in western Asia Minor represented a substantial movement with early control over many of the churches in the area. This fits the pattern that is characteristic of what I call the Bauer Thesis: first, heresy is generally strong and is the *dominant* form of Christianity in area after area; and second, heresy is generally early and represents the *original* form of Christianity in most areas. Such was the case Bauer argued in detail for Edessa and Egypt; it differs little from his reconstruction of Christianity in western Asia Minor[14] and other areas of the early Christian mission.

B. Critique of Bauer's Reconstruction

Robert Kraft and Gerhard Krodel, the editors of the English edition of Bauer's work, ask the critic to refrain from certain kinds of criticism. They appear frustrated, in particular, by critics who dismiss certain suggestions of Bauer as "conjectural," since Bauer himself was conscious of the hypothetical nature of parts of his reconstructions.[15] There is some basis for their concerns, though

---

13. Bauer, *Orthodoxy and Heresy*, 65/ET:61, says that Ignatius portrays, not the actual situation, but the ideal. Yet, for two reasons, it is an ideal situation that could be brought quite quickly to actuality. One, the orthodox's candidate for the office of bishop apparently has some special aura that gives him credibility in the eyes of the heretical majority (66/ET:62); and two, the heretics are disunited (67/ET:63). (See chapter 5 §III for a detailed discussion.) Given that a separate assembly for the schismatics probably existed in Smyrna [even on Bauer's own admission (73/ET:69)], the move of the orthodox to institute and control the monarchical office in the area seems well under way. Once the orthodox gained control of the assembly through their bishop, Bauer thought the orthodox would either bring the heretics to heel, or failing to do that, would force them out of the community (66/ET:62).

14. Although Bauer admits a form of Pauline Christianity early in western Asia Minor, his reconstruction of Christianity in that area posits a Pauline Gnosticism as the dominant form of Christianity apparently as early as the Jewish War, for that is the time of the *anti*-gnostic alliance Bauer suggested, and this alliance was in the minority. The gnostic Paulinists, by implication then, were strong by the early seventies.

15. Bauer, *Orthodoxy and Heresy*, 311, 316 (English edition only). Note Bauer's statement at the beginning of his work (2/ET:xxii): "Perhaps—I repeat, perhaps—certain manifestations of Christian life that the authors of the church

not all would agree that the limitations requested by the editors are reasonable. But I am myself prepared to control my criticisms of Bauer by a somewhat flexible observation of the following limits. I will focus only on those aspects of Bauer's reconstruction that are clearly key issues for the question of the character of primitive Christianity. I will pass over other statements, no matter how tendentious or exaggerated, without comment. I will directly criticize Bauer only where he failed to take account of material available to him or where he grossly exaggerated the weight of the evidence claimed in his favour. My focus, then, will be limited to the crucial junctures in Bauer's reconstruction, and my examination of these will be as generous as possible.

C. Crucial Junctures in Bauer's Reconstruction

Bauer's detective work—never dull, sometimes ingenious, occasionally brilliant—suffers from defects more serious than the sporadic overstatements and tendentious claims that even his disciples have had to acknowledge.[16] Overstatements and un-supported claims are not the problem; if anything, in Bauer's work, they are the spice that provokes attention to often unnoticed possibilities. Far more fundamental and less easily corrigible, the defects of Bauer's argument are structural.

Specifically, his reconstruction of early church history in western Asia Minor is collapsible at its three structurally critical points:[17] (1) the hypothetical alliance of "ecclesiastically oriented" Paulinists with Palestinian immigrants against gnosticizing Pau-

---

renounce as "heresies" originally had not been such at all..." At the same time, however, the charge can be laid against Bauer that he did not allow the "perhaps" of his introduction to be reflected clearly enough in the body of his work.

16. In Appendix 2 of Bauer, *Orthodoxy and Heresy,* 296, the editors have admitted that a number of scholars have found Bauer's treatment of the evidence from Ignatius "especially open to question." Later they say: "The situation in Asia Minor...is admittedly more complex than Bauer indicated" (p. 315). Arnold Ehrhardt, "Christianity Before the Apostles' Creed," *HTR* 55 (1962): 102, says that Bauer's thesis on Asia Minor is a "challenging, if not wholly convincing scrutiny."

17. Norris, "Asia Minor Before Ignatius," 365, is dead on target when he points to three fundamental problems of Bauer's reconstruction of western Asia Minor.

linists; (2) the alleged strength of heresy in the area; and (3) the proposed cause for the rise of the monarchical episcopate. These three parts of the argument work together in Bauer's determined effort to show that a non-catholic form of Christianity was to be found early in western Asia Minor, and that this form was stronger than catholic Christianity. It parallels Bauer's claims for all other areas of the church's expansion, except for Rome: non-catholic, or heretical forms of Christianity were both early and powerful. For western Asia Minor, I intend to show that neither claim is defensible, and in so doing I intend to call into question the soundness of the Bauer Thesis.

II. The Anti-Gnostic Alliance

As we have seen, Bauer argued that the emphasis on a distinction between Jewish Christians and gentile Christians gave way in western Asia Minor to an emphasis on the distinction between "orthodox" Christians and "heretical" Christians. This, he said, occurred after the Palestinian immigrants arrived in the area and aligned themselves with the anti-gnostic, ecclesiastically oriented Paulinists (91/ET:87). In other words, Pauline Christianity split, and one side joined forces with a Jewish element with which it had not been affiliated in the past. Bauer was not perfectly clear here. He did not say what led some of the Paulinists (or most of the Paulinists) to go in the direction of Gnosticism, and he did not indicate how large the gnosticizing group was, except to say explicitly that in a number of churches Gnosticism was the majority view by the nineties (82/ET:78), and to imply that it was so even in the seventies when the Palestinian immigrants came. Some scholars have argued that Paul's churches almost as a whole went in the direction of Gnosticism,[18] but this is not what Bauer had argued. Bauer thought that at least an element in the Pauline movement rejected the trend towards Gnosticism and worked to defeat it (91-3/ET:87-9).

---

18. Cf. Haenchen, *Acts*, 596-7.

The anti-gnostic alliance is *crucial* to Bauer's theory, for it serves as the earliest evidence for a considerable heretical element in western Asia Minor. As we have seen, Bauer believed that heretical movements were both strong and early throughout the Christian mission. If in western Asia Minor—the only area for which information is relevant, extensive, and early—no evidence can be found for a strong and early heretical element, that would be a considerable loss of support for a theory such as Bauer's.

Although I shall argue against Bauer's reconstruction of the primitive church in western Asia Minor, let us for the moment suppose that there were such groups as Bauer proposed in this area in the seventies and eighties. Let us suppose, too, that such an alliance between Palestinian immigrants and anti-gnostic Paulinists did occur. A basic question arises. It is this. Why did this realignment occur? What was it about the trend towards Gnosticism that caused Pauline-founded churches to find more in common with Palestinian-Jewish Christians than with fellow gentile Paulinists of a gnostic bent? Bauer did not give even passing attention to this question. But surely this is a probing question in any attempt to discover an early consciousness of "orthodoxy" in the church, for the shift just considered would seem to indicate that the self-understanding of the ecclesiastically oriented Pauline group was such that it excluded the possibility of Gnosticism but was open to a Jewish element new to it. Had Bauer dismissed the shift as a political one or one involving a clash of personalities, his failure to see in this shift implications of an early sense of orthodoxy could be excused. But Bauer believed theological issues to have been at stake (i.e., Gnosticism: 91/ET:87; 93/ET:89).[19] This implies that the issue is truth. The question arises, in short, whether orthodoxy has here become a thematic issue. But Bauer turned a blind eye to this tantalizing implication, speaking of this shift and new alliance against Gnosticism as though it were a most natural occurrence, seeming not to recognize the serious problem that this shift might bring against his primary theory that a consciousness of orthodoxy

---

19. Bauer did not explain what issues were at stake other than to indicate that what was at the heart of the problem was the trend towards Gnosticism.

was late. He did not entertain the new question that had arisen. If he was aware of the issue, he dodged it. This is troubling.

Bauer did recognize, however, that the radical realignment he proposed was problematic. Paulinists and Jewish Christians were, on Bauer's own admission, strange bedfellows.[20] In order to lessen the objection to this hypothetical alliance, Bauer argued that the two groups were prepared to undergo radical modification in order to bring about this unheard of Pauline/Jewish-Christian alliance against the gnostic Paulinists. The anti-gnostic Paulinists became more tolerant of Jewish customs; the Jewish Christians became less rigorous in regard to the ceremonial law. As Bauer put it:

> In exchange for having sacrificed the law for their orthodox gentile Christian brethren, Asian Jewish Christianity received in turn the knowledge that henceforth the 'church' would be open without hesitation to the Jewish influence mediated by Christians, coming not only from the apocalyptic traditions, but also from the synagogue...(91-2/ET:87-88).

But that explanation raises more questions than it answers. What, one wonders, made this new tolerance and flexibility possible? There was, of course, the threat from Gnosticism. But the gnostic factor was simply what made the alliance necessary. The question is: what made the alliance possible?

It was in the destruction of the temple that Bauer found his explanation for this new tolerance. He argued that "the catastrophe in Palestine forever erased the demand that the gentile Christians of the diaspora should be circumcised and should to some extent observe the ceremonial law" (91/ET:87). The fence separating

---

20. The major tension in the early church seems to be between Paul and Jewish Christians. Bauer believed that there was, in fact, little sympathy anywhere for the Jewish Christian version of Christianity. The exception, he thought, was in the western part of Asia Minor (90/ET:86), a strange place to find an exception, one might point out. If western Asia Minor was more open to Jewish Christians than other areas were, then this might indicate a loss of Pauline influence, according to Paul, for that area had been at one time the area of Paul's primary mission. The idea of a loss of Pauline influence thus becomes part of Bauer's reconstruction.

Jewish and gentile Christians had been torn down. But Bauer did not bother to explain in what way the destruction of the temple would have "forever erased" the demand for circumcision and the observance of the ceremonial law for gentile Christians of the diaspora. This is a serious gap in Bauer's argument, for it is anything but obvious that the destruction of the temple would have removed these demands. Such new tolerance on the part of previously conservative Jewish Christians simply cannot be permitted into our reconstruction without more convincing grounds than Bauer has provided.

Admittedly, if Judaism came to be centred on the synagogue rather than on the temple, the uncircumcised might possibly then participate more fully in the Jewish religion: the temple was forbidden to the uncircumcised; the synagogue was not. But Judaism in the diaspora was always more centred on the synagogue than on the temple simply due to practical considerations. The question is whether the destruction of the temple would have brought about a markedly more liberal position in regard to circumcision and food laws than already had existed in the diaspora. We have no evidence that any new toleration occurred within Judaism. That it happened within a liberal Jewish Christianity is certainly possible, but if it did happen, there is no reason to relate this particularly to the destruction of the temple. It was a matter worked out by one element in Jewish Christianity during Paul's ministry, and nothing suggests that a group of Jewish Christians who disagreed with the freedom promoted by Paul suddenly had a change of heart on the matter after the temple had been destroyed.

Further, the destruction of the temple would have carried weight in terminating the old order of things only if the destruction had been viewed as permanent. With the strong apocalyptic tone within Judaism at the time (the Jewish War and the later Bar Kochba War are evidence of this emphasis), no permanent loss of the temple would have been envisioned by Jews. Nor would the attitude have been markedly different for those Jews who were Christians and who held a positive view of temple and cult. All this threatens Bauer's reconstruction—a reconstruction that requires a Jewish-

Christian group whose views are made more liberal by the destruction of the temple.

Bauer thought he had evidence of one Jewish-Christian group that had taken steps to give up the requirement of circumcision and features of the ceremonial law, learning more to synagogal structures than to the temple. This was the community to whom the Apocalypse was addressed (88/ET:84). But Bauer's example is not convincing. This group did not depreciate the temple and exalt the synagogue; rather, the opposite. The synagogue is the synagogue of Satan (Rev 2.9; 3.9). True, the temple in Jerusalem is not mentioned, and there is said to be no temple in heaven, but that is only because God and the Lamb have become the temple (Rev 21.22). This does not make the group radically antitemple. It is doubtful, then, that the destruction of the temple can provide for Bauer's hypothesis an adequate explanation for the realignment he proposed. At least the example of the Apocalypse cannot carry Bauer's thesis here.

Bauer's theory of an increased Jewish colouring in the anti-gnostic alignment in western Asia Minor is further to be faulted because it fails to do justice to the increased Jewish colouring throughout the spectrum of Christianity in the area. It is not just the catholic element that reflects a Jewish colouring, it is the gnostic element as well. Bauer himself had to admit that this seemed to be the case, but he dismissed all the evidence that would challenge him. The Jewish elements in the "gnostic" position are problems enough for the way Bauer perceived the lines to have been drawn. But Bauer must face another problem. Not only are there Jewish strains in the gnostic position, there are *anti*-Jewish strains in the Jewish/Pauline alliance against the gnostics. This complicates Bauer's theory, in which the lines seem more clearly specified. Bauer only weakens his theory regarding the alliance each time he is forced to dismiss the Jewish traits in the gnostic group and each time he passes over in silence the anti-Jewish strains in the Jewish influenced anti-gnostic alliance.

Let us look carefully at Bauer's special pleading and his troubling silences in dealing with Jewish features of Gnosticism and anti-Jewish features of the alliance against Gnosticism.[21] For the Apocalypse, Bauer failed to note the Jewish colouring of the heresy (which, according to Bauer's reconstruction, was gnostic [88/ET:84]), and he failed to mention the sharply critical attitude of the Apocalyptist towards Judaism (Rev 2.9; 3.9). Troubling for Bauer's thesis is that one would have expected somewhat different emphases from the anti-gnostic alliance proposed by Bauer. In regard to the Ignatian material, Bauer admitted that Ignatius did charge the heretics with the practice of Judaism, but he dismissed the substance of this charge by claiming that it was merely a reflection of Ignatius's own "complex personality" and not of the nature of the heresy opposed (92/ET:88). For the Pastorals, we find again Bauer's admission that the writer did charge his opponents with some aspect of Judaism, but Bauer refuses to accept the substance of the charge as valid. According to Bauer, the peculiar heresy described in the Pastorals stemmed from "the perspective of the mentality of the pseudonymous letter-writer—as Paul he was forced to deal with the 'teachers of the law' (1 Tim 1.7) and the 'circumcision party' (Titus 1.10), but as a second century churchman, he opposed Gnosticism" (92-3/ET:89). In other words, the real heresy opposed by the author of the Pastorals had no Jewish colouring; the admixture was simply a creation of the confused perspective of a pseudonymous letter writer trying to address his own situation in language that reflected Paul's.

Bauer did not do justice to the material by this rather off-handed treatment. There is a considerable amount of early literature (the Pastorals, the Apocalypse, the letters of Ignatius) and reports about people like Cerinthus[22] that identifies a Jewish element in the heresies of this period. Bauer contends—and must contend for the sake of his thesis—that all these authors gravely misrepresented the Jewish character of the heresies. But the strained explanations put forward by Bauer to convince us are extreme, and insulting both to

---

21. Norris, "Asia Minor Before Ignatius," 376, observes that Bauer rejected the evidence of 1 Timothy and Ignatius that pointed to a possible connection between Judaism and Gnosticism. Bauer's dismissal of this evidence is troubling.

22 See Raymond Brown, *The Epistles of John*, AB 30 (Garden City: Doubleday, 1982), 768-771.

the ancient authors and to the modern readers. The charge of the Jewish tendency in the heresies cannot be so easily dismissed. Bauer, of course, could not have permitted such widespread Jewish influence in the Christianity of the area, for his reconstruction had played a Jewish-Christian/anti-gnostic Pauline alliance against a *purely gentile* gnosticizing tendency.

Bauer's strained handling of the Jewish element in the heresies is suspicious. A non-Jewish heresy was precisely what his thesis demanded—but what none of the evidence supplied—until Bauer got his hands on it and twisted it to fit the context of the purely gentile heresy he had proposed for his reconstruction. If a clear Jewish element was found in the heresy, as most scholars think,[23] then a Jewish alliance against the heresy would be only half the story. It would leave unaccounted for the Jewish element in the gnosticizing group—a group Bauer thought was totally gentile.

But is this much ado about nothing? Should we perhaps let Bauer off the hook? Is this period not among the most obscure in all of the history of the church, requiring of any reconstruction certain liberties? One could, I admit, be somewhat generous towards Bauer's reconstruction here, except for the fact that this is a crucial juncture in his reconstruction. It serves as the primary basis from which to make credible his argument that heresy was a significant, if indeed not the dominant, force in western Asia Minor when Ignatius passed through (as will be discussed later). It is not so much Bauer's reconstruction of the church between 60 and 90 that is objectionable (any reconstruction of this obscure period will be not completely compelling); it is what Bauer did with his reconstruction of this early period that is objectionable.[24]

---

23. For a discussion of the problem, see n. 1 of Appendix A.

24. Bauer's thesis as a whole would have been more credible had he not argued for this early, radical alliance—and, in fact, he need not have argued for it. He could have easily argued that serious problems with heresy arose considerably later than in the three decades between A.D. 60 and 90. On his own reckoning with the evidence, the heretics were, for the most part, still in the church when Ignatius passed through in the second decade of the second century. Bauer generally spoke simply of minorities and majorities struggling for control of the same assembly (81-4/ET:77-80), though for Smyrna, he was prepared to admit a counter-bishop (73/ET:69). (Exactly in what way this counter-bishop was related to Polycarp's assembly was not made clear, but then, it is not made clear in the Ignatian

Bauer's reconstruction of the years from 60-90 is really a secondary feature of his work. It seems to have come to mind only after Bauer had already made a decision about the state of affairs in the church at the time of the writing of the Apocalypse. The idea of an early alliance seems to have become attractive to Bauer after he had first decided to use the Apocalypse as evidence for a massive heretical movement in western Asia Minor at the end of the first century. (Bauer needed a massive heretical movement at this time to support his particular reading of the Ignatian material).[25]

Bauer's argument at this point must be followed closely, for he used the material in a curious way. The evidence for a significant heretical movement at the time of the Apocalypse was not, as we might have expected, the references to the Nicolaitans or to Balaam and Jezebel in three of the seven letters of the Apocalypse (Rev 2:6, 14, 15, 20).[26] For Bauer, the evidence for the presence of heresy was less explicit but considerably more striking. The explicit references to Nicolaitans, Balaam and Jezebel were thought to reflect *only the tip of the iceberg!*

Two features suggested to Bauer the presence of a much more significant heretical movement. First, certain other churches are

---

material either.) None of the earlier literature would have forced Bauer to admit an early alliance. The Pastorals, with their clearly expressed polemic against heresy, were dated by Bauer somewhat later than the Ignatian material (88/ET:84). The Apocalypse does, admittedly, suggest that the church was having a problem with heretics, but given the disdain that Bauer had for the Apocalyptist (81-2; 88/ET:77-8; 84), Bauer could have dismissed the Apocalypse as evidence of nothing more than the grumbling of a malcontent (81-2/ET:77-8). Thus Bauer could have argued that the problems with heresy surfaced much later than the sixties or seventies of the first century, and the radical alignment, so suggestive of a self-understanding reflecting a consciousness of orthodoxy, could have easily been placed later. Yet, it is an early alignment that Bauer proposed. What led Bauer to this reconstruction is unclear. He offered no unambiguous evidence from the literary materials for the alliance; his main argument related to the immigration of Palestinian Christians to the area around the time of the fall of Jerusalem. Yet, surely he could have admitted such an immigration without having been forced to admit as well the radical alignment he proposed.

25. If there is not a strong heretical movement in western Asia Minor by the late first century, it would be difficult to explain how the heretics have come to control so tightly the churches in the area by the time Ignatius passes through in the early second century. See discussion in §V of this chapter.

26. That evidence simply does not lend itself to any numerical calculation of the heretical element in western Asia Minor.

known to have existed at this time in the area, but the Apocalyptist did not address them (Bauer mentioned the churches at Colossae and Hierapolis). The omission of these churches, argued Bauer, could best be explained by a heretical majority so powerful there that the Apocalyptist could not hope for a hearing in these assemblies (82/ET:78). Second, Bauer argued that even in several of the seven churches addressed by the Apocalyptist, heresy was a serious problem. The Apocalyptist, Bauer concluded, could not find even seven churches free of heresy. The credible sphere of influence for the Apocalyptist was thus limited to something less than seven churches for the entire province of Asia (82/ET:78).

Once Bauer had begun to think in terms of spheres of influence as early as the writing of the Apocalypse, he would have been forced to think of two fairly distinct movements existing sometime prior to the mid-nineties. By the mid-nineties, according to Bauer, one group already controlled a number of churches, and the Apocalyptist was aware that those churches were beyond his sphere of influence. This would indicate a clear "them/us" distinction, and such a distinction would have required some time to have become so clearly defined. Roots in the eighties or seventies would be required to account for such clear distinctions in the nineties.

The problem Bauer had to face was that he found nothing in the literature prior to the time of the Apocalypse that gave any indication of credible heretical movements.[27] Bauer made an effort to resolve this lack of history for the heretical movements by pointing to a supposedly significant immigration of Palestinian Jewish-Christians to western Asia Minor around A.D. 70. By proposing a split in the Pauline movement and an alliance of one group of the Paulinists with these newly arrived Jewish Christians, Bauer had at least the beginnings of two distinct and competing elements within the church. The problem is this: Bauer failed to pay even minimal lip service to the problems raised against his thesis by such an alignment; he simply stated that such an alliance did occur. Besides

---

27. Although there is a widespread tendency to speak of a gnosticizing Pauline movement during this time, the situation reflected in the Ignatian letters strongly argues against any such movement being significant in the latter part of the first century. My discussion throughout this and the following chapter is crucial here.

the obvious initial question as to whether there was, in fact, such a split, a number of other questions should have been addressed. Were the "ecclesiastically oriented" Paulinists always ecclesiastically oriented? Which of the Paulinists, the gnostics or the ecclesiastics, better represented Paul's original message? Could the ecclesiastical group have gone in the direction of Gnosticism had other personalities been involved? (This question is important because it recognizes that a distinction must be made between forces that are theologically significant and those that are not.) But Bauer considered none of these questions.

The most disturbing observation to be made here is not that Bauer failed to prove an early Gnosticism, or that he failed to prove the radical alignment he proposed. As I have said earlier, the period being considered is among the most obscure of the early church, and some speculation can be allowed and some hypotheses lacking clear support considered. What is disturbing is that Bauer could disregard completely the potential of such a radical shift to indicate an early, and perhaps discriminating, sense of "orthodoxy" for a significant segment of the church. One wonders what, precisely, would have served to convince Bauer of an early consciousness of orthodoxy on the part of some element within the church. Bauer seems to have placed unreasonable demands on what he would admit as evidence of this kind of self-understanding among the Jewish-Pauline alliance. And this is disturbing, since that issue is the heart of the matter.

III. A Gnostic Trajectory?

The golden calf of the last few years has been the use of the concept of trajectory as a means for filling in significant gaps within the history of primitive Christianity.[28] The idea is this: if we can

---

28. J.M. Robinson and H. Koester, *Trajectories through Early Christianity* (Philadelphia: Fortress, 1971). The authors acknowledge the roots of this concept in the work of Walter Bauer (p. 16). See the cautions expressed in the following reviews: R.McL. Wilson, review of *Trajectories through Early Christianity*, by Robinson and Koester, *JTS* 23 (1972): 475-7; and R.H. Fuller, "New Testament

identify the probable source of an idea that we find clearly expressed at some later time, we can then plot a path from the point of origin to the present position. This path (though established only by an early "vector" and a later "vector") provides clues to what we might expect for the points between. James Robinson speaks of trajectory as the attempt to show how, in terms of an "overarching movement," an idea comes "successively to expression as one moves downstream from the point of departure."[29] Numerous illustrations could be used other than that of trajectory. Sunrise or sunset could be used. If we know how dark it was at 5 a.m. and we know how light it was at 7 a.m., we can come to some reasonable conclusion about the probable degree of light at 6 a.m. Or consider the growth of a plant. If we know the stage of growth at an early point and at a later point, we can reasonably draw conclusions about the stage of growth at a point between the two known points. All that is essential for an illustration to work is that there be some sequential development or decline in the process. There must be some sense of a controlled path or line. The idea of explosion would be the antithesis of the idea of trajectory.

But the problem with this paradigm is that it may misrepresent the way ideas develop or decay. The human dimension complicates the paradigm. As E.P. Sanders has argued against the idea of trajectory: "A lot of things do not move in trajectories...and the trajectory paradigm may mislead one into attempting to impose sequential development where none exists."[30]

Let me illustrate the failure of the trajectory paradigm for one well known period of history: the Protestant Reformation. If we did not have a firmly dated history of the first century of the Protestant movement, the concept of trajectory, rather than aiding us in our historical reconstruction, would hinder us. Would we place the Anabaptist Movement within a few brief years of Luther's Ninety-

---

Trajectories and Biblical Authority," in *Studia Evangelica* 7 (Berlin: Akademie-Verlag, 1982), 189-99.

29. Robinson, *Trajectories*, 17.

30. E.P. Sanders, *Paul and Palestinian Judaism: A Comparison of Patterns of Religion*, (Philadelphia: Fortress, 1977), 23. Sanders devoted a special section to a criticism of Robinson's idea of trajectory (pp. 20-24).

Five Theses? Or would we trace two trajectories from Luther (or Zwingli), one ending in Protestant Scholasticism and one in the Anabaptist movement, placing both a century or more after Luther? Safe money is clearly on the latter. But, of course, we would be wrong. There simply is no trajectory running from Luther to the Anabaptists. What we have is an explosion. We have men who create; not men who mould. And that is why the concept of trajectory may be mute or, worse, misleading. It is better able to take account of refinement and controlled development than of explosive and original thought.

I wonder too whether the idea of trajectory is more appealing to those whose roots are in a more mainline tradition, in which change is more gradual and controlled. Speaking as someone without such a background, the idea of trajectory does not strike me as the most convincing paradigm for the way in which change and development occurs in new religious movements.[31]

When we come to the question of Gnosticism, we must be particularly cautious. It is not clear that the trajectory paradigm will provide a reliable schema upon which to reconstruct those silent periods for which no documentary evidence exists.[32] Possibly the paradigm of "explosion" is a better one for Gnosticism. For the purposes of this present study, however, I will use neither. I will simply look at the explicit documentary evidence that we have for the late first and early second centuries, and on the basis of that

---

31. I reflect upon the history of Pentecostalism, the religious tradition in which I have roots. The essence of its history is not one of gradual development; it is one in which there were a handful of explosive ideas at various points in its history, not all of which made a lasting impact on the movement. Nothing prepared one for these explosions. They were explosions because they were not part of some line of gradual development. And the history of the movement was one either of solidification (not development) of these explosive ideas or of a decline from these ideas. Frequently, a call would be made to return more intensely to one of these primary ideas, but little about such a call would aid in providing chronological or geographical clues from which to plot such a call. A sermon in a 1980's Pentecostal church may be almost identical to a sermon in a 1920's Pentecostal church; in fact, it may be considerably closer to the 1920's situation than to a 1950's situation that reflected a new explosion of thought, which after some time died out.

32. I am assuming here that we do not possess documentary evidence for the period from 60-90 that would convincingly demonstrate a gnostic movement within the church.

evidence I will argue that the early and strong gnostic movement required for Bauer's reconstruction of western Asia Minor is a fiction. Even a generous use of the paradigm of trajectory cannot convincingly fill the silent years of the late first century with Bauer's necessary gnostics.

IV. The Loss of Pauline Influence

Although it has now become a commonplace to speak of the loss of Pauline influence in western Asia Minor,[33] Bauer's arguments for this loss in late first century Ephesus are particularly suspect. According to Bauer, the author of the Apocalypse, by emphasizing the twelve Apostles as the foundations of the new Jerusalem and by not mentioning Paul in the letter to the church at Ephesus, either deliberately suppressed or had no recollection of Paul's connection to western Asia Minor (87/ET:83). But Bauer's "either/or" options are so starkly contrasting that it is doubtful that they came to mind as a result of a careful analysis of the situation. If the writer is suppressing the historical connection of Paul with Ephesus, the context is one where that connection is widely known, and from the perspective of the seer at least, in need of some measure of discrediting. If, on the other hand, the seer has no recollection of Paul's connection with Ephesus, the context is one where Paul's connection with Ephesus is not even faintly known. If an examination of the material cannot direct us to one or the other option, the material is too mute a witness to be of any use, and should beckon us to silence rather than to conjecture.

---

33. A good review article concerning opposition to Paul is found in E. Earle Ellis, "Paul and His Opponents: Trends in the Research," in *Christianity, Judaism and Other Greco-Roman Cults: Studies for Morton Smith at Sixty,* ed. J. Neusner, (Leiden: E.J. Brill, 1975), 2:264-98. Brown and Meier, *Antioch and Rome,* vii-vii, are explicit in their intentions: they want to "severely" test the assumption that Paul's thought "won out." Ernst Käsemann agrees with Brown and Meier: Paul lost. [This is the thesis of Käsemann's article, "Paul and Early Catholicism," in *New Testament Questions of Today,* Philadelphia: Fortress, 1979), 236-51. Käsemann disagrees with Brown and Meier in thinking that such loss was a bad thing, not a good thing.

But is the witness quite so mute? Bauer himself noted that the seer recalls an earlier time when the community in Ephesus had been better off (87/ET:83). Bauer was referring to the statement in Rev 2.4, where the loss of the "first love" by the Ephesian church is mentioned. This statement certainly would make sense on the background of historical memory that associates Paul with Ephesus.[34] That there could have been such a memory of Paul's connection to this area is suggested by several things: one, by the growth of the post-Pauline literature, which is for the most part tied to the western Asia Minor area; two, by the Acts material, whose author is familiar enough with western Asia Minor, and who makes Paul his hero; and three, by the presence in the church of people who might themselves have become believers when Paul was in Ephesus. Only forty years separate Paul's presence in Ephesus from that of the Apocalyptist. A founder who continued to be the subject of the church's literature and who was, during his life, a close friend of present church members is not readily forgotten.[35]

---

34. The term *"first love"* most naturally would recall the days of the *founding* of the church, and this would root the positive era of that church in Paul's own mission. The only way to avoid this conclusion is to argue that the churches addressed by the Apocalyptist were not Pauline churches (cf. Daniélou, *Christian Centuries*, 1:39-44). But this would not help Bauer's theory. We would have a Pauline church in western Asia Minor along with a Johannine church, and the Apocalypse could not be used to enlighten us as to the state of Pauline Christianity in late first-century Ephesus (as is crucial to Bauer's theory), nor could the evidence from the "Johannine" Apocalypse be linked to evidence from the Pauline Ignatius in an attempt to specify the growth of heresy (as, too, is crucial to Bauer's theory).

35. W.H.C. Frend, *The Early Church* (London: Hodder and Stoughton, 1965; Philadelphia: Fortress, 1982), 35, said: "The years that followed the fall of Jerusalem are among the most obscure in the life of the primitive church." Helmut Koester, *Introduction*, 2:279, said that we do not know the name of a single Christian from A.D. 60-90. He continued: "the second Christian generation has thus become completely anonymous for us." Koester's remark is merely an exaggerated rephrasing of Frend's observation and needs to be substantially qualified because it implies that the late first century is more obscure than what it actually was, and it fails to take into account the younger co-workers of Paul who would have outlived him. To say that we do not know the name of a single Christian in this period reflects a disturbing tendency to grant to persons mentioned in the New Testament records no history beyond those documents that mention them. This is fine for characters like Little Red Riding Hood: we need not speculate whether she went to college and married and raised little basket-carrying children of her own. But we can, and perhaps must, speculate about

Admittedly, Bauer pointed to other evidence for a considerable loss of Pauline influence in the area in the late-first and early-second centuries (88-9/ET:84-5). In particular, Bauer has in mind the situation of the church of western Asia Minor that is reflected in the Pastoral Epistles and the presence of the gnostic Cerinthus in the area in the early second century. (Bauer did not seem to notice that Cerinthus should have been pro-Pauline according to his thesis.) It is difficult to know how to assess this material. Many scholars are comfortable with the use of this material to demonstrate that heresy was wide-spread in the early part of the second century, but that is not the only possible reading of the material.[36] We must caution ourselves against measuring the strength of heresy in terms of the decibel of the polemic used against it: for the same situation, mild men may write mildly; intolerant men may write wildly. We must attempt to filter all polemical material through some more neutral screen. I contend that a better measure of the strength of heresy is the concrete situation of various areas as reflected in the parts of the literature that is less clearly polemical, and it is to those parts that I direct much of my attention.

---

persons mentioned in the New Testament record. From Paul's letters written in the fifties, we know, by extension, the names of some, if not numerous, Pauline Christians in the last decades of the first century, and we can assume the existence of numerous others—the unnamed Paulinists who populated the Pauline communities. From all indications, the early Christian preaching attracted young people as well as old. Twenty-year-old converts under Paul in Ephesus in the early fifties would be only in their late fifties in the last decade of the first century. If the Pastorals are from the last years of the first century, the structure of the church, with a ruling body of elders, may have had as the most credible members of that body persons who had been converted under the ministry of Paul himself. Consider Timothy, for example. He had a life outside of the records that mention him; so, too, Titus and the various other characters mentioned, or assumed, in the Pauline letters. This is often forgotten, with the result that too much obscurity is granted to this period. The last third of the first century is hopelessly obscure only if all of Paul's converts and assistants followed Paul, Jim Jones-like, to their deaths.

36. Cf. Norris, "Asia Minor Before Ignatius," 371.

V. Determining the Strength of Heresy in Western Asia Minor

A. The Last Decade of the First Century

Bauer contended that in many churches in western Asia Minor, the heretics were in the majority. As we have already seen, Bauer argued that by the time of the writing of the Apocalypse, heresy was so widespread that the Apocalyptist, unable to find an adequate number of orthodox churches to fill out his scheme (in which the number "seven" was prominent), had to include churches in which the majority were committed to heretical tendencies (82/ET:78).

It is surprising to find Bauer calculating the strength of heresy in terms of those not within the sphere of the Apocalyptist's influence. For one thing, Bauer thought that the Apocalyptist was peculiar, so peculiar, in fact, that he was unlikely to have been a leader of the western Asia Minor churches (81-2/ET:77-8). Further, Bauer said that in this period orthodoxy came in several quite different forms, and he recognized that the Apocalyptist would not have spoken for all of them (81/ET:77). But given these conditions, one is certainly not compelled to conclude that the Apocalyptist was limited in the number of churches he could address because he happened to be orthodox and most of the churches were not. It is more likely, given Bauer's portrait of the seer, that the Apocalyptist was limited by his peculiar message, which had no appeal to any significant segment of the church, whether orthodox or heretical. Yet Bauer attempted to determine the number of heretics in the area by counting all those who would not have come under the influence of the Apocalyptist. Even by Bauer's own reckoning, a considerable number of the orthodox (i.e., the non-gnostic community) must have been part of this group.

What of this supposedly large group of heretics controlling the churches of western Asia Minor and minimizing the influence of the Apocalyptist? Most commentators conclude that only one group was being opposed by the seer: a group called the Nicolaitans, apparently active in Smyrna and Thyatira and known in Ephesus.[37] Whoever the Nicolaitans were, they were numerous enough to be identified as a distinct group, though if they were followers of a well-known person, it may have been the stature of the leader, not the size of the group, that drew the attention of the seer.

The only reliable information we have about the Nicolaitans is from the Apocalypse.[38] Bauer's theory requires that we know more. For one thing, it is essential that the Nicolaitans have their roots in the earlier gnosticizing Pauline movement that Bauer had proposed.[39] Such a connection is needed in order to explain how the heresy opposed by the Apocalyptist could be as widespread by the mid-nineties as Bauer had argued. If the heretics of the Apocalypse were of recent origin, the strength of this movement proposed by Bauer would be difficult to explain. If, however, the heretics stood in line with a successful gnosticizing Pauline movement from the sixties or seventies, a strong movement by the nineties would not be particularly problematic. But one is caused to ponder whether Bauer came up with the idea of this radical post-70 realignment of gnostic and anti-gnostic parties mainly because he had already convinced himself that there was a significant (and in many cities dominant) heretical movement in the nineties in western Asia Minor. An earlier movement towards Gnosticism would provide the credible history Bauer needed for his thesis of a strong and dominant gnostic movement in the nineties.

But an early move towards Gnosticism raises one problem for Bauer's thesis. Although an early gnosticizing movement, if

---

37. That is not to say that the precise nature of the heresy has been agreed upon, or that the relationship of this group to earlier and later groups has been settled.

38. See Norbert Brox, "Nikolaos und Nikolaiten," *VC* 19 (1965): 23-30; and G.B. Caird, *A Commentary on the Revelation of St. John the Divine*, HNTC (New York and Evanston: Harper & Row, 1966), 31. Stephen Gero, "With Walter Bauer on the Tigris: Encratite Orthodoxy and Libertine Heresy in Syro-Mesopotamian Christianity," in *Nag Hammadi, Gnosticism, and Early Christianity*, ed. Charles W. Hedrick and Robert Hodgson, Jr. (Peabody: Hendrickson, 1986), 303-5, suggests a longer history for the Nicolaitans.

39. One might argue that the roots of the Ignatian heretics could have been in a group of similar character to the Nicolaitans, rather than in the Nicolaitans themselves. That hardly enlightens. The Nicolaitans are difficult enough to get a handle on; we gain little by proposing an even less accessible group.

successful, could explain the widespread influence of the Nicolaitans (assuming that one is related to the other and that the
Nicolaitans are really widespread), Bauer's thesis cannot adequately
explain why the rejection of this movement did not occur until the
nineties if, as he himself claimed, an alliance was formed against
this movement in the early seventies.[40] The Nicolaitans are
comfortably a part of the church that the Apocalyptist addresses.
Separating lines between "orthodox" and "heretic" are just being
drawn; the lines are not part of the fabric of a twenty-year old split
that Bauer proposed.

There is a further problem. It is not enough to say that Paul's
churches tended towards Gnosticism after his death. We must
allow, too, for the probability of continued Pauline influence in the
form of the younger co-workers of Paul, who, even after Paul's
death, would have continued to feel a sense of responsibility to the
churches over which they had laboured with Paul.[41] Unless we
make Paul himself a leader in the movement towards Gnosticism,[42]
we perhaps should not assume a widespread move towards
Gnosticism in the Pauline churches at an early date. The leadership
in those churches must have stood close to Paul's own thinking and
should not be thought to have moved in mass to some other
viewpoint unless that move can be explained.[43]

Admittedly, some argue for a considerable gnosticizing
movement in the first century.[44] The issue is complex enough. We

---

40. Bauer did not state clearly when the alliance was formed, but it seems that
he related the alliance to the immigration of Jewish Christians to the area about
the time of the destruction of Jerusalem and not to some later period (89-
91/ET:85-7).

41. Whether we want to argue for a Pauline school or for something less
concrete, we must recognize a period after the death of Paul of continued Pauline
influence through his co-workers. The long lists of co-workers and trusted friends
in responsible church positions repeatedly reflected in the Pauline corpus make it
improbable that the death of Paul was the end of the Pauline movement.

42. Cf. Dunn, *Unity and Diversity*, 279, who argues that Paul tolerated
Gnosticism.

43. Much will depend here on whether we view Paul as tolerant to features that
later became characteristic of Gnosticism. If we do, then we can attribute to Paul
himself the tendency of some Christians in western Asia Minor towards
Gnosticism.

44. There are really two questions here. The first is whether Gnosticism in
some form or other was pre-Christian. The most thorough discussion of that

do have several documents from the late first century that make certain beliefs the object of their attack, and all seem to have essentially the same group in mind.[45] We have, as well, the warning in Acts 20:19-31 that after Paul's death, heresy would arise in the church at Ephesus. And there is the statement in 2 Timothy 1:15 that all Asia had forsaken Paul. Both the passage in Acts and that in 2 Timothy are taken by many scholars to indicate either extensive heresy or widespread desertion of Paul in the late first century[46]—the time frequently proposed for the composition of these documents. If one adds to this the trouble with the Nicolaitans in the mid nineties, Ignatius's trouble with schismatics fifteen years or so later, and the stories about a Cerinthus in Ephesus, it appears to many scholars that one can soundly infer from these that a widespread heretical movement was in place by the turn of the century. But such an inference is, in fact, questionable.

The problem is that the references to heresy in first-century literature is offset by the overall picture of the church of this period painted by the documents. Bauer had to disregard completely the most natural reading of the material: the seer is charged with exaggerating his authority (82/ET:78), the writer of the Pastorals is considered to be almost schizophrenic (92-3/ET:88-9);[47] and

---

question is Edwin Yamauchi, *Pre-Christian Gnosticism: A Survey of the Proposed Evidences*, 2nd ed. (Grand Rapids: Baker, 1983). This edition differs from the first edition, published in 1973 by Tyndale House, by the addition of a sixty-two page chapter twelve, titled "A Decade Later," and with updated bibliography and indexes. The second question, assuming that there was a pre-Christian (or a first-century Gnosticism), is to what degree that Gnosticism affected the church in its early period. I indirectly address this question at various points in my criticism of Bauer's reconstruction of the primitive church in western Asia Minor.

45. Docetism is an issue in the Johannine epistles. Not much can be said about the Nicolaitans, unless they are related to the opponents in the Johannine epistles. The opponents of Ignatius are docetic as well (see Appendix B), as is that early opponent, Cerinthus (see Brown, *Epistles of John*, 766-771).

46. Against the conclusions of Bauer on this matter, see the discussion in Norris, "Asia Minor Before Ignatius," 366-71.

47. Bauer thinks the author of the Pastorals reflects two different situations: as a pseudonymous letter writer, he writes as Paul; as a second-century churchman, he writes as himself. Bauer argues in this way because he wants to keep Gnosticism as free of Jewish elements as possible, for his theory is that Jewish Christianity aligns itself with *non-gnostic* Paulinism against *gnostic* Paulinism. If the gnostic element itself reflects Jewish traits, Bauer's realignment is called into question.

Ignatius is made into a man whose mind is gripped by an unhealthy passion and who fails to reflect the real situation (65/ET:61). The charge that these men exaggerated or misunderstood the situation wears thin with repeated use and generally seems to stem primarily from a lack of sympathy for the concerns close to the seer and to Ignatius.[48]

Consider the seer. Bauer's portrait of a man without power is hardly what is reflected in the Apocalypse. The Apocalyptist wrote as someone who expected to be taken seriously. Certainly, he did call repeatedly for repentance, but that call could come from a respected church leader just as easily as from a malcontent. The significant point here is that, though the seer did criticize (sometimes very sharply), he wrote as though the majority were on his side and could respond in an effective way to silence the heretical minority. Heretics were present in certain churches, not because they are in the majority, but because the majority had failed to act in a responsible way against the heresy.

The church at Ephesus had apparently rejected the Nicolaitans (Rev 2.6), while the church at Pergamum (Rev 2.15), and if there is a common heresy, the church at Thyatira (Rev 2.20-6) were tainted by the Nicolaitan teaching (though the charge was not precisely for holding Nicolaitan doctrine but for tolerating Nicolaitan teachers). The seer may have been trying to make the best of a bad situation; he may have been pulling his punches. But if he was, it is one of the rare times that he exercised such moderation. The kinds of things he said to the other churches (and to the churches at Pergamum and Thyatira) gives the impression that the seer could be quite blunt. The seer did address the congregation at Pergamum and Thyatira, in which the Nicolaitans were active. He called on those churches to take a specific course of action against the Nicolaitans. Such a request is hardly what we would expect if the orthodox were in a

---

48. Bauer had little sympathy for the position of the Apocalyptist (88/ET:84) or of Ignatius (81-2/ET:77-8). There is a long list of scholars who have held Ignatius in low esteem. Christine Trevett, who wrote her dissertation on Ignatius (Sheffield, 1980) and continues to publish frequently on that subject, noted that "there is almost universal agreement concerning the existence in Ignatius' work of aberrant and even abhorrent elements." [Trevett, "The Much-maligned Ignatius," *Exp Tim* 93 (1982): 299.] Trevett, herself, is sympathetic.

minority. Nor is such a request what we would expect some twenty years after the lines had been drawn and the struggle engaged against the gnostics (as Bauer saw the situation). It is only by making some prior judgment that the seer (in order to fill his seven-part structure) had been forced to address churches outside his sphere of influence that we would seriously question the seer's right to address these churches authoritatively.

B. The First Decade of the Second Century
1. Bauer's Argument

We have already seen how Bauer made his case for widespread heresy in the nineties seem more credible by positing a schism and defining polemical sides in the obscurity of the seventies and eighties. After arguing for widespread advance of heresy in western Asia Minor at the time of the writing of the Apocalypse, Bauer then noted that four of the churches addressed by the Apocalyptist were not addressed by Ignatius. Noting that those four were churches especially troubled by heresy when the Apocalyptist had written to them some twenty years earlier, Bauer concluded that the trend towards heresy that was evidenced in the Apocalyptist's polemic had reached a stage by the time of Ignatius where it was no longer possible for anyone as orthodox as Ignatius to hope to influence these communities (83/ET:79). Koester agrees with Bauer's idea of an increase of heresy from the time of the Apocalyptist to Ignatius.[49] But is a theory of the rapid growth of heresy in several prominent west Asia Minor churches supported by the evidence?

2. Bauer's Faulty Method

Bauer depended much too heavily on his assumption that churches were omitted by the Apocalyptist and by Ignatius mainly because of the rampant heresy within those churches. The first third of Bauer's chapter four, "Asia Minor Prior to Ignatius," dealt with what churches were addressed by particular ecclesiastical leaders and what churches were not. No doubt, the presence of heretical majorities in these churches might have made them less likely

---

49. Koester, *"Gnomai Diaphoroi,"* 310.

addressees for orthodox leaders, but that explanation should not be accepted until some other evidence of significant heretical presence in a particular church has been found or until all other reasonable explanations have been exhausted.

Bauer consistently avoided other explanations for the omission of particular churches by orthodox writers. If a church was not addressed, that in itself, in Bauer's view, was sufficient to prove significant heretical presence in that church. Working from this rather limited perspective, Bauer was prepared to outline the spread of heresy based *solely* on what churches addressed by the Apocalyptist were not, some twenty years later, addressed by Ignatius. If the Apocalyptist addressed a particular church, that showed a core of orthodox believers; if Ignatius failed to address that church, that showed that even this core was gone: heretics controlled the church; there was no longer any use for an orthodox leader to attempt to influence them.

Let us consider other possible explanations for the address to particular churches—explanations at least as reasonable as that suggested by Bauer. In the case of the Apocalypse, seven churches were addressed. Bauer was probably correct to argue that other churches would have existed at this time in the general area. As early as the fifties, churches had been established at Colossae, Hierapolis and Troas (1 Cor 2.12). But one should not assume that these cities possessed significant churches in the nineties. The church at Troas never strikes us as significant. Colossae did have a bishopric at a later time, but as Sherman Johnson argued, this may not mean much, for we know the name of only one of the bishops there.[50] In fact, the assumption that the church at Colossae was important may stem from a false impression made by the canonical status of Paul's letter to that church.[51] Further, Colossae may have

---

50. Sherman E. Johnson, "Laodicea and its Neighbours," *BA* 13 (1950): 7.

51. The question of the authenticity of the letter is relevant here. If the letter was inauthentic, one might argue that the church at Colossae must have been somewhat significant in the eighties or nineties to have had such a letter addressed to it. Perhaps. But we know so little about the purpose of pseudonymous letters in primitive Christianity. We certainly do not know that they would not have been addressed to a small church. For this particular letter, we do not know for certain that it was pseudonymous; scholarship is about split on the question.

experienced an earthquake around this time and perhaps would not have offered the seer a credible assembly to address.[52] A similar situation may have been the case for Hierapolis. Johnson argued that the city was destroyed by an earthquake between A.D. 60-110.[53] It is possible, then, that Hierapolis was uninhabited at the time the Apocalypse was written.

But there is enough uncertainty concerning these matters to grant the point to Bauer: it is probable, if not certain, that churches other than those addressed, did exist at the time of the writing of the Apocalypse and of the Ignatian correspondence. And it is reasonable for Bauer to have raised the question why certain churches were addressed, and others not. But some hesitation regarding his conclusion is in order, for it has not been convincingly demonstrated either by Bauer or his followers that those churches which were not addressed were already under the control of heretics, and that this was true, too, for some of the churches that were addressed.

Bauer knew of an alternative explanation—the one offered by William Ramsay[54]—but he dismissed it, without explanation, as irrelevant (82/ET:78). Although Ramsay's theory may have been forced in places, that does not improve the probability of Bauer's contrary view. If anything, Ramsay's view could be criticized because it slighted the importance of some of the cities addressed, not, as Bauer apparently thought, because it exaggerated the importance.[55]

---

52. Bo Reicke, "The Inauguration of Catholic Martyrdom according to St. John the Divine," *Augustinianum* 20 (1980): 281.

53. Johnson, "Laodicea and Its Neighbours," 13.

54. William M. Ramsay, *The Letters to the Seven Churches*, (London: Hodder and Stoughton, 1904; Grand Rapids: Baker, 1985). Maurice Goguel, *The Birth of Christianity,* trans. H.C. Snape (New York: George Allen & Unwin, 1953), 412, prefers Bauer over Ramsay. Goguel was heavily influenced by Bauer at numerous places in his reconstruction of primitive Christianity. Some more recent writers are returning to Ramsay. See Reicke, "Catholic Martyrdom," 281-3; and Colin J. Hemer, *The Letters to the Seven Churches of Asia in their Local Setting,* JSNTSup 11 (Sheffield: JSOT Press, 1986), 14-5.

55. See Reicke, "Catholic Martyrdom," 282. Also, Hemer, *Letters to the Seven Churches,* 14-5.

The seven churches of Asia addressed in Revelation were located in major cities. Several things point to the prominence of these cities. First, the cities served as the seven chief postal stations of Asia Minor.[56] Second, six of the seven cities were members of the seven-membered religious council of the province.[57] Third, the governor of the province held his court in twelve cities of the province,[58] and five of these cities were addressed by the Apocalyptist. Thus, even from a pagan standpoint, the seven cities addressed by the writer of the Apocalypse were chief cities of Asia.

That does not mean that the churches in the seven cities were the seven chief churches of Asia Minor. A relatively unimportant city could have experienced phenomenal Christian successes. We have, however, no evidence that other churches were more important than the ones addressed by the Apocalyptist.[59] It seems, then, that the author may well have addressed the churches he did because these were, in fact, the important Christian centres of the area and could represent other churches in less important cities. By addressing the churches he did, the Apocalyptist was able to spread his message in such a way that no church, regardless of where it was located in the general area of his address, would have been more than a day's journey from one of the churches addressed.[60] While it would be speculation to say that the churches addressed were considered the chief among the churches of their area, nevertheless, what we know of any other church in the area does not seriously challenge that

56. J. M. Ford, *Revelation*, AB 38 (Garden City: Doubleday, 1975), 382. Of Ramsay's argument here, Norris, "Asia Minor Before Ignatius," 374, says that, though at times pretentious, it is as plausible as Bauer's. Norris then points to Zahn's observation that an ancient geographer used a similar arrangement of cities.

57. Kirsopp Lake, ed., Eusebius: *The Ecclesiastical History*, LCL (Cambridge, Mass.: Harvard/London: William Heinemann, 1926), 1:332.

58. A.M. Jones, *The Cities of the Eastern Roman Provinces* (Oxford: Clarendon, 1937), 61.

59. I have just noted above that insufficient evidence exists to argue that Colossae, Hierapolis and Troas are important Christian centres in the nineties. It should also be noted, on balance, that we have little evidence that the churches in Philadelphia, Thyatira, Pergamum or Sardis were important either, other than that they were selected by the seer as members of his "Seven Churches of Asia."

60. A day's journey is not an exact distance. W.M. Ramsay, "Roads and Travel," in *A Dictionary of the Bible*, ed. James Hastings, 5:386, thought a day's journey was between sixteen and twenty Roman miles.

idea. Bauer gave no attention to this. This makes his argument for significant heretical majorities in western Asia Minor at the turn of the century inadequate.

Bauer's argument for widespread heresy in the time of Ignatius is no more compelling. The main problem is that Bauer failed to recognize the occasional nature of the Ignatian letters. He was puzzled why several churches in the area were not addressed by Ignatius, just as he was puzzled by the omission of particular churches in the address of the Apocalypse. His solution was that Ignatius avoided churches he could not hope to influence—churches in which heretics were in control—a solution identical to the one he proposed for the Apocalypse. Then he noted that the churches avoided by Ignatius were the very churches that were most troubled by heresy when the Apocalypse was written. This, Bauer thought, indicated the continued growth of heresy in the churches of Pergamum, Thyatira, Sardis and Laodicea (82-3/ET:78-9). But, as with frequent arguments in Bauer's work, the case is weakened by the muteness of the evidence. True, Ignatius did not write to four of the churches addressed by the Apocalyptist. But that tells us little about the situation in those churches. It may be that heresy was rampant there, but the mere absence of letters from Ignatius to those churches cannot be put forward as a basis upon which to determine that.

Bauer considered other churches too. He was particularly interested in Ignatius's failure to address the churches in Laodicea, Hierapolis and Colossae[61] (84-5/ET:80-1), the latter two of which were not addressed by the Apocalyptist either. But the question that needs first to be answered is not why Ignatius did not write to the churches in these three cities; rather, it is whether we can be certain that Ignatius did not write to these churches. It must be recognized that the seven-letter Ignatian corpus generally judged to be authentic does not contain the entire epistolary corpus that stemmed from Ignatius's journey, and any argument assuming that it does is

---

61. These three cities were clustered together near the source of the Maeander River.

misleading.[62] I am not pleading here for the admission of some of the discarded six letters of the traditional Ignatian corpus back into the corpus of Ignatius's authentic works.[63] I am merely attempting to take into account explicit statements in the authentic seven-letter corpus itself that letters which we do not now have were, in fact, written.

Note Ignatius's request to Polycarp that he write to a number of churches (ISmyr 8.1). Assuming that Polycarp did fulfill Ignatius's request (we have no reason to believe that the request was disregarded), these letters are no longer extant: only Polycarp's letter to the church at Philippi has survived. If some of Polycarp's letters were lost (or simply were not preserved), that should caution against hasty conclusions that a similar fate could not have happened to some of Ignatius's letters. In fact, the survival of the letters of Ignatius that we now possess may have resulted simply from a quirk in the history of the church at Smyrna.

All but one of the seven Ignatian letters can be tied directly to the church at Smyrna: four were written from Smyrna; two were addressed to Smyrna.[64] The only letter lacking such close connection to the church at Smyrna is that to the church at Philadelphia. This letter was written in Troas (IPhil 11.2) by Burrhus, a deacon from Ephesus who was supplied to Ignatius at the expense of the churches at Ephesus and Smyrna (IEph 2.1; IPhil 11.2). Whether Burrhus returned to Ephesus when Ignatius sailed from Troas is not

---

62. Cf. Norris, "Asia Minor before Ignatius," 374-5. Of course, the question is not really whether Ignatius knew the Apocalypse. He must have had knowledge of the existence of the major churches in the area, and this knowledge could have come from a number of sources. The crux of the issue is why some churches were addressed by Ignatius while others were not. And as for Norris's comment (p. 375) that Ignatius might have intended to write more letters if he had the time, I wonder whether we can really say that Ignatius did not write more letters (see my argument following).

63. The question of the authenticity of the seven-letter corpus as against that of the traditional thirteen-letter corpus is addressed briefly in the recent work of William R. Schoedel, *Ignatius of Antioch*, Hermeneia (Philadelphia: Fortress, 1985), 3-7. Three modern dissenters from the scholarly consensus are reviewed there.

64. Written from Smyrna: Ephesians (21.1); Magnesians (15.1); Trallians (12.1) and Romans (10.1). Written to Smyrna: one letter addressed to the church there and one letter addressed specifically to the bishop of that church.

known (he may have accompanied Ignatius all the way to Rome). If he did return immediately, he would most likely have gone by way of Smyrna and have delivered the letters that Ignatius had written in Troas to Polycarp and to his church. Undoubtedly, he would have carried the letter to the church at Philadelphia at least as far as Smyrna, for that too had been written in Troas (IPhil 11.2). If, on the other hand, Burrhus continued with Ignatius, the letter-carrier sent from Troas with the letters written there would probably have passed through Smyrna on his way to Philadelphia. In either case, it is not difficult to see how the existence of a letter to the church at Philadelphia might have come to the attention of the church at Smyrna.

Now at this point it is important to recognize that the corpus of the Ignatian letters that we have is more accurately described as the *Smyrnaean* corpus of the Ignatian letters. Apparently the church at Smyrna made a collection of Ignatius's letters shortly after Ignatius had departed their city—perhaps no more than days after. A collection was complete even before the Smyraean church had received word of Ignatius's execution (PolPhil 13.2).

We need not assume that the church in Smyrna had kept on file copies of the letters written by Ignatius while he was there. All we need assume is that the church at Smyrna would have been aware that Ignatius had written letters to Ephesus, Tralles and Magnesia (the churches addressed from Smyrna). The Smyrnaeans themselves would have had copies of two letters: the one to their church and the one to Polycarp, their bishop. I have already accounted for their knowledge of the existence of a letter to the church at Philadelphia. Having decided to make a collection of Ignatius's letters, they could have quickly contacted the other four churches and made copies. This is probably what we should assume to have happened, since it seems that the letter to the Romans was originally not part of the corpus,[65] and this would suggest that copies of the letters had not been kept on file when Ignatius wrote them, since, had that been the case, the church at Smyrna would have had a copy of the letter to the Romans, which had been written in Smyrna.

---

65. See discussion in Lightfoot, *Apostolic Fathers*, II.1.423-430.

Since all seven letters of the collection can be tied quite closely to the church at Smyrna, we should be cautioned against assuming that the corpus collected in Smyrna represented the complete literary production of Ignatius during his journey from Antioch to Rome. Bauer's assumption that Ignatius had no support in the churches of an area stretching from Antioch to western Asia Minor rests solely on the assumption that the church at Smyrna would have been able to locate (and would have desired to locate) every letter that Ignatius had written to churches over some seven hundred miles of roads.[66] But in reality, the collection made in Smyrna was probably intended to be much more limited. Except for the letter to the Romans, which does not seem to have circulated with the other letters originally, all the letters were to churches within seventy-five miles of Smyrna. That is just one-tenth the distance that Ignatius had travelled up to this point. Add to this the observation that all the letters in the collection are closely tied to the church in Smyrna. Should that not caution us against thinking that the Smyrnaean collection of Ignatius's letters is even closely a complete collection of Ignatius's correspondence? Yet, Bauer's theory is crucially tied to the assumption that it is.

But it might be objected that, had Ignatius written other letters, they would have been preserved. Unfortunately, we can have no such certainty about the literature of the early church; the surprising thing about this literature is not that some of it was lost but, rather, that some of it was preserved. Given the occasional nature of much of this material, a letter might be preserved and valued by a local church but be otherwise unknown, in time to be lost and forgotten even by the recipients. A letter of Paul to the Loadiceans was apparently lost, and perhaps letters to the church at Corinth. These are letters we know to have been written but which have since dis–

---

66. This is the approximate distance involved if Ignatius took the overland route from Antioch through Loadicea to Smyrna. If Ignatius took a ship from Antioch to Attaleia on the south coast of Pamphylia, he would have travelled somewhat under three hundred miles through areas which may have had churches Still, that distance is considerable enough.

appeared.[67] Other letters could, and indeed did, experience a similar fate.

Even supposing—and that without good grounds—that Ignatius wrote only the seven letters that we now possess, that hardly makes Bauer's explanation of Ignatius's selection of churches any more attractive. A fairly compelling explanation for Ignatius's selection of churches comes out of an examination of Ignatius's historical situation, which Lightfoot was careful to note.[68] Three of the letters (to Ephesus, Tralles and Magnesia) were written to churches that had sent delegates to visit Smyrna. These three churches must have heard in advance that Ignatius was on this way to Rome via Smyrna. The route through Smyrna would probably have been decided in Laodicea. From there, a messenger could have been sent down the Maeander Valley to announce this to the churches at Tralles, Magnesia and Ephesus.[69] A group from these churches could have then made the trip north to Smyrna, arriving there about the same time Ignatius would have, and perhaps even before, if Ignatius was delayed along the way.[70] Ephesus and Smyrna were competing seaports for the trade that used the road system connecting the eastern and western parts of the Roman Empire. Undoubtedly, inhabitants of the area would have been familiar with the customary delays in getting passage at the ports and may have hoped to catch Ignatius in such a delay.[71] At any rate, delegates from the three churches did manage to meet with Ignatius, in spite of Ignatius's itinerary being at the whim of his armed escort, who, on Ignatius's own testimony, were anything but friendly towards him (IRom

---

67. The existence of a letter of Paul to the church at Loadicea depends to some extent on the authenticity of Paul's letter to the Colossians, for it is in that letter that a letter to the Laodiceans is mentioned.

68. Lightfoot, *Apostolic Fathers*, II.1:33-4.

69. See Lightfoot, *Apostolic Fathers*, II.2:34; William R. Schoedel, "Theological Norms and Social Perspectives in Ignatius of Antioch." In *JCSD*, 43.

70. Ignatius had opportunity to meet with people in Philadelphia, but it is not possible to determine whether this stay was brief or extended.

71. They assumed that they would likely be able to meet with Ignatius, and they came to see him with a fairly large company of ten church officers from the three churches [five from Ephesus (2.1); four from Magnesia (2.1); and one from Tralles (1.1)].

5.1).[72] That Ignatius chose to write to these three churches, which had sent delegates (and aid), tells us nothing of the presence of heretics in churches which did not send delegates—nor, for that matter, of the absence of heretics in those churches that did.

As for the letters to Polycarp and to the church at Smyrna, these can be explained from Ignatius's stay with them while waiting for passage to Rome.[73] And the letter to the church at Rome is explained simply from Ignatius's need to urge that church not to make efforts to prevent his execution.[74] The letter to the church at Philadelphia is also explained quite naturally. Ignatius seems to have written the letter after the arrival in Troas of Philo of Cilicia and Rheus Agathopous of Syria. Both had visited the church at Philadelphia and had brought word to Ignatius of some incidents there. Ignatius writes in response to this new knowledge of the situation in that church (IPhil 11.1). That may explain why that particular church was addressed and others were not.

Of the western Asia Minor cities Ignatius did not address, only Sardis might be considered a problem. Pergamum and Thyatira lay to the north, off the route taken by Ignatius, but not so Sardis; it lay on the road Ignatius took to Smyrna. But simply because Ignatius passed through that city does not mean that he was able to meet with the church there. And even if he did meet with the church there, we should not assume that he would have later felt any need to write to

---

72. Bauer did not always pay adequate attention to Ignatius's status as a prisoner under guard. Bauer sometimes spoke as though Ignatius were free to come and go as he pleased (84-5/ET:80-1), assuming that if Ignatius did not meet with a particular church along the route, the choice would have been one Ignatius himself made, and one he made solely on the grounds of whether he thought there would be sufficient support for his position in that assembly. Even if we had a complete record of what churches Ignatius visited and what churches he did not, we would have no basis for saying that those he visited had a credible orthodox element and those he bypassed had none. Surely, the plans of the guards would account in part for the selection.

73. Apparently the stay was extended, and a number of people in Smyrna became quite well known to Ignatius (ISmyr 9.2; 10.2; 13.1-2; IPoly 1.1; 8.2-3).

74. This is the theme of the entire letter. Some have questioned whether Ignatius's life was really in serious jeopardy in light of the possibility that the church at Rome could, in some way, have had the sentence of death revoked (see Appendix B).

it—unlike the case for Philadelphia, of which he had received further, and somewhat disturbing, news.

Further in regard to the corpus of Ignatius's writings, it should be noted that Ignatius had a consuming desire to write. He made it plain that he had wanted to communicate with more churches than the seven addressed from Smyrna and Troas. He was prevented from writing to such churches at this time (IPoly 8.1), and thus appealed to Polycarp to take up this task.[75] Furthermore, the provision of a secretary for Ignatius would seem to confirm that correspondence was a consuming concern of Ignatius. This may indicate the importance Ignatius was placing on correspondence even before his arrival in Smyrna.

Putting aside this aspect of Bauer's unconvincing argument, we find that Bauer's method for determining the strength of heresy is suspect for another reason. When he spoke in terms of "spheres of influence" of the Apocalyptist and of Ignatius, he defined those spheres in terms of cities. The church in Colossae was closed to the Apocalyptist; the church in Laodicea, though open to the Apocalyptist, was closed some years later to Ignatius (82-3/ET:78-9). But Bauer failed here to give attention to the basic unit of corporate worship—the house church. Any city that experienced a successful Christian mission would have had several, if not scores, of these small assemblies.[76] Surely some of these units in every city would have been open to the Apocalyptist and to Ignatius.[77]

---

75. This passage does not imply that Ignatius was interested in addressing only the churches that lay ahead of him, even though his specific request is that Polycarp would write to the churches that lay ahead. This request reflects only what Ignatius felt to be most pressing; it does not reflect the full scope of his interests or the complete list of churches to which he might have written.

76. See chapter 3 §IV.B.

77. Admittedly, the phenomenon of the house church has not been given its due until recently, and Bauer cannot be faulted for not having considered it. And even had Bauer taken into consideration the phenomenon of the house church, he probably still would have wanted to think of a central city presbytery exercising control over each house church. The tendency now is to think that there was no such central authority: each theological group is thought to have exercised its authority over its own little collection of house churches. According to my reading of the Ignatian materials, Bauer may have had the better understanding of the situation. But even granting one presbytery controlling all the house churches of a city, the seer and Ignatius surely would have been able to find reception in some of those smaller units, in spite of what the presbytery would

VI. Summary

The purpose of Bauer's close analysis of the Apocalypse and the Ignatian material was to determine the strength of heresy in western Asia Minor around the beginning of the second century. In this chapter, I have tried to analyze Bauer's arguments with the same close detail Bauer applied in his investigation of the literature of the period. I believe I have demonstrated that Bauer's explanation of the selection of churches by the Apocalyptist and by Ignatius is far from compelling. This is a serious matter, for it is the selection of churches that plays the key role in Bauer's conclusions about the strength and growth of heresy.

I turn now to the relation between the schismatics and the orthodox that is reflected in the Ignatian material. This chapter, along with the one just presented, is intended to make a case for the contention that Bauer's thesis fails for western Asia Minor. Unlike Bauer thought, heretics are neither early nor are they strong.

---

have wished, for according to Bauer the presbytery consisted of both heretics and orthodox. Surely one of the orthodox presbyters would have welcomed Ignatius.

Chapter Five

Analyzing the Relationship between the Schismatics and the Orthodox

I. Bauer's Theory

In the previous chapter, we discussed Bauer's arguments for his contention that heresy was widespread in western Asia Minor by the late first century. In this chapter, we look at one of the most distinctive arguments Bauer presented in support of his theory. It is the rise of the monarchical episcopate.

Bauer thought that the *rise* of the monarchical office in western Asia Minor suggested widespread heresy in the area. This was based on the assumption that, in a society with a number of diverse elements, it would be a minority group that pressures for a restructuring of authority so that one man, rather than the majority, makes the final, binding decisions. As it was the ecclesiastically oriented group in western Asia Minor that pressed for the monarchical office, it must have been, according to Bauer, the ecclesiastically oriented group that was in the minority (66-7/ET:62-3). This conclusion served as the primary basis for Bauer's contention that heresy was widespread in the area.

The hypothesis is not without its logic. It is undeniable that a minority is less likely to be heard where the voice of the majority determines the final decisions than where the final decisions are made by one man, who is himself directed by, or is in sympathy with, the views of the minority. Further, it is not unreasonable to expect that a minority element might press for the concentration of power in one office if they believed they could control that office.

Many scholars find Bauer's theory attractive at this point. They assume that before the effort made by Ignatius, the office of the monarchical bishop in western Asia Minor and in Antioch was recognized by only a small element within the church. The larger element, which the bishop hoped to bring under his control, had no sense of an obligation of loyalty to either the bishop or to his office.[1] Some have even argued that the office did not exist until the

---

1. W.M. Ramsay, *The Church in the Roman Empire before A.D. 170*, Mansfield College Lectures (New York/London: G.P. Putman's Sons, 1912), 370-1, describes Ignatius as not "a historian, describing facts" but "a preacher, giving advice on what ought to be." Ramsay continued: "[Ignatius] insists, then, that the bishop should guide the community; but he says that this principle is a special revelation, and his reiteration seems a proof that urgency was necessary. I can find in Ignatius no proof that the bishops were regarded as *ex officio* supreme in Asia...The really striking development implied by Ignatius is, that a much deeper distinction between bishop and presbyter had now become generally recognized. This distinction was *ready to become* [emphasis mine] a difference of rank and order; and he first recognized that this was so. Others looked at the bishops under prepossessions derived from the past; he estimated them in view of what they might become in the future." William R. Schoedel, "Theological Norms and Social Perspectives in Ignatius of Antioch," in *JCSD* 1:33-4, holds a similar position. He said: "We need not believe with Walter Bauer that Ignatius virtually invented the monarchical episcopate to feel that he invested it with unusual importance. For his views on the subject stand out strikingly from the literature of the period, and the letters are too emphatic on the point to reflect what everyone took for granted." C.P. Hammond Bammel, "Ignatian Problems." *JTS*, n.s. 33 (1982): 77, agrees that, at least for Antioch, Ignatius was leader of a minority element. Robert Joly, *Le Dossier d'Ignace d'Antioche* (Brussels: Editions de l'Université de Brussels, 1979), recognizes that the figure of bishop in the letters is an impressive one, but Joly was able to dismiss the significance of that by arguing that the figure is an anachronism of a midsecond-century forger. Helmut Koester, *Introduction to the New Testament* (Philadelphia: Fortress, 1982), 2:284, says that though Ignatius is the first witness to the monarchical office, we do not know "to what degree this new structure was a reality at this time." See too John P. Meier, in Raymond E. Brown and John P. Meier, *Antioch and Rome: New Testament Cradles of Catholic Christianity* (New York/Ramsey: Paulist, 1983), 75, n. 166. But H.W.C. Frend, *The Early Church* (London: Hodder and Stoughton, 1965; Philadelphia: Fortress, 1982), 41, thinks that the office of monarchical bishop was established before Ignatius's travel through Asia, and Leonhard Goppelt, *Apostolic and Post-Apostolic Times*, trans. Robert A. Guelich (London: A. and C. Black, 1970), 144, says: "The tendency which appeared in Ignatius bearing his own personal stamp had already existed in the Church prior to and contemporary with him, since it was conditioned by the particular situation of

effort by Ignatius on his way to martyrdom.[2] But, in spite of the logic of Bauer's hypothesis, the hypothesis is improbable. An examination of the historical situation indicates something quite different: the monarchical office did not arise out of a group in search of some effective power structure that it did not possess; rather, it rose out of a group fully aware of its own position of strength and rightful leadership. In the following discussion, I will attempt to counter the arguments by which Bauer hoped to advance his thesis.

II. The Problem of the Evidence

A. The Earliest Evidence

The problem we face when dealing with the monarchical office in western Asia Minor is that Ignatius's letters seem to be the earliest evidence for an office of a bishop clearly set off from a subordinate presbytery.[3] It must be from these letters, then, that we attempt to determine the date for the introduction of this office. Our problem is complicated by Ignatius's obvious bias: he was clearly an advocate of the monarchical office, and he made no attempt to hide this.[4] Some have suspected that this caused Ignatius to misrepresent the situation before him: he was so driven by the need for the office that

---

that age; for example, Ignatius found the monarchical episcopate already at hand in Asia Minor." James F. McCue, "Bishops, Presbyters, and Priests in Ignatius of Antioch," *TS*, n.s. 28 (1967): 828-34, argues that, though the offices of bishop and presbyter were regarded as permanent, there was not a permanent subepiscopal eucharistic ministry. See general discussion in E.G. Jay, "From Presbyter-Bishops to Bishops and Presbyters. Christian Ministry in the Second Century: a Survey," *SC* 1 (1981): 125-162.

2. That conclusion seems incomprehensible, given Ignatius's frequent use of the concept in a way that clearly assumes some understanding and acceptance of the concept (if not also of the office) by the recipients of his letters. See Frederick W. Norris, "Ignatius, Polycarp, and I Clement: Walter Bauer Reconsidered," *VC* 30 (1976): 35.

3. The assumption is that the Pastoral Epistles, if dated earlier, do not distinguish between "elders" and "bishops" in the clear way done in the Ignatian letters.

4. This is clear not only from Ignatius's repeated praise for the bishops and from his calling the church to submission to the bishop, but also from the specific point of contention Ignatius had with the schismatics (see Appendix B).

he reflected more often an ideal situation than the actual one.[5]

Those who argue that Ignatius exaggerated the significance of the office share this much with my reading of the material: we both agree that in the Ignatian material we are presented with a monarchical office not unlike the strong monarchical office well-established throughout the Great Church a few decades later. Our disagreement lies in the extent to which we find that Ignatius portrayed the actual situation. In the following discussion, I attempt to show not only that the letters of Ignatius reflect a strong monarchical office (for which Ignatius's own wishful thinking might have been the cause) but that such a strong monarchical office is what Ignatius actually found in western Asia Minor. In this, I part ways with many scholars of the Ignatian material.

B. The Situation Reflected in the Ignatian Materials: Antioch or Western Asia Minor?

Scholars who have discussed the Ignatian materials, and who have accepted the authenticity of the seven-letter corpus,[6] are divided in their conclusions regarding the primary context reflected by the letters. Some argue that the letters reflect the situation of the church in Antioch, the city where Ignatius was bishop and where his theological position was shaped.[7] The polemic so central to the letters is said to be one with deep roots in the Syrian ecclesiastical situation—a situation perhaps more fully developed than that in

---

5. As Bauer thought (65/ET:61); so, too, B.H. Streeter, *The Primitive Church* (London: Macmillan, 1929), 163, 165, 259, who emphasized the neurotic disposition of Ignatius. See, too, the comments of Ramsay (n. 1 above).

6. For a recent review of the issue, see William R. Schoedel, "Are the Letters of Ignatius Authentic?" *RelSRev* 6 (1980): 196-201. Schoedel concludes that the recent attack on the authenticity of the seven-letter corpus does not succeed. That leaves us with the work of T. Zahn, *Ignatius von Antiochien* (Gotha: Perthe, 1873) and J.B. Lightfoot, *The Apostolic Fathers,* basically intact.

7. Bammel, "Ignatian Problems," 84; Paul J.Donahue, "Jewish Christianity in the Letters of Ignatius of Antioch," *VC* 32 (1978): 81; Virginia Corwin, *St. Ignatius and Christianity in Antioch,* Yale Publications in Religion 1 (New Haven: Yale University Press, 1960), 3. But note the caution of L.W. Barnard, "The Background of St. Ignatius of Antioch," *VC* 17 (1963): 194-8, who criticizes Corwin for her use of the Ignatian material in reconstructing the nature of the church in Antioch. Barnard's comments are particularly noteworthy because he himself saw Ignatius against a Syrian background (pp. 194-5).

western Asia Minor.

The other view is that the polemic of the letters reflects a focused attack on a distinct and fairly well organized movement in western Asia Minor—a movement opposed to the ecclesiastical element and especially to the bishop or his office. This was, with some qualifications, Bauer's view, and a host of respected scholars consent.[8] The latter view perhaps has the advantage of taking seriously the intense concern expressed in each of Ignatius's six letters to the churches or church leaders in western Asia Minor— letters that frequently reflect the concrete situation of one of the churches.[9]

Both views of the basic context of the church situation reflected in the Ignatian letters are credible, and neither has been able to win a consensus. This, of course, makes the use of this literature difficult in a discussion of the situation in western Asia Minor, the area of my primary interest. Even granting that in western Asia Minor opposition was expressed to the bishop, the extent of that opposition depends ultimately on the basic context one assumes for the letters. For example, Peter Meinhold thinks that the opposition had become so intense that separate communities, or at least distinctive groups, had been formed in each of the five cities in western Asia Minor addressed by Ignatius.[10] But Meinhold believes that the letters reflected the situation in western Asia Minor. If, however, Ignatius was merely warning of a possible situation (in light of his ex-

---

8. Bauer, *Orthodoxy and Heresy*, 67-71/ET:63-7, used the Ignatian letters for his brief discussion of Antioch, but the more serious use was in the discussion of western Asia Minor (81-88/ET:77-83). Although Bauer thought Ignatius did not always reflect the real situation, he did believe that Ignatius faced a real opposition in western Asia Minor and that the concerns expressed in his letters relate to this opposition. Schoedel, "Theological Norms," 30-56, took the Ignatian material to provide some insight into the western Asia Minor situation, and he continues with this perspective in his recent commentary on Ignatius [*Ignatius of Antioch*, Hermeneia (Philadelphia: Fortress, 1985)]. Peter Meinhold, *Studien zu Ignatius von Antiochien* (Wiesbaden: Franz Steiner, 1979), 19-36, uses the letters to provide a detailed picture of the situation in each of the five western Asia Minor cities addressed.

9. See §V of this chapter for a discussion of how closely the letters to Magnesia, Philadelphia and Smyrna are tied to the concrete situation of these churches.

10. Meinhold, *Ignatius*, 19-36.

periences in Antioch), then perhaps we must qualify a conclusion like that of Meinhold's about the extent of the opposition to the ecclesiastical structures in western Asia Minor.

Ignatius does warn the Trallians of heresy, but he tells them he does so only to make them aware of snares of the devil that might come, not because there is heresy already among them (ITral. 7.1; 8.1). To the Ephesians, Ignatius reports that he has heard that heresy does not dwell among them (IEph. 6.2; 8.1), and that they have successfully avoided the wandering heretics who had attempted to sow evil doctrine there (IEph. 9.1). Likewise to the Smyrnaeans: Ignatius describes his warnings as warnings in advance to a church not yet affected by the problem (ISmyr. 4.1).

The difficulty with these reports (and a point in favour of a view like Meinhold's) is that Ignatius may have been overly generous in his description of the stability and good order of these churches. We hear the same kind of compliments to the churches in Philadelphia and Magnesia, yet it is almost beyond doubt that separate assemblies of some sort had been formed or that some kind of specific opposition to the bishop had been expressed in these two churches. To the Philadelphians, Ignatius warned of "specious wolves" but added, "they will find no place if you are in unity" (IPhil. 2.2). Yet Ignatius admitted the existence of a separate assembly of some sort; in fact, it was probably the chief issue of discussion during Ignatius's short stay in that city (IPhil. 7-8). Even so, he was able to say that he had not found division among them, though he had to add a significant qualification—which in essence admitted division—"I have found...filtering" (IPhil. 3.1). So, too, in the letter to the Magnesians. After extensive warnings, Ignatius concluded: "Now I say this, beloved, not because I know that there are any of you that are thus, but because I wish to warn you...not to fall into the snares of vain doctrine" (IMag. 11.1). But, clearly, Ignatius's concern over those who were Christians merely in name, who showed respect to the bishop in their words but not in their actions,[11] does not hark back to some earlier, unknown

---

11. There is a question of the intended meaning here. See pp. 185-6 for a full discussion.

situation in Antioch but relates specifically to the concrete situation of the young Damas, bishop of Magnesia, who had encountered opposition (IMag. 3-4).

If Ignatius was more generous than the situation called for (he perhaps himself admits this in ITral. 3.3), then the churches of western Asia Minor may already have been extensively fractured. Given the specific details of some of the problems (separate baptisms and *agapes*)[12] and the varied charges and warnings from letter to letter, perhaps Ignatius was reporting a fairly clear picture of the actual fractured state of the churches in western Asia Minor, in spite of his qualified denial of this.

For this present discussion, the lack of a clear resolution to this problem is rendered less significant by the fact that my main questions are most clearly answered by an examination of the letters to the Philadelphians and the Magnesians, and it is in these churches that the argument for the existence of separate assemblies is most convincing.[13] The letter to the Smyrnaeans and the one to its bishop are of some importance, too. A separate assembly of some sort may have been formed there, for an extensive range of ecclesiastical activity conducted separate from the main body is described.

III. The Orthodox: A Weak Minority?

A. The Problem

As we noted at the beginning of this chapter, Bauer had contended that the orthodox minority pressed for a restructuring of the power base because, as a minority, they were usually defeated in

---

12. The comment in IEph 5.2 may hint at a separate Eucharist, and depending on the extent to which ecclesiastical activity was conducted in separation from the bishop at Magnesia (IMag 4), perhaps separate Eucharists, baptisms and *agapes* were conducted there. The situation in Tralles may have developed into a separate Eucharist (ITral 7.2), as in Philadelphia, where a schism had clearly occurred (IPhil 3-4). The most explicit reference to a separate eucharist is the comment in ISmyr 8.1 (but note the qualification in 7.1). It is most likely that Ignatius's charge that some abstain from the Eucharist is a polemical charge and means simply that the Eucharist in which they participated was not under the control of the bishop (Schoedel, "Theological Norms," 33).

13. See Appendix A.

decisions made by the common assembly, in which the heretics were in the majority (66/ET:62). The assumption that the orthodox pressed for a restructuring of the power base in order to gain control in the church requires the additional assumption that the orthodox were a weak minority without control to begin with—if they had been already strong, why the need for a change in the power structure? But then a new problem arises. If they are weak, how does one explain the success of the weak minority in effecting a significant change in the power structure? Briefly put: if they are strong, why the need? if they are weak, how the success?

Bauer's view that the orthodox were weak does not do justice to the strength that the orthodox seem to have had, for they apparently were able to push through a decision radically altering the structure of power in their favour, so that the chief authority came to rest in the hands of one of their own members. This does not seem to be the kind of action that a browbeaten, usually overruled minority, could effect. Bauer's theory is thus weakened, for it is required by that theory that the orthodox element be in the minority, and that that minority be weak. The kind of minority that radically alters the structure of power, as we find even in Bauer's reckoning, is hardly an ideal candidate.

Bauer recognized that the weak orthodox minority he proposed was difficult to reconcile with the strength suggested by their radical altering of the structure of power. He put forward two factors that he thought might account for the success of this minority. One was that the heretical groups were disunited (67/ET:63); the other was that the man put forward for this chief position by the orthodox had a special "aura," which apparently eased whatever opposition that normally would have been expressed to this new power structure (66/ET:62). Neither explanation, however, is credible.

B. The Disunited Heretics

Consider the disunity of the heretics. If the orthodox were able to bring about a restructuring of authority as radical as the restructuring of the power base—and a restructuring clearly in their favour—it is puzzling why they felt the need for such a restructuring of authority at all. Surely for other issues too, most of which would have been far less radical than that of the office of a monarchical bishop, the orthodox must have been able to push through their wishes against the disunited heretics. We could speculate about which group might align with which group (if we could be certain there were a number of heretical groups, rather than just one or two, as is usually thought),[14] but the fact remains that the orthodox were able to push through a most radical restructuring of power to their own advantage. This threatens Bauer's thesis regarding the weakness of the orthodox group.

Bauer's thesis suffers too from a lack of evidence for numerous, disunited heretical groups. The view we get from reading Bauer here is of a church divided into several factions so at odds with each other that they were unable to unite against a common enemy posed in the orthodox group. If there was one large heretical element, or several smaller, but united, heretical elements, the shift of power to the orthodox simply could not be explained. Yet, when we look for evidence of numerous, disunited heretical elements (so essential to Bauer's thesis), such evidence simply cannot be found.[15]

It does not seem that Bauer himself expected to find disunited heretical groups either. He had a non-gnostic Pauline group align itself against the gnosticizing Paulinists; other groups are not mentioned, nor is the gnostic group said to be divided until Bauer was forced to say this in order to explain the power of the orthodox minority over the larger gnostic group. One might say that Bauer evoked the division within the gnostic group "out of thin air." It comes as a surprise to discover that the gnostic group of Bauer's reconstruction was itself splintered. Bauer offered nothing to support his theory of a fractured gnostic movement at the time of Ignatius. But the gnostic movement must be fractured if Bauer is to

---

14. Apart from Christine Trevett's attempt to identify three heresies opposed by Ignatius, scholars have been divided regarding whether there was one heresy or two: Trevett, "Prophecy and Anti-Episcopal Activity: a third Error Combatted by Ignatius?" *JEH* 34 (1983): 1-18. The question of whether there was one or two heresies cannot be resolved until it is first resolved whether there can be a heresy with both Jewish elements and gnostic elements, for it seems that Ignatius was forced to fight against both. For a discussion of the problem, see Appendix A.

15. See §VII of this chapter.

explain the success of the orthodox minority in introducing the monarchical office. It is precisely at this point that Bauer informs us that the gnostic movement was, in fact, splintered. But the split among the heretics proposed by Bauer appears a little too conveniently out of thin air at precisely the point that Bauer needed it for one not to be a little suspicious of this explanation. Bauer expects too much when he asks his readers to accept without question—and without even a thread of proof—that the gnosticizing Paulinists were already hopelessly fractured. At such a crucial juncture in Bauer's argument, that is simply too much to ask.

At a later point in his work, Bauer did argue that it is not possible to imagine an alliance of Marcionites, Jewish-Christians and Montanists against the orthodox group (233/ET:231). One must agree with Bauer on that point, but that argument, at best, might explain the success of Roman orthodoxy. It has nothing to do with the rise of the monarchical office in western Asia Minor, and it is for this period that Bauer needed to provide some evidence for a splintered gnostic movement. Not to charge Bauer unfairly here, Bauer did not claim that these diverse groups of the late second century illustrated a similar inability in the groups of Ignatius's time to unite effectively against a common catholic enemy. But not to let Bauer off the hook too easily either, the reader might make that connection, for Bauer simply says that the groups in the time of Ignatius were unable to unite (67/ET:63)—he offers no evidence that this was, in fact, the case. The little we know about the groups of early second-century Asian Christianity prevents us from judging whether or not such groups could have united against the catholic movement. More importantly, as I have just argued above, it is unlikely that we even have several competing groups. At least the evidence for such groups is not compelling.

Even taking the not-uncontested contention of some scholars that the heretics did form two distinct groups (one gnostic and one Jewish, of some sort)[16], Bauer's explanation for the rise of the monarchical office remains unattractive. Even if there were two distinct groups of heretics, the orthodox would have had as much

---

16. See Appendix A.

claim as either of these to a primary position and may have been the strongest of the three. For Bauer's thesis, the orthodox group must be more seriously discredited.

C. The Special "Aura" of the Orthodox's Candidate

Bauer's second explanation for the success of the orthodox minority in altering the power structure is equally problematic. Bauer claimed that the man put forward by the orthodox had a special "aura" that made him a credible candidate for office even in the eyes of the heretical elements (66/ET:62). But that picture of the orthodox's candidate is sharply at odds with the picture reflected in the Ignatian materials, which is the earliest evidence we have for the monarchical episcopate. According to Ignatius, the bishops of western Asia Minor did not hold their office because of a special aura; they held their office in spite of lacking any such aura. The bishop at Magnesia was too young and thus discredited,[17] and in several cities the bishops were discredited because of their "silence." Whether this silence relates to their lack of charismatic phenomena— contrasted to the charismatic activity of the heretics—or to some-

---

17. IMag 3.1. The same concern was expressed by the author of the Pastorals. Timothy, who held the chief position in the church, was young, and his youth was, to some extent, a mark against him (1 Tim 4.12). Polycarp himself may have been only thirty-five or forty at the time of Ignatius's visit (given Polycarp's death at the age of eighty-six sometime around A.D. 155 or 160). It is difficult to determine precisely what the concrete situation was that placed young men in powerful offices. One would expect the bishops to have been older, and that must have been generally so, since in those churches where the leader was young, their youth became a matter of contention and possible grounds for disregard. If the monarchical office developed out of the presbytery, and if the presbytery generally consisted of older men in the community, a young man holding the supreme office is surprising. Perhaps where the appointment was made by some "word of the Lord," a young man might have been appointed to the position. Another possibility is that the previous leader may have exercised some direction in the appointment of his successor, thus allowing for the appointment of a young assistant. The latter option would seem to require that the appointment be made by someone of outstanding authority (perhaps a figure with apostolic connections)—one can imagine Paul or John with this kind of authority. But if not a man of apostolic authority, then the man who directed the appointment of a young assistant as his successor must be viewed as a man of bishop-like powers himself, and this, in either the case of Damas or the situation of the Pastorals, would place a powerful bishop-like figure as early as the last decade of the first century.

thing more obscure, it serves sufficiently as evidence that bishop after bishop in the west Asia Minor churches lacked any special aura.[18] This throws suspicion on Bauer's explanation for the rise of the monarchical office. The special aura of the orthodox's candidate was what Bauer offered (*and required*) to lend credibility to his less-than-convincing contention that the minority orthodox group was able to get their candidate placed in the bishop's office. But the contention that the orthodox's candidate had some special aura is less than convincing itself and, in fact, contradicts the detailed picture of the bishops reflected in the Ignatian materials.

Other questions come to mind about this supposedly special aura of the orthodox's candidate. Did the heretical groups have no one who could compete with the orthodox candidate? Note that all the churches addressed by Ignatius in western Asia Minor had a bishop who was judged to be orthodox by Ignatius. If the heretics did not have a credible candidate for the episcopal office, why did they not? If there was some special aura that the orthodox's candidate had, what could this quality have been? And why does it seem to be restricted to the orthodox camp? Further, would this special quality not have provided weight in the church for the orthodox position even prior to the establishment of the monarchical office? And if so, would this not call into question Bauer's contention that the orthodox were without power and felt forced to rectify the situation by introducing a monarchical office? To focus the question: if we grant that the orthodox were the ones pressing for the monarchical office, must we not also grant that the orthodox knew they could offer a candidate who could not be seriously challenged for the office (in spite of their candidate not seeming to have any special aura), and that they knew, as well, that they could carry the vote? Bauer failed to give these issues serious consideration.

Yet, all of this undermines Bauer's hypothesis. For some reason, Ignatius seemed to have assumed that the bishop would always be on the orthodox side.[19] F.F. Bruce noted that "the idea that the bishop might himself sponsor heresy does not seem to have

---

18. IEph 6.1; ITral 3.2; IPhil 1.1. Schoedel, *Ignatius of Antioch*, 56-7.
19. See Appendix B.

occurred to Ignatius."[20] True. But the astounding thing is why this did not occur to Ignatius. It would not be sensible to encourage almost unquestionable obedience to an office if that office could be controlled just as easily by a heretic as by an orthodox leader. It might be argued, in reply, that Ignatius did not really understand the situation, but that argument weakens with each appeal to it. Whatever the case, from Ignatius's perspective at least, orthodoxy appeared to be the significant force, and Ignatius apparently saw no reason to think that it would soon be otherwise. Only in light of this does his call for submission to the bishop make sense.

IV. The Call for Obedience to the Presbytery

Bauer noted Ignatius's repeated appeal for obedience to the bishop. He believed that the intense effort by Ignatius to encourage obedience to the monarchical office could only be explained if the office had not yet been firmly established in western Asia Minor (65-6/ET:61-2), and many scholars follow Bauer in this reasoning.[21] The argument has its logic: if the office is established and generally accepted, why should obedience to this office be the recurring theme of the Ignatian material?

Yet, in spite of its logic, the argument is weak. It is weak because it gives a strikingly one-sided view of the situation. Bauer's repeated emphasis on Ignatius's support for the office of the bishop stands in sharp contrast to Bauer's failure to mention Ignatius's equally frequent support for the presbytery. It was not an orthodox bishop at the head of a fractured presbytery to which Ignatius demanded the obedience of the church; it was to the whole presbytery that such obedience was demanded. The unity between the bishop and the presbytery was so healthy that repeatedly it

---

20. F.F. Bruce, *New Testament History* (Garden City: Doubleday, 1972), 418.

21. See n. 1 of this chapter. Streeter, *The Primitive Church,* 164, while believing that Ignatius exaggerated the importance of the bishop's office, draws the lines between church officers and the laity, not between bishops and presbytery, as Bauer did.

received Ignatius's approval.[22] This simply cannot be accounted for under the terms of Bauer's thesis.

The call for obedience in the letter to the Ephesians is a call for obedience to both bishop and presbytery (2.2). In the letter to the Magnesians, the call is the same (2.1; 6.1, 2; 7.1; 13); indeed, it it a commonplace of Ignatius's letters (ITral 2.1-2; 7.2; 13.2; IPhil Intro.; 7.1; ISmyr 8.1; IPoly 7.1). To these passages could be added a number of other passages which, though not speaking specifically of obedience, link bishop and presbytery positively. When Ignatius wished to define the church, for example, he did so, not in terms of the bishop alone but in terms of bishop, presbytery and deacons (ITral 3.1). Of the presbytery in Philadelphia, they were, as was the bishop, "appointed according to the mind of Jesus Christ and...established...in security...by [the] Holy Spirit" (IPhil. Intro.). In IPhil 4, Ignatius argued not *for* a presbytery united with the bishop, but *from* a presbytery united with the bishop, in order to discredit separate assemblies.

This stands as solid evidence that, for Ignatius, the presbytery was basically free of error and clearly in harmony with the bishop, neither of which would be expected under Bauer's hypothesis. Such repeated calls for obedience both to the bishop and to the presbytery are, in fact, unintelligible on Bauer's framework. For Bauer, the monarchical office was a development forced by the orthodox minority in order to seize the reins of power. Prior to the establishment of the monarchical office, power would have been in the hands of the presbytery. This presbytery would have been controlled by the heretics, for they would have had a greater number of representatives. The orthodox, as a minority, would not have been so well represented. But the call by Ignatius for obedience to the presbytery as well as to the bishop makes little sense if the presbytery was divided between heretical and orthodox representatives, and it makes even less sense if the heretics had the

---

22. Even in those churches in which separate assemblies had been formed, Ignatius found no opposition to the bishop in the presbytery. It is not the presbytery who oppose the young Damas in Magnesia (IMag 3.1). In Philadelphia, Ignatius called the church to unity under the bishop *and* the presbytery (IPhil intro.).

majority of presbyters—the very situation that Bauer seemed to visualize, though he did not state this explicitly.[23] Whatever conflict and division Ignatius saw in the churches, it was a conflict and division not reflected in the presbytery. The presbytery was clearly united. In fact, Ignatius used the concord of the presbytery with the bishop to encourage similar concord on the part of each lay member with the bishop and presbytery.[24] This stands in marked contrast to Bauer's reconstruction.

Further evidence that the presbytery did not include leaders of the heretical movement is that the heretical element seems to have started to conduct independent assemblies, which Ignatius labeled as "outside the sanctuary."[25] Admittedly, independent meetings indicate a challenge of some sort to the authority of the bishop. Ignatius himself made such a charge.[26] But too much attention has been given to the "fact" of independent meetings; too little to the significance. That opposition to the bishop was expressed in the form of independent assemblies suggests that the faction was unable to find effective means of opposition to the bishop within the structures of the church. Yet, had a number of presbyters been from the heretical camp, one would have expected that opposition to the bishop would have been channelled through these presbyterial representatives. But we hear nothing of opposition at this level; we hear only positive comments. It would seem, then, that the heretical faction was not only unable to get their own man elected to the office of bishop, they were unable to get effective—if, in fact, they were able to get any—representation within the presbytery.

---

23. Bauer thought the orthodox were generally in the minority and that this minority pressed for the monarchical office in order to control the assembly (66/ET:62). Power would normally have been in the hands of the presbytery, and both the minority status of the orthodox and their desire to establish the monarchical office would, given Bauer's reconstruction, indicate that the orthodox were outnumbered in the presbytery.

24. Ignatius described the relationship of the presbytery to the bishop in Ephesus as "attuned...as the strings to a harp" (IEph 4.1). There is no indication that he had a less positive opinion of the presbytery in the other churches.

25. Separate assemblies of some kind have been formed at least in Magnesia and Philadelphia (IMag 4; IPhil 7), but Ignatius's criticism of activities that are "outside of the sanctuary" is found throughout his correspondence.

26. See Appendix B.

This point should be emphasized for it is central to Bauer's thesis. This thesis requires, as I have said, that the presbytery be weighted in favour of the heretics. Bauer's contention was that the old structure of power was controlled by the heretics, and the orthodox, in order to gain power, pressed for the novel monarchical office. Ignatius was supposed to be the driving force behind this move. The old power structure was, of course, simply the presbytery, without a monarchical office. Yet, according to all the evidence of the Ignatian letters, the presbytery was not a problem at all. Presbyters were, as the whole church ought to have been, properly united with the bishop, and Ignatius as unhesitatingly called for loyalty to the presbytery as he called for loyalty to the bishop. The tension between the presbytery and the bishop that must have existed, by any accounting of Bauer's thesis, simply is not there, even at the time when this tension ought to have been the sharpest—at the time of the introduction of the monarchical office. But search as we will, we cannot find heretical presbyters. Whither, we might ask Bauer, has this large heretical presbyterial element suddenly disappeared?

What we see reflected in the Ignatian letters is a heretical faction with no claim on the sanctuary, no claim on the bishop, and no claim on the elders or the deacons. The picture is one of an existing system of orthodox leaders being challenged on the perimeter by heretics. The heretics cannot have been at the centre, for on that supposition, Ignatius's appeal for obedience to the presbytery would not make sense.

Bauer knew he had to find tension between the bishop and the presbytery, but his argument for this tension is particularly disappointing. He did not deal with any of the many statements that posits a positive relationship between bishop and presbytery; worse still, he overestimated the significance of the rare statements that might be construed to reflect some tension within the presbytery towards the bishops. Let us consider Bauer's points.

First, Bauer called attention to the introduction of the letter of Polycarp to the church at Philippi. There Polycarp identified the senders of the letter as himself and "the presbyters with him."

Bauer argued that what Polycarp meant was that the presbytery was divided and only those presbyters on Polycarp's side actually issued the letter. Bauer went so far as to say that there was an antibishop in Smyrna, leading the opposition against Ignatius (73-4/ET:69-70).

Some years previously in his commentary on the Apostolic Fathers, Bauer had translated the phrase Πολυκαρπος και οἱ συν αυτῷ πρεσβυτεροι τῃ ἐκκλησια (PolPhil intro.) in such a way that the whole presbytery was on Polycarp's side.[27] In his study on orthodoxy and heresy, Bauer "confessed" that this translation was a mistake (74/ET:70). But was Bauer's revised translation a better one? Grammatically, the phrase could refer either to a presbytery fully behind Polycarp (as Bauer had translated it at first) or to a divided presbytery. Only by an examination of other passages can one determine which of the two is the better translation in this passage.

Bauer's revised translation implies that no credible monarchical office existed in Smyrna: the presbytery was divided and a significant number of presbyters did not support Polycarp. The problem with this picture of the presbytery at Smyrna is that it cannot make sense of the rather generous comments that Ignatius, only days earlier,[28] had made about that very presbytery. We find those comments in the letter to the Smyrnaeans and in the letter to Polycarp. There Ignatius had called the church to follow the bishop "as Jesus Christ follows the Father, and the presbytery as if it were the Apostles. And reverence the deacons as the command of God" (ISmyr 8.1). And in closing that letter, he wrote: "I salute the godly bishop and the revered presbytery..." (12.2). Speaking to the church in the letter addressed specifically to Polycarp, Ignatius

---

27. Walter Bauer, *Die Briefe des Ignatius von Antiochia und der Polycarpbrief,* Handbuck zum Neuen Testament, ed. H. Lietzmann (Tübingen: Mohr, 1920). Bauer had translated the phrase "Polycarp and the presbyters with him." When he was writing his commentary, Bauer meant to imply that all the presbyters were united behind the bishop. In his *Orthodoxy and Heresy,* no such unity is argued for by Bauer. In fact, the opposite. Cf. Robert M. Grant, "Scripture and Tradition in Ignatius of Antioch," in *After the New Testament* (Philadelphia: Fortress, 1967), 53-4.

28. Polycarp wrote to the church at Philippi before he had news concerning Ignatius's execution (PolPhil 13.2). That allows for a few weeks, at most, from the time of the composition of Ignatius's letters to Polycarp's own writing.

stated that he was "devoted to those who are subject to the bishop, presbytery and deacons" (IPol 6.1).

Clearly, Ignatius viewed the presbytery at Smyrna positively, so much so that he called for obedience to it. If the presbytery was divided, such an unqualified call for obedience is hardly intelligible. That call by Ignatius for obedience to the presbytery as a whole indicates that Ignatius believed that the presbytery was not split into two camps but rather was united fully behind Polycarp.

Any reconstruction that must deny Ignatius's accuracy here requires an excessive distrust of Ignatius's ability to recognize open factions within the church. Ignatius offers us some assurance that he was not so loose witted: he did recognize opposition within the church, in spite of that opposition being disguised,[29] yet he believed that the presbytery was not involved in the faction, and in his attempt to stabilize the situation in favour of Polycarp, he even called for submission to the presbytery. Considering Ignatius's first-hand dealing with the situation in Smyrna, his approval of the presbytery must be allowed as evidence for a presbytery fully behind the bishop. This clearly subverts Bauer's reconstruction.

Only one other passage in the Ignatian material might be taken to indicate a tension between bishop and presbytery. In ITral 12.2, Ignatius said that "it is right that each of you, especially the presbytery, should refresh the bishop." He went on to entreat them to listen to him lest he become a witness against them (12.3). Is this a warning directed especially to the presbytery, as Bauer argued (72/ET:68-9)? It seems unlikely.[30] Throughout the letter, Ignatius

---

29. If ISmyr 5.2 refers to people Ignatius met while in Smyrna, we have, then, an instance where Ignatius exercised sharp judgment, recognizing a dangerous stance of those who praised him.

30. Cf. Schoedel, *Ignatius*, 159-160, n. 3. James Moffatt, "An Approach to Ignatius," *HTR* 29 (1936), 1-38, offers a detailed analysis of the situation in Tralles. He believes that the presbyters are posed against the bishop, with the deacons aligning with the bishop against the presbyters. Moffatt claims that the presbyters receive no praise from Ignatius (p. 14), but he fails to explain the call that Ignatius made for obedience to both the bishop *and* the presbytery (ITral 2.1-2; 7.2; 13.2). This is a telling point against Moffatt's reconstruction. Moffatt attempts to support his reconstruction further by pointing out that the bishop of Tralles comes to Smyrna alone, while presbyters or deacons come with the other bishops. "We suspect," says Moffatt, "that the presbyters at Tralles were not quite so good colleagues as they were elsewhere" (p. 14). But surely someone

has given every indication that the presbytery stood firmly behind the bishop. In 2.2, the church was called to obedience to the bishop and presbytery (subjection to the presbytery as to the Apostles), and a paragraph later, the church was defined in terms of bishop, presbytery and deacons (3.1). And in 7.2, again the bishop and the presbytery were linked in a way that does not suggest tension. Given these positive comments, it seems unfair to the thrust of the letter as a whole to contend that the reference in 12.2 indicates significant opposition to the bishop within the presbytery.

One might argue that the heretical presbyters had already separated themselves from the body controlled by the bishop. Admittedly, some kind of separation within the community had indeed occurred,[31] and there could have been a presbyter or two who had joined or even led it. But the break with the bishop by presbyters must have been rare: Ignatius's attitude towards presbyters is too positive for it to have been otherwise; his belief in their loyalty to the bishop too firm. An appeal to Ignatius's ignorance of the situation to explain this has little to commend it.

If presbyters did desert the bishop, they apparently had given up any hope of holding power under the monarchical office. That suggests a well-established monarchical office, not one just being introduced by Ignatius. Further, if a number of presbyters have deserted, they apparently were already discredited, perhaps by their very leaving. Ignatius could, and did, appeal for loyalty to the presbytery. That suggests that if there were both heretical and orthodox presbyters, Ignatius believed that his call for loyalty to the presbytery would be understood by the church as loyalty to those presbyters who were themselves loyal to the bishop.

Unless, then, Ignatius was markedly ignorant of the situation in the churches he was writing to, only two options remain. The presbytery was united behind the bishop, or the presbytery was

---

besides the bishop was in sympathy with the bishop's position in Tralles. That only the bishop came from Tralles may indicate more about the financial situation in the church there than about the political or theological situation. Moffatt should have noted that, of the three cities, Tralles was the most distant, and thus would have involved the greatest expense and inconvenience.

31. See §V following.

divided, and those against the bishop were already discredited. The first seems to take better account of the evidence, though either will undermine Bauer's reconstruction.

In light of these observations, we cannot but conclude that the position of the orthodox was notably more favourable than Bauer has acknowledged.

V. Signs of Token Recognition of Ignatius and of the Bishops by the Schismatics

Bauer spoke of the "inherent contradiction of a monarchical bishop with only partial recognition" (67-8/ET:71-2). What he was referring to were the frequent references within the Ignatian letters themselves regarding opposition to the authority of the bishop.[32] Some critics have objected that no bishop at any time in the history of the Christian church has had the pleasure of ruling without opposition,[33] and Bauer's failure to accept as monarchical any office to which opposition was expressed is an obvious weakness in his hypothesis. That, however, should not be made the significant point for debate. What is crucial is an understanding of the character of this opposition, quite apart from the question of whether opposition can be envisioned within a genuinely monarchical sphere.

That opposition of some sort did exist is the most natural reading of the Ignatian letters. Ignatius not only knew of opposition, he seems to have known some of the opponents by name, and he had a large and unflattering stock of polemic terms with which to describe them.[34] That element of Ignatius's polemic is universally recognized. What needs to be resolved now is the nature of that opposition.

---

32. See Appendix B.
33. Norris, "Ignatius, Polycarp and 1 Clement," 34-5.
34. The schismatics are described as "haughty" (IEph 5.3), "ravening dogs" (IEph 7.1), "unbelievers" (ITral 10.1), "wicked offshoots which bear deadly fruit" (ITral 11.1), "evil growths" (IPhil 3.1), "tombstones and sepulchers" (IPhil 6.1), "beasts in the form of men" (ISmyr 4.1)—a list to which a number of other terms could be added.

It is usually assumed that the opposition to the bishop in western Asia Minor at the time of Ignatius was blatant and sharp. I wish to argue against this view, taking the position that the opposition was not so open, and if not hidden, certainly it was underhanded. I will attempt to establish two points in support of my reconstruction. First, the schismatics continue to recognize the bishop (though perhaps only in some token way), and such recognition, I contend, is unintelligible in a context of open opposition. Second, the separate assemblies may have been viewed as valid options under a monarchical framework (at least, Ignatius seems to have considered the separate assemblies a more serious matter than the churches had before his arrival); again, such a relationship is unintelligible in the context of open opposition. If either point can be established, Bauer's theory that there is open and widespread opposition to the monarchical office will need to be modified.

One feature of Ignatius's polemic not given its due is that, in spite of Ignatius's obvious hostility towards the opponents, Ignatius was forced, on occasion, to admit that some of the opponents rendered token recognition to both himself and the bishops. Passing notice has been paid to this on the rare occasion. Virginia Corwin, in her Yale dissertation on Ignatius, suggested that the opponents in Magnesia had not yet separated from the bishop's church, for they seem, nominally at least, to have acknowledged the bishop. Corwin held that the bishop represented the centrist (and majority) position.[35] William R. Schoedel, with less sympathy for Ignatius's side, noted the respect that the Docetists seem to have had for Ignatius. Schoedel observed a peculiar feature of the relationship. Ignatius had been starkly critical of the Docetists at several points in the letter to the Smyrnaeans. Schoedel wrote:

> ...it would be natural to conclude that the Docetists must have viewed Ignatius from afar with disapproval. And yet that was not so. For Ignatius lets slip a remark that changes the picture entirely. He asks, "What does a man benefit me if he praises me but blasphemes my Lord, not confessing that he is a bearer of flesh"? (Smyrn. 5.2) The implication is that the Docetists admired him but he is unwilling to

---

35. Corwin, *St. Ignatius*, 52, 64.

accept their admiration. Clearly it is Ignatius who polarizes the situation.[36]

I agree with one point of Schoedel's observation. Given Ignatius's general hostility towards the schismatics, it is surprising that he nevertheless admitted that the opponents rendered at least token recognition to himself or to the bishops. But the admission is a forced one. It is the last thing that Ignatius wanted to admit, and the fact that he did mention it speaks for its truth, especially since Ignatius seemed uncomfortable in admitting it, and once having admitted it, sought quickly to discount it by claiming that the recognition was in some way defective: the obedience was hypo-critical (implied in IMag 3.2); the recognition of the bishop was not with good conscience (IMag 4). If we grant the probable and admit that there was such recognition, we will find that this recognition of the bishop by the schismatics (whether token or genuine) is puzzling, especially on Bauer's accounting of the evidence. From Bauer perspective, the opposition is supposed to have been ranged against the monarchical office, and Ignatius is supposed to have been the chief promoter of that office against the schismatics (65/ET:61-2). But even token recognition in this context would be unintelligible. For western Asia Minor, we have at least token recognition of the bishop, and this challenges Bauer's recon–struction.

A detailed discussion of the schismatics' relationship with the bishops and with Ignatius follows. If it can be established that the opponents rendered some kind of recognition to the bishops and to Ignatius, such recognition will not find compelling explanation within the framework of Bauer's hypothesis.

In analyzing the relationship between the bishop and the schismatics, our primary question is what to make of the recognition that the schismatics are prepared to render to the bishop. The crucial question is not whether the recognition was genuine or merely token; it is why there should have been any recognition at all.

---

36. Schoedel, "Theological Norms," 32.

A. Magnesia (Key Passage: IMag 3-4)

1. The Opposition: Open or Hidden?

There was, at the time of Ignatius, a separate assembly in Magnesia (IMag 4.1; 7.1-2). It is difficult to determine to what extent the separate assembly was seen as a rival assembly; the schismatics may have joined with the bishop's church for some of their activities (Ignatius could have been exaggerating in IMag 4).[37] But when Ignatius spoke of this faction, the vocabulary that came to his mind is unexpected. He spoke of the group as having tried to lead their bishop astray ($\pi\lambda\alpha\nu\alpha\omega$), and he warned in this context that those who were trying to deceive the bishop were not dealing with men but with the invisible one—the God who sees even hidden things ($\kappa\rho\upsilon\phi\iota\alpha$). This seems strange language to describe open opposition to the bishop.

Further, Ignatius called for obedience without hypocrisy, and the context seems to demand that he had in mind the hypocritical obedience rendered by some, especially since in the proceeding paragraph he spoke of those who apparently gave token recognition to the bishop but yet did everything without him (IMag 4). The Greek behind this phrase is not difficult to translate, but it is difficult to determine the precise intention of Ignatius. Ignatius said that some "name" ($\kappa\alpha\lambda\epsilon\omega$) the bishop but do everything without him. Lightfoot translated the verb as "respect";[38] Lake translated it as "recognize";[39] Schoedel translated it as "acknowledge."[40] Perhaps none of these words is entirely suitable, all being less ambiguous than Ignatius's own comment. Yet, in spite of the ambiguity of the phrase "they name the bishop," it was clearly intended as some kind of contrast to what follows: "they do everything without him." This would seem to require that Ignatius intended $\kappa\alpha\lambda\epsilon\omega$ to indicate some kind of recognition of the bishop by the schismatics (though perhaps

---

37. Some activities must have occurred outside of the normal structures of corporate worship over which the bishop was responsible. But it is possible that these activities were not viewed as negatively by the local assembly as by Ignatius. See too p. 194n50.

38. Lightfoot, *Apostolic Fathers*, II.2:115.

39. Kirsopp Lake, ed., *Apostolic Fathers*, LCL (Cambridge, Mass: Harvard University Press/London: William Heinemann, 1925), 1:201.

40. Schoedel, *Ignatius*, 109.

only token recognition). This reading of the phrase is particularly attractive, given the context in which Ignatius has spoken of deception and hidden things and has implied a hypocritical obedience from the schismatics. The thrust of the passage would seem, then, to strike at an opposition that was more hidden than blatant.[41]

One might argue that blatant opposition seems to be implied by Ignatius's charge that the schismatics "do everything without the bishop." But it does well to note here that of the two phrases (they name the bishop; they do everything without him), the former is more likely a nonpolemical description of the schismatics; the latter more likely something that flows from Ignatius's polemic and, of the two, is the less likely to describe the schismatics fairly. That both statements are equally descriptive of the schismatics is unlikely: the contrast between the two is too stark.

If Ignatius's comments have any application at all to the situation in Magnesia (and they seem to, since they are grounded in the concrete situation of young Bishop Damas),[42] blatant opposition to the bishop is highly unlikely. All of Ignatius's comments seem to indicate that the opponents in Magnesia had been rendering at least token recognition to the bishop. It is difficult to see how the word "deceive," for example, is appropriate to describe a situation in which opposition was blatant; it is difficult to see how "secret things" and "hypocrisy" and "naming the bishop" (unclear, admittedly, but positive nonetheless) fit the scene of a divided

---

41. This Bauer himself recognizes, speaking of the "lip service" that the schismatics pay to the bishop (72/ET:68). Bauer's failure to discuss the significance of this lip service is troubling, for it strikes at the heart of Bauer's understanding of the situation in western Asia Minor, as I argue in this section.

42. The attempt to dismiss the accuracy of Ignatius's knowledge of the status of the bishops is not convincing. Bauer, *Orthodoxy and Heresy*, 65/ET:61, says that "one must be especially careful in evaluating the accuracy of [Ignatius's] statements." And what is Bauer's reason for this caution? Bauer says that for some of the communities, Ignatius knows the situation primarily from the bishops of these communities, and these bishops would have had "no reason to place themselves and their influence in an unfavourable light." But the impression one receives from reading Ignatius's letters is exactly the opposite: the bishops have not exaggerated their role. I find no difficulty in taking Ignatius's knowledge of the situation in Damas's Magnesia to be accurate enough to lend itself to confident reconstruction of the situation there.

church, where lines were clearly drawn and the authority of the bishop openly challenged.

2. The Introduction of the Monarchical Office: A Cause for the Schism?

The problem that faces us respecting the situation in Magnesia, then, is how to make sense of those phrases that seem out of place (if not unintelligible) in the context of flagrant opposition to the bishop—a situation demanded by Bauer's reconstruction. If we find that the evidence points more convincingly to hidden opposition than to flagrant opposition, the implications will be far-reaching. For one thing, it makes nonsensical the view put forward by Bauer that the schismatics started their own assembly because of the introduction of the monarchical episcopate, for had that been the reason for their separation, the deference they continued to show to the very office that caused them to separate would be unintelligible. That point cannot be overstressed.

Not only is it unlikely that the separate assembly was formed because of the introduction of the monarchial office, it is unlikely too that the rise of the monarchical office and the formation of the separate assembly occurred at the same time. If that had been the case, we would be confronted with the introduction of a radically new structure of authority in the church at the very time of the break of one element from the main body, and it would be almost impossible to believe that one was not related to the other—and related negatively at that.

It is, thus, not easy to make sense of the recognition of the bishop (which, even if not genuine, nevertheless seems to reflect a prior positive relationship) if, at the core of the break, there was opposition to a newly promoted office of monarchical bishop. The recognition of the bishop by the schismatics when Ignatius passed through would seem to demand that, at some time *prior* to the break, a relatively positive relationship had existed between the two groups then meeting, at least for some functions, separately. Even *token* recognition would seem to require that a positive relationship had existed between this group and the bishop prior to the formation of the separate assembly. We can, for instance, make sense of lip-service paid to a king prior to a republican revolution; it is much harder to make sense of such lipservice after the revolution, and impossible to make sense of it if the rise of that particular dynasty was what caused the revolution in the first place. A similar situation confronts us in the lip-service paid by the schismatics to the bishop.

If we cannot, then, date the introduction of the monarchical episcopate at the time of the break in the community, we have only two options left. Either the office was established before the break, and well-established at that, or the office was introduced after the break, perhaps, but not necessarily, in reaction to the break. Let us consider the latter possibility first.

If the monarchical office was introduced after the schism in Magnesia, the recognition the schismatics are prepared to render the bishop would seem to indicate an attempt of the part of the schismatics to establish closer links with the main assembly—they were prepared to go so far as to show respect to a man or an office which had been without authority over them in the past. The problem with this analysis was that the schismatics were charged with the opposite tendency: according to Ignatius, they were guilty of opposition to the bishop and guilty of shearing their links with the bishop's church (IMag 3-4; 6.2; 7). Ignatius was a generous enough man to have given a more friendly welcome to a group desiring closer links with the bishop's church.[43]

To my knowledge, no one promotes the theory that the factions were moving towards a more positive relationship with the main church. All the evidence points to a group tending away from the authority of the bishop and minimizing its participation in the corporate activities of the bishop's assembly. Yet we are considering no straw man when we consider the possibility that the dissident faction was seeking a more positive relationship with the main church. That would have been precisely the situation if the introduction of the monarchical office occurred after the initial separation.

---

43. IEph 10 and especially Ignatius's instructions to Polycarp in IPoly 1.2-2.2.

Returning to our chief problem, how do we explain the recog—nition—even if only token recognition—that the schismatics con—tinued to grant to the bishop in spite of a move on their part from the jurisdiction of the bishop? Neither the suggestion that the monarchical office was introduced at the time of the schism nor the suggestion that it was introduced after the schism can make sense of such recognition. We are left, then, with the likelihood that the monarchical office was introduced before the separation of the faction, and sufficiently before the separation for the monarchial office not to have been the ground for the break.

Exactly how long a bishop held a monarchical position in Magnesia prior to the break is difficult to determine, but we have some clues. We do know that the bishop there was *young* at the time of Ignatius (IMag. 3.1).[44] That he himself introduced the office is unlikely since that would place the split in the church about the time of the introduction of the office, for the schism seems itself recent and the break not fully achieved. Yet, as I have already argued, it is not possible to explain the recognition that the schismatics render to the bishop if they broke off prior to, or about the time of, the introduction of the monarchical office, or if they broke off because of the introduction of this office.

The office of the monarchical bishop would seem to have been introduced in Magnesia, then, at some time prior to the appointment of young Damas to the bishop's position. The opposition to Damas would have been, then, an attempt to take advantage of the *youth* of the bishop—the very thing Ignatius charges (IMag 3.1).

---

44. Schoedel, *Ignatius*, 109, says that youthful bishops seem to be an exception: if the main leadership of the community was appointed from the presbytery and if this presbytery was open to only the older men in the community, a youthful bishop is unlikely to have been appointed from the presbytery. From this Schoedel concludes that the office is in an important state of transition. The problem with that conclusion is that it rests on the assumption that the office of bishop was viewed in the early church as merely a chief office within the presbytery. Although that assumption is widespread, we really know so little about the rise of the episcopal office that more caution would be wise. Given that Damas as a young church leader is not an exception (see n. 17 above), membership in the presbytery may not have been the main qualification for appointment to the episcopate. Perhaps being an aide to the chief leader was of considerable significance.

We must date the introduction of the monarchical office at least as early as the leader in the church before Damas's appointment. The most compelling analysis of this situation is one that posits a strong church leader prior to Damas, who functioned, if not in name, certainly in essence as a monarchical bishop. Whatever opposition to the bishop there might have been prior to Damas's appointment, the opposition did not (and perhaps dared not) form independent assemblies, and it was only with the appointment of a new leader, and particularly a young leader, that the opponents attempted a clearer independence from the main assembly.

At this point it is useful to consider the references to angels in the letters to the seven churches of the Apocalypse. A few scholars have argued that these angels are the bishops, though most scholars are uncomfortable placing the monarchical office so early.[45] It is difficult to resolve the question, but for the purposes of my argument, it is not crucial to do so. Whether the angels refer to bishops or to some spiritual entities, the point nonetheless stands: the author views the Christian movement in each city under the authority of one figure, and this idea is at the heart of the monarchical episcopate.[46] The reality of a monarchical office in

---

45. See Colin J. Hemer, *The Letters to the Seven Churches of Asia in their Local Setting*, JSNTSup 11 (Sheffield: JSOT Press, 1986), 32-34. Bammel, "Ignatian Problems," 92, mentions the tradition that John reorganized the churches in Asia Minor by introducing monarchical bishops (see too p.89 n. 2). Arnold Ehrhardt, "Christianity Before the Apostles' Creed," *HTR* 55 (1962): 90; and Bo Reicke, "The Inauguration of Catholic Martyrdom according to St. John the Divine," *Augustinianum* 22 (1980): 281-2, agree that the "angels" of the seven letters are like the bishops of Ignatius's correspondence. For those who believe that Ignatius institutes a new office, see n. 1 of this chapter.

46. Note should be taken of another feature of the structure of the church in western Asia Minor that could have made the assemblies comfortable with an individual at the head of a collection of churches within a city. I am speaking of the role that men like Timothy and Titus played in the supervision of the Pauline assemblies (both in reality and in the understanding of the author of the Pastorals). It matters little that Timothy and Titus are seen to function in semi-apostolic roles rather than in precisely the role played by the later bishops; their role nonetheless lends weight to a structure that places authority in the hands of one individual, and this could aid in a quick acceptance of the monarchical episcopate. Cf. Raymond E. Brown, "*Episkope* and *Episkopos:* The New Testament Evidence," *TS* 41 (1980): 330-32; and Streeter, *The Primitive Church*, 104-5. Later Streeter considers men like John the Elder and Aristion, whose leadership roles may have served as a pattern for other churches (p. 135). But one might ask: are John the Elder and Aristion the *cause* for the rise of the monarchical office or do they reflect the prior

Magnesia in the early second century (if not earlier) is not unlike the sense that the author of the Apocalypse has for the structure of authority in neighbouring churches in the late first century.

Summarizing the situation, then, for Magnesia, Ignatius's letter confirms not a weak monarchical office, nor a recent introduction of that office, nor a strong antimonarchical faction. In each case, the letter suggests the opposite.

B. Philadelphia (Key Passage: IPhil 7)

When we turn to the letter to the Philadelphians, we find that here, as in the letter to the Magnesians, when Ignatius spoke of the separate meetings, words like πλαναω and κρυπτα[47] came to his mind. In this case, the matter of deception concerned Ignatius himself rather than the bishop, as seems to have been the case in Magnesia, but the problem is similar.

Lightfoot noted the attempt to deceive Ignatius but thought the reference too obscure to allow for resolution.[48] But perhaps the reference is not so oblique. The immediate context of the charge that some had tried to deceive Ignatius concerned Ignatius's knowledge of the separate meetings. The structure of the argument seems to offer some clarification concerning precisely what the attempt at deception involved. The argument runs thus: Ignatius claimed that some have tried to deceive him, but the Spirit (which knows all things—even secret things) could not be deceived, and it was by the Spirit that Ignatius had censored the separate meetings. Knowledge of the separate meetings was the matter in question; the deception and the hidden things, if they relate to the situation in Philadelphia (as surely they do), must have had something to do with those separate meetings.

Yet such terms to describe the situation are strange if the faction stood in blatant opposition to the bishop. Blatant opposition is not

---

establishment of the monarchical office? Either is possible. Too, some consideration must be given to the position of Diotrephes (3 John 9-10). Also see n. 45 above.

47. This word is a cognate of one of the words used to describe the situation in Magnesia (κρυφια: IMag 3.2).

48. Lightfoot, *Apostolic Fathers*, II.2.266.

intelligibly described as deceptive or hidden, yet these are precisely the terms that came to Ignatius's mind when he spoke of the faction at Philadelphia, just as had been the case for Magnesia.

An objection might be raised. Ignatius is referring specifically to his own knowledge of the faction: could it not be that for those within the church at Philadelphia, the matter of the faction was more blatant than deceptive? Several considerations make this unlikely. First, even if the schismatics blatantly opposed the bishop, they apparently wished to appear loyal to the bishop when Ignatius was present. At least, Ignatius charged certain ones with an attempt to deceive him, and it was specifically in regard to the separate meetings that Ignatius laid the charge. The problem here is to reconcile a blatant opposition to the bishop prior to Ignatius's coming with a desire to hide that opposition when Ignatius was present. Certainly it makes implausible the theory that the lines were clearly drawn and that the office of the bishop was precisely what is at issue.

In the context of blatant opposition to the bishop, neither Ignatius's charge that some have tried to deceive him about the separate meetings nor his claim to know of the schism only through the Spirit makes sense. If Ignatius did not know about the division (or if he could credibly claim not to have known about the division), the situation was not likely to have been one of open and widespread opposition to the office of the bishop. Had that been the case, there would not have been any question of how Ignatius had come to know about the separate assembly—it would have been assumed that everyone knew. But, clearly, there did seem to be some question concerning how Ignatius had come to know about the division. The schismatics, to be sure, were probably not convinced by Ignatius's claim that his knowledge had come from the Spirit, but they appear to have had no proof by which to challenge that claim. The whole weight of Ignatius's argument depends on their not having such proof, and Ignatius's description of the opponents as οἱ ὑποτεύσαντες (IPhil 7.2) would seem to emphasize further the schismatics' uncertainty about the source of Ignatius's knowledge.

For the situation in Philadelphia, there are two sources by which

Ignatius might have come to know about the division in the church (excluding the prompting of the Spirit). Either will quite easily refute Ignatius's claim that his knowledge came solely from God.

The first is the common assembly. But we can rule this out here. The common assembly could not have offered any obvious indicators of a division, for it seems to have been within the common assembly that Ignatius revealed his knowledge of the division (to the surprise of those present, it seems).[49] What is to be noted here is that this indicates that common assembly could not have reflected the schism in any obvious way. If it was clear that Ignatius knew of the division before he spoke, his whole argument would have been rendered unintelligible. There had to have been some question of how Ignatius had come to learn of the schism, and this rules out the presence of obvious indicators of the schism in the assembly where Ignatius's address was given.

Perhaps it should not be expected that the common assembly would have reflected the schism. That some Christians in the area were not in attendance or that some who were in attendance participated, as well, in separate meetings would not necessarily have been obvious to Ignatius. Even so, the point needs to be made: as a source of Ignatius's knowledge of the faction, the common assembly must be ruled out.

Nor is it likely that Ignatius learned of the schism from the bishop or the bishop's supporters. These are, of course, the most likely people who would have reported the matter to Ignatius—and especially so if the separate meetings were formed in open opposition to the bishop. But Ignatius denied that his knowledge came from any man. Admittedly, the schismatics may have suspected that the bishop's supporters had informed Ignatius of the faction, yet they apparently could not refute Ignatius's denial that these men informed him. We must take seriously Ignatius's claim that the bishop's supporters had not informed him of the faction. If

---

49. The passage does not indicate clearly that the schismatics were in the assembly when Ignatius addressed the group. They may simply have heard about Ignatius's comments from some who had attended. Yet it is probable enough that they were themselves in the meeting, especially in light of evidence that a radical break had not already occurred (as I have argued in this section).

they had, Ignatius becomes less than frank in his specific statement that he had learned of the schism from no man.

Furthermore, Ignatius's claim not to have received his knowledge from man appears credible in light of the fact that the schismatics had made an attempt (or could be charged with having made an attempt) to deceive Ignatius regarding the schism. That they would have made an attempt to keep the matter hidden suggests that there was at least the possibility of success in keeping the schism hidden. In other words, the situation had to be such that the schismatics could have counted on the possibility that Ignatius could be in their midst without their schism being reported to him, and this implies that they could have expected (or reasonably hoped) that the bishop's supporters would not draw attention to the schism. Unless that was a possibility, their attempt to hide the schism was a grand exercise in futility. That would not have made the attempt impossible, but it certainly would have made it unlikely.

All this makes the situation fairly complicated, especially for a theory that posits open opposition to the bishop in Philadelphia at the time of Ignatius. How could it have happened—in a situation of open opposition to the bishop—that the bishop and his supporters made no mention of the schism to the chief supporter of the bishop and critic of schism, Ignatius himself? Or how could Ignatius have claimed—in a situation of open opposition to the bishop—that his knowledge of the faction came only from the Spirit? Or how could the schismatics have hoped—in open opposition to the bishop—to deceive Ignatius about the schism?

It will not do to argue that Ignatius was mistaken in thinking that the schismatics had been concerned to hide their meetings from him. Even if that were not their concern, one serious problem nonetheless remains. Suppose that the schismatics believed that their separate assembly was a valid option under a monarchical framework, and suppose that the matter was not brought to Ignatius's attention because even the bishop did not see these meetings as blatant challenges to his authority—neither bishop nor schismatic understanding the gravity of the separate assemblies.[50] Under such

---

50. William R. Schoedel, "Ignatius and the Archives," *HTR* 71 (1978): 105-6,

a reading of the situation, we would not only have no blatant opposition to the bishop, we would not have even hidden opposition. But unless there was opposition of some form to the bishop, then respect for the bishop on the part of the schismatics would have been natural. We might go so far to say that unless the schismatics themselves sensed that they stood in opposition to the bishop, there would be no reason to think that the schismatics would not have recognized the bishop. Thus we can take the schismatics' recognition of the bishop at Philadelphia as a given. And the problem for Bauer's thesis remains: the schismatics' recognition of the bishop is difficult to fit on a framework of open hostility and opposition required by Bauer.[51]

We are left, then, with no evidence for open opposition to the bishop. And this corresponds exactly with the situation we found in Magnesia. Whatever opposition there was to the bishop, it was not blatant; at least token recognition was given to the bishop. And all the implications for the situation in Magnesia follow us to Philadelphia. First, the schism could not have resulted from the introduction of the monarchical office. If that had been the case, why, then, did the schismatics show deference to the very office that had caused them to separate? Second, the monarchical office must have had some authority (if not considerable authority) for some time prior to the separate meetings. If that had not been the case, why, then, did the schismatics bring themselves under a new authority they had not previously recognized and to which they had no real commitment?

C. Smyrna

The two letters to Smyrna, one to the church and one to the bishop, are the most detailed regarding both the belief and the structure of the opposition to the bishop. The belief was clearly

---

argues that Ignatius drew sharper lines than those in the bishop's church: those whom Ignatius opposed were an accepted part of the community.

51. Bauer, *Orthodoxy and Heresy*, 73/ET:69, recognizes that Ignatius met with the dissenters in the "community gathering." These people apparently "consciously" avoided the leadership of the bishop. But Bauer failed to note what this implied about the relationship between the schismatics and the orthodox community.

docetic (ISmyr 1; 2; 3; 7); the structure was one of independent meetings involving the Eucharist, *agapes* and baptisms (ISmyr 7; 8.2). The spectrum of ecclesiastical activity conducted apart from the larger body was so extensive that Bauer even argued for a counter-bishop, of sorts, in Smyrna (73/ET:69).[52]

But this schismatic faction, so separate from the main body for many elements of the corporate life of the Christian community, received Ignatius not as an enemy but as a friend (ISmyr 5). Further, they appear to have been still sufficiently a part of Polycarp's church to have had the opportunity to meet with Ignatius, who was the guest of some more faithful members of Polycarp's church.[53] If the group had been involved in a conscious and open opposition either to Polycarp, the bishop, or to the monarchical office, their acceptance of and their access to the chief proponent of that office is puzzling.[54]

Polycarp himself may have been partly to blame for the independence of the group in Smyrna. The case is not entirely compelling, but I offer here two points for consideration. First, Ignatius told Polycarp to allow nothing to be done without his approval (IPoly 4.1). This suggests that Polycarp had not exercised his full authority; he had allowed what he perhaps could have censored. If that assessment of the situation seems to give Polycarp too much authority, it should be observed, on the other hand, that Ignatius's charge to Polycarp is out of place in a situation where the lines are clearly drawn, and the battle engaged. A second point: Ignatius spoke of those who apparently appeared plausible but, in

---

52. Schoedel, "Theological Norms," 34, allows for the possibility of a presbyter heading the docetists but thinks the leader could hardly have been a bishop, for, as Schoedel says (p. 221 n. 10), "Ignatius would have had more to explain than he does."

53. The closing of both the letter to Polycarp and that to the church at Smyrna carry greetings to several people whom Ignatius had come to know. In ISmyr 13, a whole house is greeted—perhaps the house in which Ignatius was a guest while in Smyrna.

54. Cf. Bammel, "Ignatian Problems," 82. She notes that in Smyrna, a schism stands in disobedience to the bishop. This she finds strange. She says: "interestingly, they apparently join the rest of the community in admiration for Ignatius himself." Both this admiration for Ignatius and the access to Ignatius that the schismatics have must be explained in any reconstruction.

some way, were seen to be overthrowing Polycarp. Again, such a statement is out of place in a situation where the parties are divided into bishop-supporters and bishop-opponents. We have here, as we had in the situation in Magnesia and Philadelphia, an indication of deception on the part of the schismatics, and this throws some suspicion on any reconstruction that makes the opposition to the bishop blatant. The situation in all three churches seems to have been one more of dialogue than of open hostility. It was Ignatius who drew the lines more sharply and censored any activity not under the strict control of the bishop, a point Schoedel recognized.[55]

We must conclude, then, that in the situation known to Ignatius firsthand (Philadelphia and Smyrna), the opposition encountered cannot be explained by a hypothesis such as Bauer's. Opposition to Ignatius was not sharp enough; lack of respect for the bishop was not open enough. Add to this the detailed picture from Magnesia about Damas and it becomes almost impossible to conclude that the monarchical office was just being introduced or that its introduction was the reason for the schism.

VI. The Conditions for Identifying a Separate Assembly as "Outside the Sanctuary"

Ignatius was able to speak of Christians who were "outside the sanctuary," or who were involved in ecclesiastical activity in some way separated from the primary sphere of the bishop's influence. In other words, in some cities separate assemblies had been formed for at least certain of the elements of corporate worship.

But to have been able to speak of the separation of an assembly, there must have been some body from which separation was possible. If, as is almost certain, there was no large assembly to which all Christians of a city came together but only scores of scattered house-church units,[56] then the mere meeting together as a

---

55. Schoedel, *Ignatius*, 12. Whether Ignatius, in drawing sharper lines, had a better grasp of the situation than the more tolerant bishops is a matter I intend to take up in a second volume.

56. See discussion in chapter 3, §IV.B.

small unit could not have, in itself, indicated a separatist tendency, for separate assemblies would have been the pattern for the regular corporate worship. In such a context, separation would be indicated, not by a visible collection of persons within some new four walls but by a challenge to some broader kind of structure that defined group unity. If we can identify what it was that provided a sense of a common body for these otherwise scattered house-church units, it may well be in terms of that to which the charge of separation was related and made sense.

The only structure we know that could have qualified at this time was one that was defined in terms of some central authority.[57] Without some central authority serving to define the primary and larger body of which all local believers—meeting in small, separate units—were considered members, it would have been impossible to have spoken meaningfully of a particular group being "outside the sanctuary" or separated from the bishop's church. Clearly, Ignatius thought he could speak meaningfully of separation of some elements; for him, loyalty to the bishop was what provided the sense of membership in a common (and, more than likely, invisible) body; a break in the loyalty to the bishop was, then, what marked a group as separatist. This is precisely what we would expect in a body where a number of visible separate units had, nonetheless, some sense that they stood within the same body.

One other option does exist, but it lends no support to Bauer's thesis. A presbyterial council might, perhaps, have served to generate some sense of unity in the context of separate house church units, but under such a structure, there would have been no reason for certain groups to separate, if, as Bauer had argued, the groups that separated had the majority of presbyters (66/ET:62). The more credible reconstruction is, I believe, one that places a bishop as head of the unit that gives a sense of membership in a common body to groups that regularly meet separately, for this makes better sense of the way Ignatius could refer to the role that the bishop played in the church. This holds even if there was some exaggeration by Ignatius on the matter.

---

57. See chapter 2, pp. 119-120.

VII. A Final Gnostic Head Count?

It is my contention, based on my arguments in this chapter and the latter, that the Bauer Thesis fails at its two most distinctive claims. The heretics were neither early nor were they strong. The Bauer Thesis requires that they be both.

My conclusions about the weakness of the heretics depend on the validity of my assumption that all major heretical groups in the area have been considered by an examination of the groups of opponents addressed by Ignatius and the Apocalyptist. If there were other significant heretical movements in this area that had nothing to do with the bishop's church (either positively or negatively), no conclusion here can be reached about the strength of heresy in the area, for my investigation of heretics will have been incomplete. How incomplete we would not know. It is therefore crucial to my argument to show that all the significant heretical elements in western Asia Minor are addressed by an analysis of the extensive literature stemming from the orthodox community of this area.

There is little question that the Nicolaitans are members of the churches that become part of the orthodox movement. Nor is there any question that the docetists who are confronted by Ignatius a few years later are rooted in the church over which the orthodox bishop is considered the head. The question, then, is to what degree such schismatics and heretics represent the main element of what comes to be called the gnostic movement. If these groups represented the majority of the "gnostics" of their day, the gnostic movement would be clearly inferior to the orthodox in numbers, in authority, and in chronological priority. If, however, these groups represent only the fringes of a vast gnostic movement that is mainly independent of the orthodox, the situation is greatly changed.

Although no consensus has been reached regarding the exact relationship between the Nicolaitans and later docetists, or of either with the later gnostic movements,[58] few would argue that the

---

58. See Raymond E. Brown, *The Community of the Beloved Disciple* (New York: Paulist, 1979), 104-6, and for a somewhat different conclusion, another work by Brown, *The Epistles of John*, AB 29 (Garden City: Doubleday, 1982), 104-6.

connections between these movements are not substantial. Consider the Nicolaitans. They are still within the orthodox community in the mid nineties of the first century, the date generally given for the writing of the Apocalypse. We have three options in extending the history of the Nicolaitans beyond their mention in the Apocalypse. They could have remained as part of the community and gained power under the bishops, but no one puts forward that unlikely hypothesis. We are left then with two options. Either the Nicolaitans were expelled from the community at the urging of the seer, or they managed to remain part of the community, and are represented in the schismatics of the Ignatian letters. In neither case do they appear the strong and credible force demanded by Bauer's thesis.

If the Nicolaitans were expelled from the churches of western Asia Minor, they apparently failed to become a significant force, as Eusebius himself reported (*E.H.* 3.29.1). I say that for two reasons. One, if they became a significant force, why have we no record of them? While it is true that they could have dropped the name by which they were identified in the Apocalypse, it is doubtful that they would have wanted to (especially if Irenaeus is correct that the name comes from Nicolas of Antioch, one of the seven deacons appointed in the Jerusalem church (*A.H.* 1.26.3; cf. 3.11.1). Even if Nicolas of Antioch was not the source of their name, once the name "Nicolaitans"[59] had been attached, the deacon Nicolas would

---

59. See Elizabeth Schüssler Fiorenza, "Apocalyptic and Gnosis in the Book of Revelation and Paul," *JBL* 92 (1973): 565-81. In particular, note the discussion on the meaning of the name "Nicolaitan" and the suggestion that the name "Nicolas" was merely the Greek counterpart of the word "Baalam" (pp. 567-8 n. 13). If the name Nicolas had been applied to this group because it could be associated with Baalam, it is clearly polemical and thus provided by the anti-Nicolaitan party. One might see how the Nicolaitans would have looked for a more positive explanation, and Nicolas the deacon would have been an ideal candidate for the root of that name. But the situation does not seem to have been like that. If the name was originally negative, it is difficult to see how the discrediting connection to Baalam would have been lost among the orthodox. The orthodox [Irenaeus, Clement of Alexandria, and Eusebius (see Caird, *Revelation*, 31)] associate the name with Nicolas the deacon, even though they take steps to disassociate Nicolas from the Nicolaitans. This suggests that the label "Nicolaitans" was one chosen by the group itself. The fact that no group is known by that name outside of the Apocalypse points to the failure of that movement to become successful. My assumption here is that the label

have been a good contact for them to point to in order to authenticate their teachings and to give them credible roots. Thus it is unlikely that we can extend the history of the Nicolaitans by keeping the movement but discarding the name.

The second reason for concluding that the Nicolaitans never became a significant force after being expelled from the orthodox community is that some fifteen years later, a docetic group was still connected to the orthodox community, or if separate, only recently so.[60] If the Nicolaitans had become a credible movement, why were the docetists of the Ignatian assemblies just attempting an element of independence from the orthodox bishop, and why did they continue to maintain links with the bishop's church when a much more accommodating home could have been found for them in the Nicolaitan movement? It will not do to argue that the Nicolaitans were not docetists (and thus an unlikely home for the docetists), for then one must decide to what else the Nicolaitans could be linked that would deserve to be considered significant by the standards of the second century.

We have, then, one final option. The Nicolaitans could have continued within the orthodox community, raising their heads again at the time of Ignatius. But the opponents we meet in the Ignatian letters do not even bear witness to a significant heretical force at the time of Ignatius—how can they bear witness to a powerful heretical movement a decade and a half earlier at the time of the Apocalypse? The strong and credible heretical movement that Bauer's thesis requires is not to be found in the opponents of the Apocalypse or the Ignatian letters. Thus the only two identifible groups we know of

---

"Nicolaitans" (chosen by the community itself and regarded as positive by the orthodox and thus most likely by the "Nicolaitans" themselves) would not have been scraped for another.

60. See pp 182-197, where I argue that the deference shown to Ignatius and the bishops by the schismatics suggests the schism is recent. Ehrhardt, "Apostles' Creed," 87, offers another reason for believing that the Nicolaitans died out quickly—none of the Fathers has any personal knowledge of the group. For an attempt to give the Nicolaitans a longer history, see Stephen Gero, "With Walter Bauer on the Tigris: Encratite Orthodoxy and Libertine Heresy in Syro-Mesopotamian Christianity," in *Nag Hammadi, Gnosticism, and Early Christianity*, ed. Charles W. Hedrick and Robert Hodgson, Jr. (Peabody: Hendrickson, 1986), 303-5.

from the early period that might be connected to the later gnostic movements fail to count as evidence for an impressive heretical movement in the early years of the second century.

Shall we then widen our search for gnostics? Although the Pastoral, Colossian, and Ephesian letters might give some evidence for a gnostic-like movement, that analysis of these documents is not entirely convincing.[61] Even allowing that the opponents of these letters are gnostics, they either stand in line with Nicolaitans and Ignatian docetists and thus fail to witness to an impressive gnostic movement, or they represent another line of the gnostic movement of which we have no other record and which is strangely associated with the same churches that are having problems with Nicolaitans and docetists.[62] That there could have been several branches of the gnostic movement in this period is certainly possible, but such an hypothesis could not explain why the orthodox polemic attempts to counter the insignificant groups of Nicolaitans and Ignatian docetists while allowing more serious branches of gnosticism to go unchecked.

---

61. Most of the information about the various groups opposed in the literature is not adequate to determine whether the groups were strong or weak. If they were weak, they do not affect my thesis. If they quickly die out, they have no connection with later groups and thus need little consideration; if they survive as a weak group, they may be connected in some way to the groups in the Apocalypse and in the Ignatian letters, but since these groups are themselves weak, little is changed. Only if some of the groups outside of the Apocalypse and the Ignatian material are strong would my thesis be threatened. But it is improbable that any such group was strong. If any were, they cannot be connected to the clearly weak groups I have argued for in the case of the Apocalypse and of Ignatian material. We would be justified in asking at this point what happened to these strong groups and why they were left unopposed by the catholic community in western Asia Minor at the turn of the century even though that community was energetic in the suppression of suspect beliefs. There seems something suspicious in arguing that a group for which we have little information was strong when the groups for which we do have information (and which drew the fire of the catholics) were weak. See Edwin M. Yamauchi, *Pre-Christian Gnosticism: A Survey of the Proposed Evidences,* 2nd ed. (Grand Rapids: Baker, 1983).

62. The post-Pauline movement has been generally considered to be part of the trend towards early catholicism, of which Ignatius is the earliest clear representative. Ignatius believed that the church in Ephesus with which he has contact is none other than the one of which Paul speaks (IEph 12.2). The churches addressed by the Apocalyptist are almost certainly the same as those addressed later by Ignatius.

Nor do individual gnostic teachers serve as useful evidence for a strong gnostic movement. Admittedly, we do know of early teachers who seem to have been propagandists of gnostic ideas,[63] and we could even admit a core of truth to the tradition that posits the roots of gnosticism in a circle around the Samaritan, Simon Magus.[64] But our problem still remains. If we associate these teachers with the gnostic-like elements attached to the church in the time of the Apocalypse and of Ignatius, they become part of an unimpressive movement. If, on the other hand, we make them leaders of a gnostic movement more detached from the catholic church, these teachers are mute witnesses to the size and significance of the movements with which they have been associated—movements about which we have no other evidence.

Too much is granted when we make these references to heretics in the early literature into a powerful gnostic movement in the early second century. The number of heretics has no proportional relationship to the decibel of the polemic raised against it. As we have seen from a close reading of the documents, it is the catholic community, not the gnostic, that represents the character of the majority in western Asia Minor in the early period (and this seems not to be any different for the later period[65]). The hypothesis of a

---

63. Simon Magus, his disciple Menander, and his disciple Saturninus were active in Ignatius's time or prior to that time (see Bauer, *Orthodoxy and Heresy*, 70-1/ET:66). Cerinthus was another.

64. Irenaeus, *A.H.* I.23.2; Justin, *First Apology* 26.1-3.

65. There is evidence that the gnostics were more anxious to function as an element (elitist, no doubt) within the catholic community than as an alternative church. Jacques Ménard, "Normative Self-Definition Gnosticism," in *JCSD* 1:142, notes that some gnostics were urging unity between the gnostic and the orthodox. No orthodox would have urged that (see Elaine H. Pagels, "Visions, Appearances and Apostolic Authority," in *Gnosis. Festschrift für Hans Jonas*, ed. Barbara Aland *et al* (Göttingen: Vandenhoeck & Ruprecht, 1978), 415-30; Gérard Vallée, "Theological and Non-Theological Motives in Irenaeus's Refutation of the Gnostics," in *JCSD* 1:261, n. 63). Norbert Brox, *Offenbarung, Gnosis und gnostischer Mythos bei Irenäus von Lyon* (Salzburg/München: 1966), 34, notes that the gnostics were not interested in representing a mainstream position; and Gérard Vallée, *A Study in Anti-Gnostic Polemics: Irenaeus, Hippolytus, and Epiphanius*, Studies in Christianity and Judaism 1 (Waterloo: Wilfrid Laurier University, 1981), 93, thinks that the gnostics were not interested in representing the mainstream position. Koester, *Introduction*, 2:207, goes so far as to say that gnostic churches, with a membership clearly distinguished from Jewish-Christian and early catholic churches, never existed. Also see Frederik Wisse, "The Use of

powerful gnostic movement, capable of overshadowing or even competing with the catholic movement of the late first and early second centuries, is neither compelling nor solidly probable.

The Bauer Thesis simply does not work for the area from which we have extensive and relevant data. Grounding the thesis in an area more obscure does not make that thesis any more convincing.

VIII. Summary

Over the last two chapters, I have attempted to demonstrate that Bauer's reconstruction of the history of the early church in western Asia Minor is faulty—not just in minor details—but at critical junctures. For one thing, the thesis does not adequately explain the alliance between Palestinian immigrants and antignostic Paulinists; for another, it does not recognize the early consciousness of orthodoxy that might be indicated by such a shift. Further, it has failed to explain how a browbeaten orthodox minority could have so radically altered the structure of power in their favour. Finally, and most significantly, it has not demonstrated that heresy was as widespread and strong as Bauer had contended. In light of these weaknesses, Bauer's reconstruction of primitive Christianity in western Asia Minor must, to a large measure, be set aside.

But the setting aside of Bauer's reconstruction of the early church in western Asia Minor points to something more seriously flawed about the Bauer Thesis. The failure of the Bauer Thesis in western Asia Minor is not merely one flaw in an otherwise coherent reconstruction. The failure of the thesis in the only area where it can be adequately tested casts suspicion on the other areas of Bauer's investigation. Extreme caution should be exercised in granting to the Bauer Thesis insight into those areas for which inventive theses appear credible only because evidence is either too scarce or too mute to put anything to the test.

What then of the Bauer Thesis? I contend that it has not served

---

Early Christian Literature as Evidence for Inner Diversity and Conflict," in *Nag Hammadi, Gnosticism, and Early Christianity*, ed. Charles W. Hedrick and Robert Hodgson, Jr. (Peabody: Hendrickson, 1986), 188.

us well if it has provided for us a *certainty* about the character of primitive Christianity in various areas. If, however, it has merely provided us with an *uncertainty* about the character of primitive Christianity in particular areas, we can live with that.

Appendix A

The Heretics
in the Ignatian Letters

One of my more important arguments against the Bauer Thesis relies heavily on a close examination of the situation in the churches at Magnesia and Philadelphia, and to a lesser extent, in the church at Smyrna (chapter 5 §V). Some scholars maintain that the situation in Magnesia and Philadelphia involved Judaizing schismatics whereas in the other churches the problem involved gnostic schismatics. The basic question is, then, whether there is one or two heresies reflected in the Ignatian material. Unfortunately, the question cannot be answered conclusively, and scholarly opinion remains divided.[1]

I am myself persuaded by those who argue for one heresy, a Gnosticism with a Jewish colouring. I am led to that position for

---

1. C.P. Hammond Bammel, "Ignatius Problems," *JTS* n.s. 33 (1982): 81-84; C.K. Barrett, "Jews and Judaizers in the Epistles of Ignatius," in *Jews, Greeks and Christians: Studies in Honour of W.D. Davies,* ed. Hamerton-Kelly and Scroggs (Leiden: E.J. Brill, 1976); L.W. Barnard, "The Background of St. Ignatius of Antioch," *VC* 17 (1963): 193-206; Paul J. Donahue, "Jewish Christianity in the Letters of Ignatius of Antioch," *VC* 32 (1978): 81-93; Einar Molland, "The Heretics Combatted by Ignatius of Antioch," *JEH* 5 (1954):1-6; J. Rius-Camps, *The Four Authentic Letters of Ignatius, the Martyr* (Rome: Pontificium Institututm Orientalium Studorium, 1979), 40-51; William R. Schoedel, "Theological Norms and Social Perspectives in Ignatius of Antioch," in *JCSD* 1:31-6; Christine Trevett, "Prophecy and Anti-Episcopal Activity: A Third Error Combatted by Ignatius?" *JEH* 34 (1983): 1-18; Kelmut Koester, *Introduction to the New Testament*, 2:204. J.B. Lightfoot, *Apostolic Fathers*, II.2.124-25; Raymond E. Brown, *The Community of the Beloved Disciple* (New York: Paulist, 1979), 155-6.

two reasons. First, I think it likely that anything attached to the Christian movement at this time would have had at least some Jewish colouring.[2] Second, in the two letters that supposedly confront a Judaizing heresy, I find several passages that are more convincingly explained against a gnostic background.[3] Scholars who have argued for two distinct heresies have found it necessary to qualify their conclusions in light of some of these more troublesome passages.[4]

The crucial question that I must deal with in the context of this work is whether my discussion of the situation in Magnesia and Philadelphia is seriously qualified by the possibility of two different heresies being combatted in the Ignatian letters. If a Jewish heresy exists in Magnesia and Philadelphia but a gnostic one in the other churches, are my conclusions about the weakness of the schismatics and their subordinate position to the bishop in Magnesia and Philadelphia applicable to the other churches? I believe that they are.

I shall not try to resolve that dilemma by attempting to convince the reader that only one heretical element is involved, for I believe my argument can succeed without engaging in that task. Furthermore, the task would likely not be successful anyway in light both of the ambiguity of some of the primary material and of the past inability of scholars to reach a consensus in spite of extensive discussion. My aim here is more modest. I wish only to specify in what way my argument regarding the situation in the churches of western Asia Minor is to be qualified if it is a Jewish heresy in the churches at Magnesia and Philadelphia, rather than a gnostic one.

Those who agree that there is but one heresy in western Asia Minor should have no preliminary difficulties with my argument

---

2. By "Jewish," I include whatever elements a Samaritan influence might leave, for I do not see any clear way to determine for many "Jewish" traits whether their immediate source was Samaritan or more directly Jewish. This observation may be important if there is any truth in the tradition that the Samaritan Simon Magus was the father of Gnosticism.

3. IMag 5.2; 9.1; 11.1; IPhil 3.3; 6.1; 8.2; 9.2.

4. Schoedel, "Theological Norms," 32, thinks IMag 9.1 and 11 were clearly docetic; Schoedel further argues that, though there were two fronts, Ignatius combined them (pp. 31-2). Bammel, "Ignatian Problems," 83, thinks that the two views might not have been entirely separate; and Donahue, "Jewish Christianity," 81, admits that conclusive proof is not possible.

against Bauer in chapter five (§V) (where I discuss the situation at Magnesia and Philadelphia), for our assumptions are similar. Even those who argue for a distinctly Jewish heresy in Magnesia and Philadelphia should find that the conclusions I have reached, based on an examination of the letters to Magnesia and Philadelphia, for the most part remain unaffected. My conclusions in that section are not tied to an analysis of the heretical beliefs of the schismatics. Whether they were Judaizing or gnostic of some sort matters little; my conclusion regarding the schismatics' relatively positive and clearly subordinate relationship to the bishop will follow in either case, as will my conclusion regarding the early date for the introduction of the monarchical office.

If there was a Judaizing heresy in Magnesia and Philadelphia and a gnostic heresy in the other churches, that helps little to strengthen Bauer's view of the impressive character of gnosticism against my objections. The clearest evidence for separation and independence is in Magnesia and Philadelphia. If the gnostics are only represented elsewhere, it would appear that the gnostics have yet to establish separate assemblies.[5] And it is the separate assemblies that Ignatius seems to have considered as the primary evidence pointing to opposition to the bishop.[6] Thus, if the gnostics did not yet have separate assemblies, one of two conclusions would seem to follow. (1) The gnostics were few in number and represented mainly by missionaries. Although they opposed the bishop, they had yet to gain sufficient adherents to set themselves up as an alternative Christian community. (2) The gnostic movement had a large number of adherents, but they had yet to break with the bishop's church, and they continued to show deference to the bishop. In either case, the gnostics at the time of Ignatius hardly were part of an independent and established movement. This would seem, at least, to be our only conclusion if there were two groups of heretics, with the gnostics found mainly in Ephesus, Tralles and Smyrna.

---

5. IMag 4.1; IPhil 7.1-2.
6. IEph 5.2-3; 20.2; IMag 4.1; 6.1-2; 8.1-2; ITral 2.1-3.3; 7.1-2; IPhil 2.1; 4.1; 7.1-2; 8.1-2; ISmyr 8.1-2; 9.1.

Whatever the case concerning the number of heretical groups in western Asia Minor at the beginning of the second century, nothing witnesses to an impressive and old gnostic movement. As I have argued extensively chapter five (§V), the separate assemblies clearly seem to have been a recent phenomenon, and the schismatics even then continued to show deference to the bishops, who held an office that was well established.

As for the other sections of chapter five, my analysis of particular issues spans the entire Ignatian corpus. Whatever can be said about the churches at Magnesia and Philadelphia can also be said about the other three churches, and a decision about the number of heretical groups confronted by Ignatius would not alter my conclusions in any serious way.

Appendix B

Ignatius's Primary Objection
to the Schismatics' Position

Ignatius was alarmed that some of the members of the churches in western Asia Minor had formed separate assemblies for particular aspects of the church's community life. The schismatics who participated in such meetings were judged to stand in opposition to the bishop,[1] though Ignatius's criticism of the separate meetings may have been much sharper than the criticism the bishop's church itself voiced against the separate meetings.[2] The question that calls for an answer here is why the separate assemblies (which, from Ignatius's perspective, constituted opposition to the bishop) should have been a matter of concern for Ignatius.

No insight is gained by answering that Ignatius rejected the separate assemblies of the schismatics because he found, at the heart of the matter, opposition to the bishop. Such an answer leaves us with the same question merely rephrased. That question is: why has Ignatius placed his loyalties on the side of the bishops and not on the side of the schismatics?

Ignatius stated explicitly a number of reasons for his call for unity under the bishop and for his rejection of the separate assemblies. The bishop is appointed by God; the bishop is a type of God and has a representative function in the church; the bishop

---

1. IEph 5.2-3; 20.2; IMag 4.1; 6.1-2; 8.1-2; ITral 2.1-3.3; 7.1-2; IPhil 2.1; 4.1; 7:1-2; 8.1-2; ISmyr 8.1-2; 9.1.

2. See pp. 194-5.

holds the chief position of authority in a structure that has a parallel on a more spiritual level.[3] And other specific arguments could, no doubt, be identified. We need not gather all such arguments; the ones just mentioned are sufficient to indicate the basic thrust by which Ignatius hoped to convince the church that the only valid place for the believer in the church was under the authority of the bishop.

The logic is sound enough. If the position of the bishop is part of God's ordained order, whatever opposes the bishop is discredited. There is, however, reason to believe that this was not the real reason for Ignatius's taking the side of the bishops and censoring separatist tendencies.

The arguments used by Ignatius to convince Christians that they should be loyal to the bishop are not necessarily the factors that caused Ignatius himself to see that loyalty to the bishop was required for the health of the church. The following discussion depends on that distinction. That is not to say that those arguments Ignatius put forward to unite the church under the bishop played no role in the shaping of Ignatius's own view of the valid ecclesiastical structure and order. Those factors probably were important. But, at the time of the writing of the letters, such factors were not the ones compelling Ignatius to action. He opposed the schismatics not simply because he saw in the separatist tendencies an opposition to a validly ordained office; he opposed them mainly because he found that they held an inadequate view of the nature of Christ.[4]

That presents a more specific question. It is this. What particular factor prompted Ignatius to judge a docetic understanding of the nature of Christ to be inadequate? His own Christology was not itself particularly thought out, and some scholars have even argued

---

3. Bishops are by the will of Jesus Christ (IEph 3.2); the bishop must be regarded as the Lord himself (IEph 6.1); the bishop presides in the place of God (IMag 6.1); the bishop is a type of the Father (ITral 3.1); the church is to follow the bishop as Jesus Christ follows the Father (ISmyr 8.1).

4. The main passages are found in ISmyr 2-7, but see too ITral 9-10.

that his thought reflects the influence of Gnosticism.[5] Why, then, was Ignatius so incensed at a docetic Christology?

Here too, as with the previous analysis of Ignatius's argument, we must distinguish those points Ignatius offered his readers to convince them that a docetic Christology was inadequate from those points that led Ignatius himself to conclude that such an understanding was inadequate. That the docetic view is not the planting of the Father (ITral 11.1) or that it is a deadly poison mixed with honeyed wine (ITral 6.2) may well have been useful points to make in a polemic against the docetists, but these tell us nothing of the *real* reason that Ignatius himself came to reject a docetic Christology. We must ask further questions. Why is it that a docetic interpretation is not the planting of the Father? What makes such a view poison? The answer seems to come from the less polemical (but more substantial) part of Ignatius's argument against the docetists.

Passing over, then, the series of slanderous remarks made by Ignatius, we look at the passages in which Ignatius was more specific (and less slanderous) in his report of the schismatics' position (ITral 9-11; ISmyr 1-7; IMag 11). In these passages, Ignatius reported errant views regarding the reality of the life, sufferings, death and resurrection of Christ "in the flesh." In light of the specific charges here against the schismatics, the repeated emphasis throughout the letters on the reality of these aspects of Jesus' life must be seen as key elements separating the thought of Ignatius from that of the schismatics.[6]

In two of the passages just mentioned, Ignatius not only identified what was defective about the beliefs of the docetists; he attempted, as well, to refute the beliefs, and he did so with arguments free from the kind of slander that seems to be reflected in some of his criticism. The substance of his argument is revealing: he offered only two counter-points, and the one that would appear to

---

5. See R.M. Grant, *Gnosticism and Early Christianity*, 2nd ed. (New York and London: Columbia University Press, 1966), 177-81; and Frederick W. Norris, "Ignatius, Polycarp, and I Clement: Walter Bauer Reconsidered," *VC* 30 (1976): 35 n. 44.

6. IEph 7.2; 18.2; 19.1; 20.1, IMag 11; ITral 9.1-2; 10; ISmyr 2-7.

be the most convincing was offered only once and is clearly of secondary significance in Ignatius's refutation of the docetic claims.

The first point: having charged that some say the passion was merely in semblance" (ISmyr 2.1), Ignatius stated:

> I know and believe that [Christ] was in the flesh even after the resurrection. And when he came to those with Peter he said to them: 'Take, handle me and see that I am not a phantom without a body.'

Then Ignatius continued: "And after his resurrection, he ate and drank with them as a being of flesh" (ISmyr 3). The argument here involves neither slander nor name-calling: Ignatius simply appealed directly to an element in the tradition to argue against a docetic viewpoint. So adequate is this point in an argument against docetic Christology, one would be tempted to say that it was tailor-made by Ignatius himself were it not for clear evidence of that theme in the tradition at Ignatius's disposal.[7]

But, for some reason, Ignatius did not use this argument repeatedly. Whether on some point the argument was weak is difficult to say, but Ignatius's use of it (if only once) would seem to suggest that it did carry some weight. There is, however, an argument Ignatius did use repeatedly. It is the significance of the sufferings and martyrdom of credible witnesses, and Ignatius made special appeal to his own position as martyr. In both passages in which Ignatius offered a reasoned refutation of the docetic viewpoint, it is Ignatius's own life as a *true* disciple that was the crux of his attack. This prominent position of his sufferings and martyrdom in the only specific refutation of the docetic christology offers some insight into the significance of Ignatius's repeated

---

7. Luke is the only Synoptic Gospel with an account of Jesus eating food after the resurrection (24.40-42). In Acts, it is assumed that Jesus ate with the disciples over the forty-day period after the resurrection (1.3-4). The Fourth Gospel seems to reflect a similar tradition (21.12-15). Whether Ignatius knew the Fourth Gospel or the Luke-Acts narrative is not the point; the tradition seems widely enough known to suggest that when Ignatius used a similar story, he was not inventing the account.

references throughout his letters to his own sufferings and fast-approaching martyrdom as marks of true discipleship.[8]

In the passage considered above (in which the tradition is appealed to in order to demonstrate the reality of Christ's *flesh* after the resurrection), Ignatius claimed that because the disciples were convinced of this, they "despised even death" (ISmyr 3.2). Here Ignatius has not only attempted to prove that Jesus was in the flesh after the resurrection (for which the appeal to the tradition should have been adequate), he proceeded to connect the reality of Jesus' flesh to the willingness of the disciples to die. The thrust of this statement is similar to Ignatius's appeal to his own sufferings and death just four sentences later. He said:

> For if it is merely in semblance that these things were done by our Lord I am also a prisoner in semblance. And why have I given myself up to death, to fire, to the sword, to wild beasts. Because near the sword is near to God; with the wild beasts is with God; in the name of Jesus Christ alone am I enduring all things that I might suffer with him (ISmyr 4.2).

The same argument is used in the letter to the Trallians, in which Ignatius also spoke in some detail of the defects in the beliefs of the schismatics. After listing seven distinct aspects of the life of Jesus in which Jesus was truly *in flesh* (ITral 9), Ignatius continued:

> But, if, as some affirm who are without God...his suffering was only in semblance...why am I a prisoner, and why do I even long to fight with the beasts? In that case, I am dying in vain (ITral 10).

Before I attempt an explanation of Ignatius's argument that makes sense of the features identified above, I offer a summary of the most important points. First, in order to discredit the schismatics, Ignatius offered a variety of arguments to prove that the bishop's office was ordained by God. But his real reason for

---

8. IEph 1.2; 3.1; 12.2; IMag 1.1; 5.2; ITral 4.2; 5.2; 10.1; 12.2; IRom 4.1; 5.1-3; 6.3; IPhil 5.1; ISmyr 4.2. See W.H.C. Frend, *Martyrdom and Persecution in the Early Church: A Study of a Conflict from the Maccabees to Donatus*, (Oxford: Blackwell, 1965; Grand Rapids: Baker, 1981), 199-200.

opposing the schismatics was not that they challenged the ordained order; rather, it is that they held an inadequate view of the reality of Jesus' existence *in flesh*. Second, Ignatius refuted this docetic Christology with two arguments. One was the appeal to statements in the tradition that challenged the docetic interpretation: Christ appears to the disciples after the resurrection and offers convincing proof that he is still *in flesh*. But this argument seems to be subordinated to another argument. Ignatius's primary argument against a docetic christology was that the sufferings and willing death of credible witnesses (he offers himself and the disciples as examples) cannot be explained unless the sufferings and death (or more generally, the whole life of Jesus) was truly *in flesh*.

The prominence given in Ignatius's antidocetic argument to the sufferings and death of credible witnesses marks this as a probable key to our understanding of what is at stake in the debate from the perspective of Ignatius. The repeated charge that the schismatics teach that the sufferings and death of Jesus were merely in semblance, side by side with the repeated claim of Ignatius that he himself suffers and embraces martyrdom because he wants to be a true disciple, makes it difficult not to conclude that what Ignatius saw as the heart of the problem of the docetic Christology was the practical impact it could have on the attitude of Christians regarding suffering and martyrdom.

The novel docetic Christology provided a foundation for a radically different option under the rubric of the Christian church. From a docetic perspective, a person could escape persecution and martyrdom without, at the same time, blatantly forsaking Christ.[9] (If, under the docetic interpretation, that option was not offered to Christians, the entire argument of Ignatius becomes incompre-

---

9. Elaine Pagels, *The Gnostic Gospels*, (New York: Random House, 1979), has demonstrated that a large section of the gnostic movement did reject martyrdom as a necessary and meaningful form of witness and that a docetic Christology was frequently what provided the theological basis for that position. See especially Pagels' chapter four, "The Passion of Christ and the Persecution of Christians," 70-101. I am not arguing here that docetism was identical to later Gnosticism. But if Ignatius even remotely knows what he is talking about, in regard to martyrdom, at least, Gnosticism and doectism seem closely related.

hensible.) This docetic perspective would have been a powerfully attractive option under the Christian rubric.

Consider the effects of persecution on a small community. We know that not every Christian rushed gladly to martyrdom. Some not only wished to escape martyrdom but actually succeeded in doing so. One way was to simply to cease to be a Christian, and many may have done precisely that.[10] But there might be another option. Suppose that the sufferings of Christ were merely in semblance. Suppose that it was not "in flesh" that Christ had appeared, and particularly, not in flesh that he had suffered. Suppose that the life in the flesh was not the realm were spiritual battles were to be fought and won. Then the grounds for the Christian enduring suffering and death could possibly be completely removed. Such an option would have been attractive enough to have competed seriously against the kind of Christianity argued for by Ignatius and those holding the office of bishop in western Asia Minor,[11] the very men Ignatius was anxious to support against the docetic schismatics.

I propose the following reconstruction for the church in western Asia Minor at the time of Ignatius. My reconstruction is based on the observations made in this appendix and in other parts of this work. First, the churches were, until a year or two[12] prior to Ignatius's visit, united under the monarchical office. Second, the theological position represented by Ignatius (and by the bishops) had recently been challenged by a new and radical interpretation (docetism) that allowed for escape from persecution and martyrdom. And third, the docetic interpretation proved sufficiently attractive that

---

10. According to Pliny (*Letters* X.96), many people exposed as Christians denied that they were still Christians, claiming to have recanted some twenty years earlier. Pliny was prepared to allow an accused to go free if he would offer a sacrifice to the emperor and would curse Christ. It does not appear to be a misuse of this evidence to say that a similar pattern of denial and escape was known elsewhere around the same time.

11. I assume that the bishops held a position not unlike that of Ignatius on this point, though we have no explicit statement to this effect by any of the bishops.

12. Although I would not want to be pressed on the exact time, I would contend that the situation appears to be a rather recent one. One to two years is a far better choice than ten to twenty years.

a strong emphasis on the validity of the older, nondocetic interpretation was required.

One question remains. It is whether persecution is likely to have been a pressing issue at the time of Ignatius. If it can be demonstrated that it was, then my analysis of the conflict between Ignatius and the schismatics would give a coherent explanation for the various features and emphases of Ignatius's argument against the schismatics.

When Lightfoot wrote his commentary, it was generally assumed that Ignatius was the victim of an organized civil persecution.[13] But the evidence for the persecution of Christians in this period is not without ambiguities. There is evidence that the Christian movement did not stand out as especially troublesome or noteworthy to the Roman government and that, in the rare cases when the civil government did act against Christians, action was neither widespread nor long in duration.[14] That kind of evidence is countered by the concern about persecution reflected throughout the Christian documents of this period and by a long list of church leaders who are known to have been persecuted or executed for their Christian confession.[15]

We gain greater clarity when we view the issue of persecution from the perspective of the Christians at the turn of the first century. It is almost without consequence that the later persecutions may have

---

13. J.B. Lightfoot, *The Apostolic Fathers* (Grand Rapids: Baker, 1981), II.1.2-22; 31-37; 50-69.

14. W.H.C. Frend, "Early Christianity and Society: A Jewish Legacy in the Pre-Constantinian Era," *HTR* 76 (1983): 60, notes that Pliny thinks Christianity can be treated mildly. A.N. Sherwin-White, *JTS*, n.s. 3 (1952): 201, also notes "the extreme insignificance of the Christian communities in the vast framework of the empire." He concludes: "Hence there arises a general improbability either that the Christians seemed important enough to the government of Nero and Domitian to require a measure of universal suppression, or that any action taken was more than local and temporary."

15. The Apocalypse and 1 Peter seem to be set in a context of persecution, and does *1 Clement*. Numerous martyrs were leaders associated with Antioch or western Asia Minor: Peter, Paul, Antipas, Ignatius, Polycarp, Justin, and the writer of the Apocalypse, who though not a martyr was nonetheless the object of imperial persecution. See Bo Reicke, "The Inauguration of Catholic Martyrdom according to St. John the Divine," *Augustinianum* 20 (1980): 275-83; also, Leon Hardy Canfield, *The Early Persecutions of Christians,* Columbia University Studies in the Social Sciences 136 (New York: AMS, 1968).

been a hundred times more severe than any that confronted the church at the time of Ignatius. The issue of persecution could have been the one shaping much of the theological thinking of Ignatius's day, even if persecution was at that time minimal by the standards of the bloody persecutions of the third century. How many Christians must be hauled off from the church to the arena before believers feel the threat of persecution? The presence of an elder at the Eucharist on one Sunday, his confinement in the city jail on the next, and his public execution a few weeks later as entertainment for the townsmen must have had an astounding impact within the Christian community, who knew that society at large looked on them as objects of contempt[16]—a contempt that could be fanned into violent attacks.[17] That is sufficient to bring the kind of issues to the forefront that we see discussed in the Ignatian materials.

---

16. Tacitus, *Annals* 15.44, and Pliny's *Letter to Trajan,* both written in the first quarter of the second century, describe Christians as objects of disgust. Frend, *Martyrdom and Persecution,* 197, notes that Christians always expected persecution.

17. Accounts of riots and beatings are frequent in Acts and, if not in detail, certainly in general must reflect the atmosphere in which the early Christians sensed themselves.

Bibliography of Works Cited

ANCIENT AUTHORS

The Apostolic Fathers. LCL. Cambridge. 1925.
Eusebius. *The Ecclesiastical History*. LCL. 1930.
Justin Martyr. *The Ante-Nicene Fathers*. 1885.
Irenaeus. *The Ante-Nicene Fathers*. 1885.
Josephus. *Jewish Antiquities*. LCL. 1927.
Origen. *Contra Celsum*. Edited by H. Chadwick. 1953.
Philo. *Works*. LCL. 1929.
Pliny. *Letters*. LCL. 1935
Suetonius. *The Twelve Caesars*. Penguin Classics. 1957.
Tacitus. *The Annals of Imperial Rome*. Penguin Classics. 1971.
Tertullian. *The Ante-Nicene Fathers*. 1885

MODERN AUTHORS

Achtemeier, Paul J. *The Quest for Unity in the New Testament Church: A Study in Paul and Acts*. Philadelphia: Fortress, 1987.

Afanassieff, Nicolas. "L'Assemblée eucharistique unique dans l'église ancienne." *Kleronomia* 6 (1974): 1-36.

Applebaum, Shim'on. "The Legal Status of the Jewish Communities in the Diaspora." In *The Jewish People in the First Century*. Edited by Samuel Safrai and Menahem Stern, 1:420-63. Compendia Rerum Iudaicarum and Novum Testamentum, 1. Assen: Van Gorcum; Philadelphia: Fortress, 1974.

_____. "The Social and Economic Status of the Jews in the Diaspora." In *The Jewish People in the First Century*. Edited by Samuel Safrai and Menahem Stern, 2:701-27. Compendia Rerum Iudaicarum ad Novum Testamentum, 1. Assen: Van Gorcum; Philadelphia: Fortress, 1976.

Arnold, Gottfried. *Unparteyishe Kirchen-und Ketzer-Historie.* Frankfurt a. M., 1699.

Bainton, Roland H. *Christendom: A Short History of Christianity and Its Impact on Western Civilization.* Harper Torchbooks. New York: Harper & Row, 1966.

Bammel, C.P. Hammond. "Ignatian Problems." *JTS.* n.s. 33 (1982): 62-97.

Banks, Robert. *Paul's Idea of Community: The Early House Churches in Their Historical Setting.* Grand Rapids: Eerdmans, 1980.

Barnard, L.W. "The Background of St. Ignatius of Antioch." *VC* 17 (1963): 193-206.

Barrett, C.K. "Pauline Controversies in the Post-Pauline Period." *NTS* 20 (1973-74): 229-45.

_____. "Jews and Judaizers in the Epistles of Ignatius." In *Jews, Greeks and Christians: Studies in Honor of W.D. Davies.* Edited by R. Hamerton-Kelly and R. Scroggs, 220-44. Leiden: E.J. Brill, 1976.

Bauer, Walter. *Die Apostolischen Vätern: II. Die Briefe des Ignatius von Antiochia und der Polykarpbrief.* Handbuch zum Neuen Testament. Tübingen: J.C.B. Mohr (Paul Siebeck), 1920.

_____. *Orthodoxy and Heresy in Earliest Christianity.* Translated by a team from the Philadelphia Seminar on Christian Origins. Edited by Robert A. Kraft and Gerhard Krodel. Philadelphia: Fortress, 1971. Originally published as *Rechtgläubigkeit und Ketzerei im ältesten Christentum.* Beitrage zur historischen Theologie 10. Tübingen: Mohr/Siebeck, 1934. Reprinted with two supplementary essays by Georg Strecker in 1964.

_____. *Griechisch-Deutsches Wörterbuch zu den Schriften des Neuen Testaments und der übrigen urchristlichen Literatur.* known in the English world as *A Greek-English Lexicon of the New Testament and Other Early Christian Literature.* Chicago: The University of Chicago Press, 1952.

_____. *Aufsätze und Kleine Schriften.* Edited by Georg Strecker. Tübingen: J.C.B. Mohr (Paul Siebeck), 1967.

Betz, Hans Dieter. "Orthodoxy and Heresy in Primitive Christianity: Some critical remarks on Georg Strecker's republication of Walter Bauer's Rechtglaubigkeit und Ketzerei im altesten Christentum." *Int* 19 (1965): 299-311.

Blackman, E.C. *Marcion and His Influence.* London: SPCK, 1948.

de Boer, Martinus C. "Images of Paul in the Post-Apostolic Period." *CBQ* 42 (1980): 359-380.

Bowman, Alan L. *Egypt after the Pharohs: 332 B.C.-A.D. 642.* Berkeley: The University of California Press, 1986.

Braude, William G. "The Church Fathers and the Synagogue." *Judaism* 9 (1969): 112-19.

Brown, Peter. "Brave Old World." *The New York Review of Books* 34 (March 12, 1987): 24-7.

Brown, Raymond E. *"Episkope* and *Episkopos:* The New Testament Evidence." *TS* 41 (1980): 322-38.

_____. *The Gospel According to John.* AB 29, 29A. Garden City: Doubleday, 1966, 1970.

_____. *The Community of the Beloved Disciple.* New York: Paulist, 1979.

_____. *The Epistles of John.* AB 30. Garden City: Doubleday, 1982.

_____. *The Churches the Apostles Left Behind.* New York and Ramsey: Paulist Press, 1984.

Brown, Raymond E. and Meier, John P. *Antioch and Rome: New Testament Cradles of Catholic Christianity.* New York and Ramsey: Paulist, 1983.

Brox, Norbert, "Nikolaos und Nikolaiten." *VC* 19 (1965): 23-30.

_____. Offenbarung, *Gnosis und gnostischer Mythos bei Irenäus von Lyon.* Salzburg and München, 1966.

_____.*Die Pastoral Briefe.* Regensburger Neues Testament. Friedrich Pustet: Regensburg, 1969.

_____. "Häresie." In *Reallexikon für Antike und Christentum.* Edited by Theodor Klauser et al. Stuttgart: Anton Hiersemann, 1984.

Bruce, F.F. Paul: *The Acts of the Apostles*, 2nd ed. Grand Rapids: Eerdmans, 1952.

_____. *New Testament History.* Thomas Nelson and Sons Ltd., 1969. Reprint. Anchor Books. Garden City: Doubleday, 1972.

_____. *Apostle of the Heart Set Free.* Grand Rapids: Eerdmans, 1977.

_____.*The Pauline Circle.* Grand Rapids: Eerdmans, 1985.

Bultmann, Rudolf. *Theologie des Neuen Testaments.* 2 vols. Neue theologische Grundrisse. Tübingen: Mohr (Siebeck), 1948-53. References are to the translation by Kendrick Grobel, *Theology of the New Testament.* 2 vols. New York: Charles Scribner's Sons, 1951-55.

Burke, G.T. "Walter Bauer and Celsus: The Shape of Late Second-Century Christianity." *SC* 4 (1984): 1-7.

Caird, G.B. *A Commentary on The Revelation of St. John The Divine*. HNTC. New York and Evanston: Harper & Row, 1966.

Canfield, Leon Hardy. *The Early Persecutions of Christians*. Columbia University Studies in the Social Sciences 136. New York: AMS. 1968.

Chapman, G. Clarke, Jr. "Some Theological Reflections on Walter Bauer's *Rechtgläubigkeit und Ketzerei im ältesten Christentum*. A Review Article." *JES* 7 (1970): 564-74.

Childs, Brevard S. *The New Testament as Canon: An Introduction*. Philadelphia: Fortress, 1984.

Conzelmann, Hans. "Luke's Place in the Development of Early Christianity." In *Studies in Luke-Acts: Essays Presented in Honor of Paul Schubert*. Edited by L.E. Keck and J.L. Martyn, 298-316. Nashville and New York: Abingdon, 1966.

Cook, J.A. *Law and Life of Rome, 90 B.C.-A.D. 212*. Ithaca: Cornell University Press, 1967.

Corwin, Virginia. *St. Ignatius and Christianity in Antioch*. Yale Publications in Religion 1. New Haven: Yale University Press, 1960.

Daniélou, Jean. *The Christian Centuries*. Vol. 1. *The First Six Hundred Years*. With Henri Marrou. Translated by Vincent Cronin. London: Darton, Longman and Todd, 1964.

Davies, J.G. *The Early Christian Church*. London: Weidenfeld & Nicolson, 1965.

Donahue, Paul J. "Jewish Christianity in the Letters of Ignatius of Antioch." *VC* 32 (1978): 81-93.

Downey, Glanville. *A History of Antioch in Syria from Seleucus to the Arab Conquest*. Princeton: Princeton University Press, 1961.

Drewery, B. "History and Doctrine: Heresy and Schism." *JEH* 23 (1972): 251-66.

Drijvers, H.J.W. *Cults and Beliefs at Edessa*. Leiden: E.J. Brill, 1980.

_____. "Facts and Problems in Early Syriac-Speaking Christianity," *SC* 2 (1982): 157-175.

_____. "East of Antioch: Forces and Structures in the Development of Early Syriac Theology." In *East of Antioch: Studies in Early Syriac Christianity*, by H.J.W. Drijvers, 1-27. London: Variorum Reprints, 1984.

_____. "Jews and Christians at Edessa," *JJS* 36 (1985): 88-102.

Duckworth, H.T.F. "The Roman Provincial System." In *The Beginnings of Christianity*. Vol. 1. Edited by F.J. Foakes Jackson and Kirsopp Lake, 171-217. London: Macmillan, 1920.

Duncan, G.S. *St. Paul's Ephesian Ministry*. London: Hodder and Stoughton, 1929.

Duncan-Jones, Richard. *The Economy of the Roman Empire: Quantitative Studies*. Cambridge: Cambridge University Press, 1974.

Dunn, James D.G. *Unity and Diversity in the New Testament: An Inquiry Into the Character of Earliest Christianity*. Philadelphia: Westminster, 1977.

Ehrhardt, Arnold. "Christianity Before the Apostles' Creed." *HTR* 55 (1962): 73-119.

Ellis, E. Earle. "Paul and His Opponents: Trends in the Research." In *Christianity, Judaism and Other Greco-Roman Cults: Studies for Morton Smith at Sixty*. Edited by J. Neusner, 2:264-98. Leiden: E.J. Brill, 1975.

_____. "Dating the New Testament." *NTS* 26 (1980): 487-502.

Elze, Martin. "Häresie und Einheit der Kirche im 2. Jahrhundret." *ZTK* 71 (1974): 389-409.

Farmer, William, and Farkasfalvy, Denis M. *The Formation of the New Testament Canon*. Theological Inquiries: Studies in Contemporary Biblical and Theological Problems. Introduction by Albert C. Outler. Edited by Harold W. Attridge. New York/Ramsey/Toronto: Paulist, 1983.

Filson, Floyd V. "The Significance of the Early House Churches." *JBL* 58 (1939): 105-112.

Fiorenza, Elizabeth Schüssler. "Apocalyptic and Gnosis in the Book of Revelation and Paul." *JBL* 92 (1973): 565-81.

Flora, Jerry R. "A Critical Analysis of Walter Bauer's Theory of Early Christian Orthodoxy and Heresy." Th.D. diss., Southern Baptist Theological Seminary, 1972.

Ford, Josephine, Massyngberde. *Revelation*. AB 38. Garden City: Doubleday, 1975.

Fox, Robin Lane. *Pagans and Christians*. New York: Alfred A. Knopf, 1987.

Frend, W.H.C. *Martyrdom and Persecution in the Early Church: A Study of a Conflict from the Maccabees to Donatus*. Oxford: Blackwell, 1965. Reprint. Grand Rapids: Baker, 1981.

_____. *The Early Church*. London: Hodder and Stoughton, 1965; Philadelphia, Fortress, 1982.

_____. "Early Christianity and Society: A Jewish Legacy in the Pre-Constantinian Era." *HTR* 76 (1983): 53-71.

_____. *The Rise of Christianity*. Philadelphia: Fortress, 1984.

Fuller, R.H. "New Testament Trajectories and Biblical Authority." In *Studia Evangelica* 7. Papers presented to the Fifth International Congress on Biblical Studies (1973). Edited by Elizabeth A. Livingstone. Texte und Untersuchungen zur Geschichte der altchristlichen Literatur 126, 189-99. Berlin: Akademie-Verlag.

Gamble, Harry A., Jr. *The Textual History of the Letter to the Romans: A Study in Textual and Literary Criticism*. Grand Rapids: Eerdmans, 1977.

Gasque, Ward W. *A History of the Criticism of the Acts of the Apostles*. Grand Rapids: Eerdmans, 1975.

Gero, Stephen. "With Walter Bauer on the Tigris: Encratite Orthodoxy and Libertine Heresy in Syro-Mesopotamian Christianity." In *Nag Hammadi, Gnosticism, and Early Christianity*. Edited by Charles W. Hedrick and Robert Hodgson, Jr., 287-307. Peabody: Hendrickson, 1986.

Goguel, Maurice. *The Birth of Christianity*. Translated by H.C. Snape. New York: George Allen & Unwin, 1953.

Goodspeed, E.J. *The Meaning of Ephesians*. Chicago: Chicago University Press, 1933.

_____. *An Introduction to the New Testament*. Chicago: Chicago University Press, 1937.

Goppelt, Leonhard. *Apostolic and Post-Apostolic Times*. Translated by Robert A. Guelich. London: A. and C. Black, 1970. Reprint. Grand Rapids: Baker, 1977.

_____. "The Plurality of New Testament Theologies and the Unity of the Gospel as an Ecumenical Problem." In *The Gospel and Unity*. Edited by Vilmos Vajta, 106-30. Minneapolis: Augsburg, 1971.

Grant, Robert M. "Pliny and the Christians."*HTR* 41 (1948):273-4.

_____. *Gnosticism and Early Christianity*. 2nd ed. New York and London: Columbia University Press, 1966.

_____. "Scripture and Tradition in Ignatius of Antioch." In *After the New Testament,* by R.M. Grant, 37-54. Philadelphia: Fortress, 1967.

_____. *Early Christianity and Society*. San Francisco: Harper & Row, 1977.

Green, Henry A. "The Social-Economic Background of Christianity in Egypt." In *The Roots of Egyptian Christianity*. Studies in

Antiquity and Christianity. Edited by Birger A Pearson and James E. Goehring, 100-113. Philadelphia: Fortress, 1986.

Gunther, John J. *St. Paul's Opponents and Their Background: A Study of Apocalyptic and Jewish Sectarian Teachings*. Leiden: E. J. Brill, 1973.

Guthrie, Donald. *New Testament Introduction*, 3rd ed. Downers Grove, Ill.: Inter-Varsity Press, 1975.

Haenchen, Ernst. *The Acts of the Apostles: A Commentary*. Translated by Bernard Noble and Gerald Shinn. Philadelphia: Westminster, 1971.

Hanson, A.T. *The Pastoral Epistles*. NCBC. Grand Rapids: Eerdmans; London: Marshall, Morgan & Scott, 1982.

Harnack, Adolf. *Marcion: Das Evangelium vom fremden Gott*. Leipzig, 1921.

_____. *What is Christianity?* Translated by Thomas Bailey Saunders. New York: Harper & Brothers, 1957.

_____. *The Mission and Expansion of Christianity in the First Three Centuries*. Translated and edited by James Moffatt. London: Williams & Norgate, 1908. Reprint. With introduction by Jaroslav Pelikan. New York: Harper & Brothers, 1962.

Harrington, Daniel J. "The Reception of Walter Bauer's Orthodoxy and Heresy in Earliest Christianity During the Last Decade." *HTR* 73 (1980): 289-98.

Harrison, P.N. *Polycarp's Two Epistles to the Philippians*. Cambridge: Cambridge University Press, 1936.

Hawkin, David J. "A Reflective Look at the Recent Debate on Orthodoxy and Heresy in Earliest Christianity." *Eglise et Theologie* 7 (1976): 367-78.

Hefner, Philip J. "Baur Versus Ritschl on Early Christianity." *CH* 31 (1962): 259-78.

Hemer, Colin J. *The Letters to the Seven Churches of Asia in Their Local Setting*. JSNTSup 11. Sheffield: JSOT Press, 1986.

Hengel, Martin. *Acts and the History of Early Christianity*. Translated by John Bowden. London: SCM; Philadelphia: Fortress, 1979.

Henry, Patrick. "Why Is Contemporary Scholarship So Enamored of Ancient Heresies?" In the *Proceedings of the 8th International Conference on Patristic Studies*. Edited by E.A. Livingstone, 123-6. Oxford: Pergamon Press, 1980.

Heron, A.I.C. "The Interpretation of I Clement in Walter Bauer's *Rechtgläubigkeit und Ketzerei im ältesten Christentum*." *Ekklesiastikos Pharos* 55 (1973): 517-45.

Hodgson, Peter C. "The Rediscovery of Ferdinand Christian Baur: A Review of the First Two Volumes of his *Ausgewälte Werke*." *CH* 33 (1964): 206-214.

Hoffmann, R. Joseph. *Marcion: On the Restitution of Christianity. An Essay on the Development of Radical Paulinist Theology in the Second Century*. AAR Academy Series 46. Chico, CA.: Scholars Press, 1984.

Holmberg, Bengt. *Paul and Power: The Structure of Authority in the Primitive Church as Reflected in the Pauline Epistles*. Philadelphia: Fortress, 1980.

Jackson, F.J. Foakes, and Lake, Kirsopp. "The Dispersion." In *The Beginnings of Christianity*. Edited by F.J. Foakes Jackson and Kirsopp Lake, 1:137-68. London: Macmillan, 1920.

Jay, E.G. "From Presbyter-Bishops to Bishops and Presbyters. Christian Ministry in the Second Century." *SC* 1 (1981): 125-162.

Jervell, Jacob. "The Mighty Minority." *ST* 34 (1980): 13-38.

Jewett, Robert. *Paul, Messenger and Exile. A Study in the Chronology of His Life and Letters*. Valley Forge, Pa.: Judson, 1972.

Johnson, Sherman E. "Laodicea and its Neighbours." *BA* 13 (1950): 1-18.

_____. "Christianity in Sardis." In *Early Christian Origins: Studies in Honor of Harold R. Willoughby*. Edited by Allen Wikgen, 81-90. Chicago: Quadrangle Books, 1961.

Joly, Robert. *Le Dossier d'Ignace d'Antioche*. Brussels: Editions de l'Université de Brussels, 1979.

Jones, A.H.M. *The Cities of the Eastern Roman Provinces*. 2nd ed. Revised by Michael Avi-Yonah et al. Oxford: Clarendon Press, 1971.

Judge, E.A. *The Social Pattern of Christian Groups in the First Century*. London: Tyndale, 1960.

Juster, Jean. *Les Juifs dans l'empire romain: Leur Condition juridique, economique, et sociale*. 2 vols. Paris: Guethner, 1914.

Käsemann, Ernst. "The Canon of the New Testament and the Unity of the Church." In *Essays on New Testament Themes*. Translated by W.J. Montague, 95-107. Studies in Biblical Theology 41. London: SCM, 1964.

_____. "Paul and Early Catholicism." In *New Testament Questions of Today*. Translated by Wilfred F. Bunge, 236-51. Philadelphia: Fortress, 1969.

Klauck, Hans-Josef. *Hausgemeinde und Hauskirche im frühen Christentum.* Stuttgarter Biblestudien 103. Stuttgart: Katholisches Bibelwerk, 1981.

Klijn, A.F.J. "Jewish Christianity in Egypt." In *The Roots of Egyptian Christianity.* Studies in Antiquity and Christianity. Edited by Birger A Pearson and James E. Goehring, 161-75. Philadelphia: Fortress, 1986.

Koester, Helmut. "Häretiker im Urchristentum." In *Die Religion in Geschichte und Gagenwart.* 3rd ed. III.14-21. Tübingen: J.C.B. Mohr (Paul Siebeck), 1959.

_____. "GNOMAI DIAPHOROI: The Origin and Nature of Diversification in the History of Early Christianity." *HTR* 58 (1965): 279-318.

_____. "The Theological Aspects of Primitive Christian Heresy." In *The Future of our Religious Past: Essays in Honour of Rudolf Bultmann.* Edited by J.M. Robinson, 65-83. London: SCM, 1971.

_____. *Introduction to the New Testament.* Vol. 2. *History and Literature of Early Christianity.* Philadelphia: Fortress, 1982.

Kraabel, Alf Thomas. "Paganism and Judaism: The Sardis Evidence." In *Paganisme, Judaisme, Christianisme: Influences et affrontements dans le monde antique: Melanges offerts a Marcel Simon.* Edited by Andre Benoit, Marc Philonenko, and Cyrille Vogel, 13-33. Paris: Boccard, 1978.

_____. "Judaism in Western Asia Minor under the Roman Empire, with a Preliminary Study of the Jewish Community at Sardis, Lydia." Th.D. diss., Harvard University, 1968.

Kraft, Robert A. "The Development of the Concept of 'Orthodoxy' in Early Christianity." In *Current Issues in Biblical and Patristic Interpretation.* Studies in Honor of Merril C. Tenney. Edited by Gerald F. Hawthorne, 47-59. Grand Rapids: Eerdmans, 1975.

Kümmel, Werner Georg. *The New Testament: The History of the Investigation of its Problems.* Translated by S. McLean Gilmour and Howard C. Kee. Nashville and New York: Abingdon Press, 1972.

_____. *Introduction to the New Testament.* Rev. ed. Translated by Howard Clark Kee. Nashville and New York: Abingdon, 1975.

Lake, Kirsopp. *Landmarks in the History of Early Christianity.* New York: Macmillan, 1922.

Lawlor, Hugh Jackson, and Oulton, John Ernest Leonard. *Eusebius, Bishop of Caesarea: The Ecclesiastical History and the Martyrs of Palestine.* 1928. Reprint. London: S.P.C.K., 1954.

Lemcio, E.E. "Ephesus and the New Testament Canon." *BJRL* 69 (1986): 210-234.

Léon-Dufour, Xavier. *Dictionary of the New Testament.* Translated by Terrence Prendergast. San Francisco: Harper & Row, 1908.

Lightfoot, Joseph Barber. *The Apostolic Fathers.* 5 vols. 2nd ed. London: Macmillan, 1889-90. Part II. *Ignatius and Polycarp.* 3 vols. Reprint. Grand Rapids: Baker, 1981.

Lohse, Eduard.*The New Testament Environment.* Translated by John E. Steely. Nashville: Abingdon, 1976.

Lonergan, Bernard J.F. *Method in Theology.* New York: Seabury, 1979.

Lüdermann, Gerd. "The Successors of Pre-70 Jerusalem Christianity: A Critical Evaluation of the Pella-Tradition." In *JCSD* 1:161-173.

MacRae, George W. "Why the Church Rejected Gnosticism." In *JCSD.* 1: 126-33.

Magie, David. *Roman Rule in Asia Minor to the End of the Third Century after Christ.* 2 vols. 1950. Reprint. New York: Arno, 1975.

Malherbe, Abraham J. *Social Aspects of Early Christianity.* 2nd ed.Philadelphia: Fortress, 1983.

Markus, R.A. Review of *Orthodoxy and Heresy in Earliest Christianity*, by Walter Bauer. *New Blackfriars* 54 (1973): 283-4.

_____. "The Problem of Self-Definition: From Sect to Church." In *JCSD.* 1: 1-15.

Marshall, A.J. "Flaccus and the News of Asia." *Phoenix* 29 (1975): 139-154.

Marshall, I. Howard. "Palestinian and Hellenistic Christianity: Some Critical Comments." *NTS* 19 (1972-3): 271-87.

_____. "Orthodoxy and heresy in earlier Christianity." *Themelios* 2 (1976): 5-14.

Martin, Brice L. "Some reflections of the unity of the New Testament." *SR* 8 (1979):143-52.

May, G. "Ein neues Markionbild?" *TheolRund* 51 (1986): 404-13.

McCullough, W. Stewart. *A Short History of Syriac Christianity to the Rise of Islam.* Chico, CA: Scholars Press, 1982.

McCue, James. "Bishops, Presbyters, and Priests in Ignatius of Antioch." *TS* 28 (1967): 828-34.

_____. "Orthodoxy and Heresy: Walter Bauer and the Valentinians." *VC* 33 (1979): 118-30.

Meeks, Wayne A. "Galilee and Judea in the Fourth Gospel." *JBL* 85 (1966): 159-69.

_____. Review of *Einfürung in das Neue Testament im Rahmen der Religionsgeschichte und Kulturgeschichte der hellenistischen und römischen Zeit*, by Helmut Koester, *JBL* 101 (1982): 445-8.

_____. *The First Urban Christians: The Social World of the Apostle Paul*. New Haven and London: Yale University Press, 1983.

Meeks, Wayne A. and Wilken, Robert L. *Jews and Christians in Antioch in the First Four Centuries of the Common Era*. Missoula: Scholars Press, 1978.

Meinhold, Peter. *Studien zu Ignatius von Antiochien*. Wiesbaden: Franz Steiner, 1979.

Ménard, Jacques E. "Normative Self-Definition in Gnosticism." In *JCSD*. 1: 134-50.

Meyer, Ben F. *The Early Christians: Their World Mission and Self-Discovery*. Good News Studies 16. Wilmington: Michael Glazier, 1986.

Moffatt, James. Review of *Rechtgläubigkeit und Ketzerei im ältesten Christentum*, by Walter Bauer. *Exp Tim* 45 (1933/4): 475-6.

_____. "An Approach to Ignatius." *HTR* 29 (1936): 1-38.

Molland, Einar. "The Heretics Combatted by Ignatius of Antioch." *JEH* 5 (1954): 1-6.

Moule, C.F.D. *The Birth of the New Testament*. 3rd ed. San Francisco: Harper & Row, 1982.

Munck, J. "Jewish Christianity in Post-Apostolic Times." *NTS* 6 (1960): 103-16.

Neill, Stephen. *The Interpretation of the New Testament 1861-1961*. The Firth Lectures, 1962. London: Oxford University Press, 1964.

Norris, Frederick W. "Ignatius, Polycarp, and I Clement: Walter Bauer Reconsidered." *VC* 30 (1976): 23-44.

_____. "Asia Minor before Ignatius: Walter Bauer Reconsidered." In *Studia Evangelica*. Vol. 7. Papers presented to the Fifth International Congress on Biblical Studies (1973). Edited by Elizabeth A. Livingstone, 365-77. Texte und Untersuchungen zur Geschichte der altchristlichen Literatur 126. Berlin: Akademie-Verlag, 1982.

Olbricht, Thomas H. "Understanding the Church of the Second Century: American Research and Teaching 1890-1940." In *Texts and Testaments: Critical Essays on the Bible and Early*

Church Fathers. Edited by W. Eugene March, 237-61. San Antonio: Trinity University Press, 1980.

Osborne, Robin. *Classical Landscape with Figures: The Ancient City and its Countryside*. London: George Philip, 1987.

Pagels, Elaine H. "Visions, Appearances and Apostolic Authority." In *Gnosis. Festschrift fur Hans Jonas*. Edited by Barbara Aland et al. Göttingen: Vanderhoeck & Ruprecht, 1978.

_____. *The Gnostic Gospels*. New York: Random House, 1979.

Pauck, Wilhelm. *The Heritage of the Reformation*. Rev. ed. Glencoe: Free Press, 1961.

Pearson, Birger A. "Earliest Christianity in Egypt: Some Observations." In *The Roots of Egyptian Christianity*. Studies in Antiquity and Christianity. Edited by Birger A Pearson and James E. Goehring, 132-59. Philadelphia: Fortress, 1986.

Pelikan, Jaroslav. "The Two Sees of Peter: Reflections on the Pace of Normative Self-Definition East and West." In *JCSD*. 1: 57-73.

Petersen, Joan M. "House Churches in Rome." *VC* 23 (1969): 264-272.

Puech, Henri-Charles. "Gnostic Gospels and Related Documents." In *New Testament Apocrypha*, by Edgar Hennecke. Edited by Wilhelm Schneemelcher (ET edited by R. McL. Wilson), I:231-362. Philadelphia: Westminster, 1963.

Quispel, G. "Gnosticism and the New Testament." *VC* 19 (1965): 65-85.

Ramsay, William M. *The Letters to the Seven Churches of Asia*. London: Hodder and Stoughton, 1904.

_____. "Roads and Travel." In *A Dictionary of the Bible*. Edited by James Hastings, supplementary volume, 357-402. New York: Charles Scribner's Sons, 1909.

_____. *The Church in the Roman Empire: Before A.D. 170*. Mansfield College Lectures. New York and London: G.P. Putnam's Sons, 1912.

Reicke, Bo. *The Epistles of James, Peter and Jude*. AB 37. Garden City: Doubleday, 1964.

_____. *The New Testament Era: The World of the Bible from 500 B.C. to A.D. 100*. Translated by David E. Green. Philadelphia, Fortress, 1968.

_____. "The Inauguration of Catholic Martyrdom according to St. John the Divine." *Augustinianum* 20 (1980): 275-283.

Richardson, Cyril C. *The Christianity of Ignatius of Antioch.* Columbia University Press, 1935. Reprint. New York: AMS Press, 1967.

Ritschl, Albrecht. *Die Entstehung der altkatholischen Kirche.* Bonn: Adolph Marcus, 1857.

Rius-Camps, J. *The Four Authentic Letters of Ignatius, the Martyr.* Rome: Pontificium Institutum Orientalium Studiorum, 1979.

Roberts, Colin H. *Manuscript, Society, and Belief in Early Christian Egypt.* The Schweich Lectures of the British Academy for 1977. London: Oxford University Press, 1979.

Robinson, James M. "Basic Shifts in German Theology." *Interpretation* 16 (1962): 76-97.

_____. "On Bridging the Gulf from Q to the *Gospel of Thomas* (or Vice Versa)" In *Nag Hammadi, Gnosticism, and Early Christianity.* Edited by Charles W. Hedrick and Robert Hodgson, Jr., 127-175. Peabody: Hendrickson, 1986.

Robinson, James M., and Helmut Koester. *Trajectories through Early Christianity.* Philadelphia: Fortress, 1971.

Robinson, John A.T. *Redating the New Testament.* London: SCM, 1976.

Sanders, E.P. *Paul and Palestinian Judaism: A Comparison of Patterns of Religion.* Philadelphia: Fortress, 1977.

Schneemelcher, Wilhelm. "Walter Bauer als Kirchenhistoriker." *NTS* IX (1962-1963): 11-22.

Schoedel, William R. "Ignatius and the Archives." *HTR* 71(1978): 97-106.

_____. "Theological Norms and Social Perspectives in Ignatius of Antioch." In *JCSD.* 1: 30-56.

_____. "Are the Letters of Ignatius of Antioch Authentic?" *RelSRev* 6 (1980): 196-201.

_____. *Ignatius of Antioch.* Hermeneia. (Philadelphia: Fortress, 1985.

Segal, J.B. "When did Christianity come to Edessa?" In *Middle East Studies and Libraries: A Felicitation Volume for Professor J.D. Pearson.* Edited by B.C. Bloomfield, 179-91. London: Mansell, 1980.

Sherwin-White, A.N. "The Early Persecutions and Roman Law Again." *JTS*, n.s. 3 (1952): 199-213.

Simon, Marcel. "From Greek Hairesis to Christian Heresy." In *Early Christian Literature and the Classical Intellectual Tradition. In honorem Robert M. Grant.* Edited by William R. Schoedel and Robert L. Wilken, 101-16. Theologie historique 53. Paris: Beauchesne, 1979.

Sitwell, Nigel, *The Roman Roads of Europe*. New York: St. Martin's, 1981.

Smallwood, E. Mary. *The Jews under Roman Rule: From Pompey to Diocletian*. Studies in Judaism in Late Antiquity 20. Leiden: E.J. Brill, 1976.

Starr, Chester G. *The Roman Empire 27 B.C.-A.D. 476*. New York and Oxford: Oxford University Press, 1982.

Stern, Menahem. "The Jewish Diaspora." In *The Jewish People in the First Century*. Vol. 1. Edited by S. Safrai and M. Stern. Assen: Van Gorcum, 1974.

_____. *Greek and Latin Authors on Jews and Judaism*. Volume one. *From Herodotus to Plutarch*. Jerusalem: Israel Academy of Science and Humanities, 1974.

Stowers, Stanley Kent. "Social Status, Public Speaking and Private Teaching: The Circumstances of Paul's Preaching Activity." *NovT* 26 (1984): 59-82.

Strecker, Georg. "On the Problem of Jewish Christianity." In *Orthodoxy and Heresy in Earliest Christianity*, by Walter Bauer, 241-85. Philadelphia: Fortress, 1971.

Streeter, Burnett Hillman. *The Primitive Church, Studied with Special Reference to the Origins of the Christian Ministry*. London: Macmillan, 1929.

Stuhlmacher, Peter. *Der Brief an Philemon*. Evangelisch-Katholischer Kommentar zum Neuen Testament, 1. Zurich: Einsiedeln, 1975.

Tcherikover, Victor. *Hellenistic Civilization and the Jews*. Translated by S. Applebaum. New York: Atheneum, 1979.

Trevett, Christine. "The Much-maligned Ignatius." *Exp Tim* 93 (1982): 299-302.

_____. "Prophecy and Anti-Episcopal Activity: A Third Error Combatted by Ignatius?" *JEH* 34 (1983): 1-18.

_____. "Approaching Matthew from the Second Century: The Under-used Ignatian Correspondence." *JSNT* 20 (1984): 59-67.

Turner, H.E.W. *The Pattern of Christian Truth: A Study in the Relations between Orthodoxy and Heresy in th Early Church*. Bampton Lectures 1954. London: A.R. Mowbray & Co., 1954.

Vallée, Gérard. "Theological and Non-theological Motives in Irenaeus's Refutation of the Gnostics." In *JCSD*. 1: 174-85.

_____. *A Study in Anti-Gnostic Polemics: Irenaeus, Hippolytus, and Epiphanius*. Studies in Christianity and Judaism/ Etudes sur le christianisme et le judaisme 1. Waterloo, Ontario:

Wilfrid Laurier University Press, 1981, for the Canadian Corporation for Studies in Religion.

van Unnik, W.C. *Newly Discovered Gnostic Writings*. Studies in Biblical Theology 30. London: SCM Press, 1960.

Veilleux, Armand. "Monasticism and Gnosis in Egypt." In *The Roots of Egyptian Christianity*. Studies in Antiquity and Christianity. Edited by Birger A Pearson and James E. Goehring, 271-306. Philadelphia: Fortress, 1986.

White, L. Michael. "Adolf Harnack and the 'Expansion' of Early Christianity: A Reappraisal of Social History." *SC* 5 (1985-6): 97-127.

Wilken, Robert L. "The Christians as the Romans (and Greeks) Saw Them." In *JCSD*. 1: 100-125.

_____. "Diversity and Unity in Early Christianity." *SC* 1 (1981): 101-110.

Wilson, R. McL. Review of *Trajectories through Early Christianity*, by James M. Robinson and Helmut Koester. *JTS* 23 (1972): 475-7.

Wisse, Frederik. "The Use of Early Christian Literature as Evidence for Inner Diversity and Conflict." In *Nag Hammadi, Gnosticism, and Early Christianity*. Edited by Charles W. Hedrick and Robert Hodgson, Jr., 177-90. Peabody: Hendrickson, 1986 PP

Yamauchi, Edwin. *Pre-Christian Gnosticism: A Survey of the Proposed Evidences*, 2nd ed. Grand Rapids: Baker, 1983. London: Tyndale, 1973.

Zahn, T. *Ignatius von Antiochien*. Gotha: Perthe, 1873.

Index of
Modern Authors

Index of
Passages Cited
(Ancient Authors)

CLASSICAL AUTHORS

Subject Index

STUDIES IN THE BIBLE AND EARLY CHRISTIANITY